Banking on Sickness:

Commercial Medicine in Britain and the USA

Ben Griffith, Steve Iliffe and Geof Rayner

LAWRENCE AND WISHART

LONDON

Lawrence and Wishart Limited
39 Museum Street
London WC1A 1LQ

First published 1987
© Ben Griffith, Steve Iliffe and Geof Rayner, 1987

Photoset in North Wales by
Derek Doyle & Associates, Mold, Clwyd,
and printed in Great Britain by
Oxford University Press.

Contents

This book is dedicated to the memory of
Pat Conroy, Martha Crossen and Louis Dahl

Preface

For the first 25 years of the National Health Service, private practice was not a major political issue. This indifference started to change in early 1970s due in large part to the growing strength of the trade unions within the NHS. Barbara Castle's 'phasing out' of NHS pay-beds brought the issue to the headlines where it has stayed ever since.

The changes in the scale and the nature of private practice since the mid-1970s have been quite phenomenal. We are mainly concerned here with two aspects of this transformation – the change of private practice from a cottage industry controlled by the medical profession to a corporation-based business better known as 'commercial medicine', and the implications of this for the health care services offered in the private sector and in the NHS.

While the changes in the UK have been profound, no discussion of commercial medicine can ignore the wider issues of the relationship between the NHS and private contractors and suppliers. Nor can the experience of other countries, especially the USA, be passed over.

The authors of this book differ in terms of writing style as well as in their politics. While this has led to a better book than any one of us could have written alone, it does mean that readers cannot fail to notice changes in tone from one chapter to another. For the record, then, the Introduction was first drafted by Geof Rayner; Chapter 1 (the historical background) by Ben Griffith; Chapters 2 (on the Thatcher era) and 3 (on the medical insurance business) by Geof Rayner; Chapter 4 (about the private hospital companies) by Geof Rayner and Ben Griffith; Chapters 5, 6 and 7 (on the nature of the public-private mix in British health care, focusing on the 'independent contractor' professions and on the pharmaceutical and medical technology industries) by Steve Iliffe; Chapter 8 (about the privatisation of hospital 'ancillary' services) by Ben Griffith; Chapter 9 (on the academic debate) by Geof Rayner; Chapter 10 (which discusses the rationale for 'going private') by Steve Iliffe; Chapter 11 (on the American experience) by Geof Rayner; Chapters 12 (setting out the arguments in favour of the NHS) and 13 (on the effects of commercial medicine on the Health Service) by Ben Griffith; Chapter 14 (on what is to be done) by Steve Iliffe and Ben Griffith; the statistical Appendix was first drafted by Ben Griffith.

While the authors have learned from each other, their thanks are also due to many others whose ideas influenced this book. Professor Brian Abel-Smith commented on an early draft. Others will find their work echoed in this book, including: John Mohan; Peter Draper; NHS Unlimited (the authors' gratitude is owed especially to its chief officers Frank Dobson, Marcia Saunders and Mike Taylor and to its chief backers COHSE, NALGO and NUPE); friends at the Health Policy Advisory Centre in New York. The authors' apologies and thanks should also be recorded to all those who helped but whose help has not been acknowledged.

The errors, the authors regret, are their responsibility alone.

BG, SI, GR – October 1986

Introduction

From one country to the next, there is enormous variety in the way health care is devised, financed and provided. There is also tremendous variation in the way people think about their health and use the services that are available. Even so, in most western countries, and in the state socialist nations, health care provision means essentially medical provision, and the main source of variation, apart from administrative details, is the degree to which the organisation of health services is undertaken by the state or through private arrangements.

Historically, there is a definite trend towards the substitution of private by public provision. However, from its beginnings, health provision has been a private, rather than public, activity. When the state did intervene in the last century it was to award monopolies to medical cliques or set standards of professional knowledge (in practice indistinguishable from the former purpose). Public health measures became increasingly significant, but these were based upon changing the environment, housing or social and work conditions. Although medical provision for the poor did grow within the Poor Law and municipal institutions, for 'respectable' society medical attention was received in the home or in the consulting rooms in London's Harley Street and its equivalent in other cities and other countries. While the appearance of an enlarged private medicine industry today is partly a return to the past, there are significant changes that make comparison with former circumstances hazardous.

Internationally, progress towards a common, public form of health provision has been slow and uneven. And as this book attests, it also suffers set-backs. Although the course of history may point us towards the development of universal and

11

comprehensive health services for all, the class character of western society resists this impulse. Modern capitalism requires a welfare state to act as a buffer against social tensions, with the proviso that it should be cheap. Obviously, lowest-common-denominator levels of provision are unsuitable for the striving professional managerial class, too rushed to suffer the indignity of queues. The result is that in Britain, and in other European countries, private medicine is not the mainstream, but to be partaken by those who can afford to step outside cheap or free public provision or who are forced to pay for medical attention due to the restrictions on the public supply.

When looked at internationally, health services in the UK are at one extreme of a continuum which stretches from mainly state provision to mainly private provision. At the opposite end are American health services, which although substantially publicly financed, are essentially private in character. The USA has long laboured with spendthrift health care policies, developing frequently unnecessary medical tasks for the few, at the cost of systematic inequality and astonishing expense. Despite half a century of reform efforts, a family's or individual's health circumstances (except for the elderly, the disabled or the very poor) are still largely individual matters of concern. By contrast, the British system runs under the Scrooge principle – health services are meant to care for increasingly deprived or elderly populations on ever-tightening budgets. Public obligations and expectations alike are very different in the two countries. In America, people expect to pay. In Britain, people expect to receive free services, and to wait.

Even if the NHS did not suffer from perennial lack of investment, there would still be a market for private medicine, just as there are those who will purchase bottled water when the same substance is literally on tap. But the change is not just one of consumer expectations. Measured by the number of private hospital beds available, the private sector has doubled in size in recent years. Measured by the number of subscribers to private medical insurance schemes, its expansion is even greater. Although it remains tiny in comparison to the National Health Service, it is now a significant component of medical provision in Britain, albeit in a defined and specialised way.

Private provision has also substantially shifted ground, from being based mainly inside the National Health Service or in charity hospitals, to becoming more clearly 'commercial' with the main market runners being hospital chains run for profit. Hence in this book we employ the term 'commercial medicine', not because every element inside private medicine is profit-directed, but because this is the leading trend. Commercial medicine is marketing-based, remorselessly in search of new areas for potential business. It is not content merely to limit its scope to minor surgery, but is developing revenue-generating services in health screening, alcoholism, in vitro fertilisation, mental health and other areas.

The new commercial medicine, unlike its old 'private' form, claims independence from the National Health Service, and in as much as it is able to construct new relatively well-equipped hospitals this is in some measure true. However, it is also inseparable from the NHS. It recruits staff from the NHS, it develops services in those areas of activity lacking in the NHS but where there is effective market demand, and it advances only because the NHS is itself under threat. Commercial medicine presents two faces to the public: that of benefactor, 'helping out' the NHS by treating its well-off clientele; that of competitor, seeking to take advantage of the NHS's difficulties.

This book mostly concerns itself with private medicine in Britain, but it also looks at the USA, both because many of the new commercial hospital companies originated there, and because, as we suggest, UK private medicine is undergoing a transformation similar in form, if not in scale, to changes occurring in America. We identify this trend as the substitution of charitable activity by commercial activity.

There are implications which stretch overseas. In the USA, as well as other countries, commercial growth lends support to the view that a public, if not collective, approach to health provision, is an anachronism in that it fails to adapt to consumer demand. Hence, when commercial medicine booms and the NHS looks sick, the argument for free, comprehensive, and equally-accessed health care in Britain, as well as elsewhere, is weakened.

Herein lies the importance of the debate surrounding private medicine in Britain. It is not ultimately about whether or not a narrow section of society can gain entry to luxurious private hospitals, or pick and choose among the most

prestigious of doctors. Nor is it even about consumer freedom.
It revolves around the question of whether or not health care is
best obtainable through the economic marketplace or through
state institutions, which, for all their weaknesses, have been
devised to cater for all, comprehensively, without the barrier
of charges.

The debate about private medicine, the argument about its
desirability or its failings, is therefore central to any discussion
about life in contemporary Britain, and, more narrowly, about
the future development of patterns of social provision which
were laid down at the end of the last war. For all its failings,
compromises and shortcomings, the NHS achieved this: it
created a climate in which every patient was equal in status to
every other patient. Equality has never existed in practice for a
whole host of reasons, but it existed in principle. The poor
person was, at worst, as entitled to join the queue as the rich
person and, at best, would receive standards of medical care
equal to those anywhere in the world.

In calling attention to the expansion of commerical
medicine, the authors are not, thereby, making the claim that
all that happens in the NHS is wonderful and all that happens
within private institutions is bad. Those of us who work within
the NHS and who agree with its principle do not need to cover
up its failures. The hierarchies within it would rival the
medieval Church of Rome.

Unfortunately, much of the discussion that has already
taken place around private provision has dwelt on the trivial
detail, for example, the fact that private patients apparently
want 'luxury' treatment, as if being in hospital was in some
way a desirable pastime. As those who work in both public
hospitals and private hospitals know, the 'quality' of care
obtainable is not something that can be described or
compared as easily as video recorders or washing machines.
What can be said is that health care, which is an enormously
varied set of tasks, usually works best when the relationships
that are established between care-giver and care-receiver are
of a non-financial kind. When the social relationship of care is
filtered through economic interests all forms of perverse
motivations are engendered. At the basest level, medically
unwarranted, profit-induced practice occurs.

The dispute about the impact of commercial medicine is

rooted in fears of the breakup and possible demise of the National Health Service. Those on the left have used public concerns over the NHS in order to attack the Conservative government, while those on the right, in the pursuit of the belief that the unfettered free market works best, have argued that the NHS is in decline due to its inherent inefficiency and inability to satisfy consumer wants. To these people the private sector, which has sustained rapid growth in the 1980s, offers them a vision of the future – health care without socialism. To the supporters of the National Health Service, the growth of private medicine, aided by a Conservative government, indicates its predatory nature. The right's enthusiasm for private medicine is rooted in its attempt to undermine the NHS as a powerful image of post-war social democracy.

However, this book is only partly concerned with the National Health Service, even if, from time to time, it necessarily touches upon it to explain the shape private medicine has taken. The first section of this book examines services before the creation of the NHS and explains how private medicine lingered on afterwards. We examine Thatcher's policies towards commercial medicine and the NHS as well as the recent pattern of commercial growth, changes in ownership and the significance of medical insurance. The second section of the book examines how public and private interrelate, and discusses the influence of the drug companies. We examine how the government has attacked the poorest workers in the NHS, while improving conditions for those at the top. In the third and final section we examine the recent debate on the commercial sector's contribution and argue that the NHS is inherently better equipped than the private sector to ration medical services. Lastly, we discuss the difficult question: should commercial medicine be abolished?

This book does not set out to exaggerate the importance of commercial medicine. We still think the crucial debate concerns the NHS, how it should paid for, controlled, managed, what services should be available and how they are assessed, and, in response to user pressure, how services can be humanised and made more appropriate to those in greatest need. We use the words 'private' and 'commercial' interchangeably throughout because they are both in common parlance, although as we have noted, we attach a rather special meaning to each term.

PART ONE
COMMERCIAL MEDICINE IN BRITAIN

Chapter 1

Private Practice Pre-Thatcher

In order to begin to understand the nature of private practice today, and of the political battle around commercial medicine, it is necessary to glance behind at the past. This helps us to understand both how the NHS came to be as it is and the ways in which it is superior to the medical mish-mash it succeeded. Looking at the history of private practice also clarifies the central position held by consultants in medical politics and in the NHS. Such a survey can also provide pointers towards an effective policy to combat the expansion of commercial medicine – or, at least, warn us away from dangerous paths.

Before the National Health Service

One hundred years ago, general practice came in a bewildering variety of forms. The well-to-do had their own doctors, whom they paid for each consultation or treatment given. Less fortunate doctors practising in working-class areas sometimes set up 'private dispensaries' where they purveyed cheap (and often dubious) medicines. Some working-class people were insured to cover consultations with their doctors. Some doctors set up 'clubs' at their dispensaries. Friendly Societies often employed other doctors to treat their members

17

(but not their members' dependents). Increasingly, the Societies got together to set up 'Medical Aid Associations' (which did cover dependents). The 'medical officers' were salaried, resented being under the authority of working men (although doctors were much less middle-class then) and argued that their 'clinical autonomy' – their right to treat and prescribe as they thought fit – was infringed. They also complained that the Associations often gave cover to the relatively well-off (and so reduced the custom available for independent GPs). Doctors and philanthropists set up 'provident dispensaries', which were like the Medical Aid Associations except that the doctors had an important say in their management and the subscibers were means-tested. The Poor Law also included a medical service, with District Medical Officers 'treating' official paupers.

Again, the doctors were salaried and looked down on many of the members of the Boards of Guardians. But many very poor people could not or would not receive Poor Law relief and they were often treated for free at the out-patient departments of the voluntary hospitals.

Drugs and advice were also dispensed by unqualified medical students, by chemists and by quacks.

In 1911, the role of public money was increased by Lloyd George's National Health Insurance (NHI). Certainly, this was a step forward but it had so many drawbacks and limitations that by 1945 there was little enthusiasm for developing and extending compulsory medical insurance.

The introduction of NHI was fiercely opposed by the medical profession and by the medical insurers. In time, the doctors became accustomed to NHI, which made them better off. About two-thirds of them would treat NHI patients – and a third of the average doctor's income would come from the NHI. Doctors were paid on a capitation basis – that is, their income depended on the number of potential patients on their list (or 'panel').

The insurance carriers were also bought off, with more disastrous consequences. Insurance Committees were set up to administer the doctors' capitation payments but the patients' cash benefits were paid out by about 7,000 insurance carriers, now called Approved Societies. These were set up by trade unions to attract new members and by commercial insurance companies to attract new subscribers (often to schemes providing 'burial benefit'). As a result of this chaotic compromise, NHI had very high administrative costs when compared with other compulsory medical insurance systems in Europe.[1]

National Health Insurance covered only a minority of the population – wage-earners and others earning less than a given amount, but not their dependents. Breadwinners falling ill were seen as a major cause of poverty and it was poverty rather than illness itself that NHI was primarily intended to combat. Working-class people – especially women – still depended heavily on out-patient departments and on doctors willing to see them for little or nothing.

The range of benefits provided by NHI was, by 1948, the most limited of any comparable system in Europe. In 1939 there were 17 million men on NHI. Only 12 million were entitled to benefit for dental treatment, only 10 million for ophthalmic treatment and fewer than 2 million received any benefit for treatment in hospitals.[2]

These additional benefits were financed out of any surplus made by the Approved Society after paying for its subscibers' basic GP treatment. As a result, the Society with the most healthy subscribers – because of its geographical location or because it refused cover to the obviously unhealthy – was also the Society able to offer the widest range of benefits. 9 per cent of NHI subscribers had their benefits administered by the Insurance Committees. These tended to be the bad risks that no Approved Society would enrol. Like many insurance systems, NHI treated the very healthy reasonably, the very ill appallingly.

Hospital Provision

Hospital care before the Second World War was provided by three types of institution – municipal hospitals, voluntary hospitals and private nursing homes.

Rudimentary medical care for paupers had been provided in the workhouse infirmaries of the Poor Law. Local authorities were also empowered to provide hospitals for the chronically ill, for the mentally handicapped and for tuberculosis sufferers. The 1929 Local Government Act enabled them to develop municipal hospitals to treat acute illness. The specialists were salaried, on a full-time basis, and some of the hospitals even included pay beds. But in general, they were shunned by those who were at all able to do so as their medical standards were low and the atmosphere of the Poor Law persisted.

While the municipal hospitals cared for the chronically ill, nearly one in two acute beds were in voluntary hospitals.

These were nearly all tiny institutions, but included a small number of teaching hospitals attached to medical schools and providing the best treatment then available. Originally, the voluntary hospitals had been financed by donations from the wealthy and the specialists had worked for nothing (or, rather, for the sake of prestige and experience). But this financial basis was withered away by rising medical costs associated with improving treatment for patients and higher wages for employees. By the mid-1930s, only 31 per cent of the income of the teaching hospitals in London came from donations and only 20 per cent in the case of the provincial teaching hospitals.

By 1940, ten of the 28 teaching hospitals were in the red. Increasingly, the voluntary hospitals had to charge their patients. The Hospital Contributory Schemes had originally funnelled donations into the hospitals, but were turning into informal medical insurance carriers for those members of the working class who wanted to avoid the stigma of charity. By 1947, the Hospital Contributory Schemes Association claimed 10.5 million subscribers and dependents were also covered.[3]

By that time, the Schemes were providing about half of the income of the voluntary hospitals. The hospitals welcomed this new source of income but the fees charged the subscribers were too low to cover the costs incurred in their treatment. So, in addition to charging their working-class patients, the voluntary hospitals introduced pay-beds in which consultants' private patients could be treated. The well-to-do were excluded from the Contributory Schemes by their maximum income limits and so began setting up their own 'provident associations' in the 1930s. But even charging patients did not solve the hospitals' economic problems – government money was needed and provided.

When the well-to-do chose not to use the pay beds in

Functions of Non-psychiatric Voluntary and Municipal Hospitals in England and Wales[1]

Type of Hospital

Speciality	Voluntary		Municipal		Total[2]	Total	Available
	Hospitals	Beds	Hospitals	Beds	Hospitals	Beds	Beds[3]
General acute	711	60,198	162	69,135	873	129,331	141,721
Special	196	16,105	31	8,543	227	24,648	26,956
Chronic	27	1,730	377	49,199	404	49,929	59,211
TB	66	7,330	134	14,389	200	21,719	27,402
Maternity	54	1,819	98	2,034	152	3,853	4,039
Isolation	3	297	636	42,725	639	43,022	43,665
Totals	1,057	87,479	1,438	185,025	2,495	273,502	302,994

Source:

Statistics held in PRO MH 80/34, as presented in John Mohan, *Private Medical Care: An Historical Comparison*, unpublished paper, 1983.
[1] Data refer to 1938 apart from those for total available beds, which are *net* figures for an unspecified date towards the end of the war – see also note 3.
[2] Since the NHS initially involved state control of over 3,000 hospitals, these figures are evidently incomplete. However, the basis on which they were gathered was not given.
[3] These figures comprise the total beds available in 1938, *plus* beds provided in Emergency Medical Service units, *minus* beds lost through wartime damage. The *net* gain in beds was therefore approximately 30,000. Though the *exact* date at which these statistics were gathered was not given, from the dates on other papers in this file it seems reasonable to infer that the data refer to late 1944 or early 1945.

voluntary hospitals, they received their hospital care in small
private 'nursing homes'. With about 40,000 beds in 1921, the
medical facilities of these nursing homes were minimal.
Indeed, one academic writer describes them in terms which
suggest how the nursing homes then grew into the private
clinics now:

'Generally, these were small hospitals, run for profit, and
frequently nothing more than adjuncts to the offices of eminent
specialists. Like most very small medical institutions they
suffered, more often than not, from lack of staff, under-equipment
and improper physical arrangements. They were scarcely an
adequate substitute for the facilities which could be offered in a
large general hospital but it was in them that most of the rich took
their institutional treatment.[4]

There was very little collaboration between the different
hospital sectors. The voluntary hospitals were parasitic on the
municipal in that they avoided the chronic sick (just as private
hospitals rely on the NHS today). The local authorities
resented this and as the same commentator observed:

The public came to associate spectacular cures and sensational
surgery with the voluntary system and treatment in municipal
institutions became afflicted with all sorts of pernicious and
self-justifying taboos.[5]

Not that the voluntary hospitals co-operated even with each
other. The competition for charitable support and for paying
patients was too severe. Nor was there much co-operation
within the municipal sector. Hospitals would refuse to treat
patients resident elsewhere. Rational planning was impossible
and the case for public control of the voluntary hospitals was
strengthened by their reliance on public money. As Aneurin
Bevan put it, the 'maintenance of voluntary hospitals and
their subvention by public funds and flag days [were]
increasingly repugnant to the conscience of the public.'[6]
   Comprehensively planned development of hospital facilities
was essential for two main reasons. First, the geographical
distribution of hospitals was ridiculously skewed. At the end
of the Second World War, for example, the London area had
10.2 hospital beds for every 1,000 inhabitants, while South

Wales had just 4.9. While voluntary hospitals were initially intended for the poor, they were set up near to the rich who made the donations and formed the clientele for the private practice on which the hospital doctors relied. The surveyors of the North-East found in 1945 that specialists flocked to Liverpool and Manchester.

> The chief determining factor is not whether there is enough work to keep a specialist busy, but whether there is enough private practice to make it worth his while to settle in the place concerned.

Not only were hospital facilities in the wrong places, there were simply not enough to go around. It was estimated that about ten hospital beds were needed for every 1,000 inhabitants, but the country had just 7.14.[7] During the war, 80,000 new beds became available. The private nursing homes were far from unique in being small and ill-equipped. One-third of voluntary hospitals had less than 30 beds; three-quarters less than 100. Municipal hospitals were generally larger (housing the chronic sick): but nearly half had less than 100 beds. Medical equipment was also short although again this would be made less severe by the war: 'The estimated number of artery forceps suddenly required by the hospitals represented over thirty years' previous demand for the whole country.'[8]

So, before the war National Health Insurance provided some primary care for a minority of the population. The limitations of its cover and its administrative complexity made it no model for a future National Health Service. The hospital service was split into three distinct sectors with little co-operation either between or within them. Medical services were unplanned, badly distributed and simply inadequate to meet needs: what Bevan called a 'patch-quilt of local paternalisms'.

The Creation of The NHS and Preservation of Private Practice

According to the dominant version of history – at least outside the labour movement – the introduction of the NHS was inevitable, merely the fruition of ideas which had been

generally accepted for many years. The Dawson Report –
produced by a committee set up by the Ministry of Health –
had foreseen a national health service of sorts in 1920.
Churchill's wartime coalition government discussed plans for a
comprehensive, planned and just medical system, and produced a White Paper in 1944 which formed the basis of Aneurin
Bevan's policy. Bevan, being too bad-tempered and not sufficiently pragmatic, antagonised the British Medical Association. In fact, the BMA had preached the need for radical
change in 1930, 1938 and 1942. According to this version, then,
the NHS was not a socialist achievement. The Labour Party
created the National Health Service only by virtue of the
historical accident that it won the 1945 General Election.

Would that progress were generally so inevitable and so
painless. Certainly, in the 1920s and 30s many members of the
medical elite came to accept that the existing medical services
were inadequate. But as important as this consensus was
another – that, in practice, nothing could be done. (Similarly
today there is broad agreement both that preventive medicine
should be massively promoted and that the cost – and the
political strength of the illness-promoting industries – makes
this impossible.) It is probably true that nothing approaching
the NHS would have emerged but for the Second World War.

Indeed, the involvement of the British state in medical care
has grown largely during and in response to war. The first state
medical service outside the Poor Law, the School Medical
Service, was a product of the Boer War. The First World War
required measures to counter TB and VD, and led to the
formation of the Ministry of Health (and the Dawson Report).

During the Second World War, an Emergency Medical
Service was set up involving *ad hoc* national planning, closer
co-operation between the hospitals, salaries for the specialists,
a blood transfusion service and other essential developments.
The voluntary hospitals became far more dependent on public
money. In 1938, 34 per cent of the income of the London
hospitals came from donors and 8 per cent from public
authorities. By 1947 the figures were 16 and 46 per cent
respectively. Also, as Eckstein noted:

> many upper- and middle-class people found themselves
> compelled, for the first time in their lives, to enter public

hospitals, the pay-beds and small wards of the voluntary hospitals now being closed to them. They thus got first hand experience of the Workhouse turned-hospital and their response generally was furious.[9]

The coalition did plan major reform of the medical services once the war was over. Compared to previous plans, the 1944 White Paper was both radical and concrete. However, it did not propose to take over the voluntary hospitals and was aptly described by Lord Woolton, the Minister for Reconstruction, as:

> a compromise scheme, but it is a compromise which is far more favourable to the Conservatives than to Labour Ministers and when it is published I expect more criticism from the left than from Conservative circles.[10]

Moreover, once the Labour Ministers left the coalition, the Conservatives backtracked fast, conceding important points on general practice and creating an administrative model of 'almost unworkable complexity'.[11] By contrast, Bevan's solution – to take over both the municipal and voluntary hospitals and integrate them in a single national system – was gloriously simple.

Bevan fought the BMA over three main issues. First, he wanted some (but minimal) control over the distribution of GPs. Secondly, he thought that a state-funded system was incompatible with GPs selling their practices to each other. Thirdly, he wanted them paid, at least in part, by salary rather than capitation. Bevan needed to fight on at least the first two issues. The third, arguably, was less important and Bevan eventually compromised and introduced legislation to forbid full-time salaries for GPs.

Not only was Bevan in the right, but the hostility between himself and the BMA was overwhelmingly the fault of the latter (aided and abetted by Conservative politicians). The BMA's pronouncements on the need for change before the war were made in the knowledge that change was not on the agenda. Even at their most radical, in 1942, the BMA's plans for a comprehensive health service were meant to be 'long-term' only. In the mean time, they favoured extending

NHI. Also, even in 1942 the BMA's Representative Body rejected even part-time salaries for GPs – and only agreed that the post-war medical system should cover everybody by 94 votes to 92. The Tories gave way on much of the 1944 White Paper and the BMA dug in its heels when Bevan tried to claw back some of the concessions. By the late 1940s – to quote Lord Moran, then President of the Royal College of Physicians – the 'extremists were in control' of the BMA. Given their intense ideological hostility to reform, the wonder is that Bevan was so tolerant and restrained his language.

So Bevan's contribution – and thus the Labour Party's contribution – to the National Health Service was substantial. Whether it is viewed as a 'socialist' achievement depends primarily on the meaning attached to the word. The radicals and socialists who produced the minority report of the Poor Law Commission in 1909, those active in the Socialist Medical Association and ordinary Labour Party members all influenced the course of events. But then so did many establishment figures who were by no means socialists. The National Health Service and the welfare state did not challenge capitalist society. They may even have helped it prosper. On the other hand, Bevan saw the NHS as a socialist achievement in that it distributed medical care according to need and was financed by general taxation. And Sir Guy Dain of the BMA did have a point when he argued:

> What the Minister appears to have done is to have the Bill which he had partly fashioned, and to have inserted into it the socialist principles of state ownership of hospitals, direction of doctors, basic salaries for doctors, and abolition of the buying and selling of practices ... The Act is part of the nationalisation programme which is being steadily pursued by this government.

But Bevan's compromises over private medicine were real enough. In the discussions during the coalition government, Labour's Attlee, Morrison and Bevin argued that GPs should be faced with the choice of working either wholly within the state medical system or wholly outside it. Indeed, under the first proposals produced by the Ministry of Health for the Cabinet, GPs at the beginning of their career would have worked solely for the state service to ensure that it was adequately staffed; Morrison pointed out that this would also please the Labour Party. After the war, however, Aneurin Bevan seems to have dropped his idea altogether and never to have questioned the right of GPs to practise privately. Arguably, the GPs' 'independent contractor status' put them in an inherently semi-private position anyway.

Bevan went even further out of his way to please the consultants (and thereby divide the profession). He accepted Lord Moran's suggestion that additional 'merit awards' could be given to top consultants. Consultants were given a major say in the administration of the National Health Service and the teaching hospitals retained some administrative independence. It was generally thought necessary to buy off the consultants by giving them the right to practise privately. Even the Socialist Medical Association saw this as a necessary compromise at least for the time being. (The SMA had accepted even the concessions to the voluntary hospitals in the 1944 White Paper.) Bevan excluded 277 hospitals from the NHS. Some were disused and unusable, such as old smallpox hospitals. Others were run by religious communities or privately. Bevan assured the BMA that the private nursing homes would be left alone (although he said the Minister would retain the right to buy land and buildings for the NHS and this could conceivably involve nursing homes). More contentious was the preservation of pay-beds, which meant that NHS facilities would be used for private practice (as the doctors were so strongly opposed to any development of state medical centres this issue did not arise in relation to general practice). Bevan argued:

> Unless we permit some few paying patients in the public hospitals, there will be a rash of nursing homes all over the country. If people wish to pay for additional amenities, or something to which they attach value, like privacy in a single ward, we ought to aim at providing such facilities for everyone who wants them ... people will want to buy something more than the general health service is providing ... If the state owned a theatre it would not charge the same prices for the different seats.[12]

(He does not seem to have foreseen that NHS waiting lists would provide the real point – and the real injustice – of pay beds.) Bevan put 'ceilings' on the fees consultants could charge pay-bed patients, although he eventually conceded that there would be no ceilings imposed for 15 per cent of pay-beds.

Bevan thought it politically utopian to try to forbid NHS consultants from practising privately. He may well have been right. But if the consultants had been faced with the choice of working privately or for the National Health Service few would have emigrated and few would have found professional pride in the private nursing homes. (Arguably, Bevan should have taken the nursing homes over – especially given the inadequacies of NHS geriatric care.) The *Manchester Guardian* certainly thought Bevan had overdone it:

> This is a false freedom that can only survive to the extent that it is abused. It must inevitably poison the doctor-patient relationship. It is the reef on which this splendid venture, with all its prospects for development, might founder at the outset.

The *Lancet*, broadly speaking, also saw the NHS as a splendid venture, removing

> from medical practice much of the mercenary element that has been growing more conspicuous for fifty years or more. The new arrangements confer a great benefit on medicine by lessening the commercial element in its practice. Now that everyone is entitled to full medical care the doctor can provide that care without thinking of his own profit or the patient's loss, and can allocate his efforts more according to medical priority.

Private Medicine – The Quiet Years

For the next 25 years, the NHS earned the continuing. and overwhelming support of the British people. The Conservatives accepted it as an essential component of the post-war consensus. Neither party was concerned to promote the expansion of private medicine but nor was its existence politically controversial.

In the 1950s, the politics of private hospital practice involved three complaints from the consultants. First, they said there were too few pay-beds. When the very low occupancy rates were pointed out, they replied that these varied greatly across the country. Secondly, they argued that pay-bed charges were too high; as private patients were relieving the NHS, they should not have to pay the economic rate. However, the Tory Minister of Health said in 1963 that it was not 'possible to justify subsidising from the Exchequer patients who have chosen to have private treatment'. Thirdly, the consultants wanted Bevan's 'ceilings' on private fees removed altogether. In fact the ceilings were ineffective, which helps explain why the Ministry never bothered to revise them to take account of inflation after 1953. But still the Conservatives would not repeal them. As the Minister said: 'Whatever might happen in the future, the time is not ripe for that.'

An important development came in 1955 when the government reached the Option Agreement with the medical profession. On the one hand, this gave consultants a rare privilege. NHS posts were to be 'open to all applicants who are prepared to give substantially the whole of their time to the post'. In other words, barring exceptional circumstances, Health Authorities were to appoint consultants without knowing whether they would hold a full-time contract or instead a 'maximum part-time' contract enabling them to practice privately. On the other hand, some argued that the Option Agreement discouraged private practice by introducing a 'differential' in favour of full-time work. This was said to arise because full-timers were paid on the basis that they worked eleven sessions or 'notional half days' each week. Maximum part-timers were paid 9/11 of the full-time salary but it was generally assumed that they would work more nine sessions. In other words, the full-timers earned more per session, at least in theory. In practice, however, the supposed differential may never have applied, for at least three reasons: full-timers too often worked longer hours than they were paid for; time spent by maximum part-timers in travelling to private hospitals or consulting rooms could count as time working for the NHS; and the self-employment status of private practice brought with it tax advantages.

Between 1964 and 1970, the Labour government made some modest changes. Firstly, the number of pay-beds was reduced. Secondly, Bevan's 'ceilings' were removed. Thirdly, the consultants' contract was adjusted and the consultants agreed that maximum part-timers could be required to work an unpaid session in addition to the nine paid sessions.

The next major political event was the report on *NHS Facilities for Private Patients* produced by the Employment and Social Services Sub-Committee of the House of Commons Expenditure Committee. Published in 1971, when the Committee's membership was predominantly Conservative, the Report did not propose any major changes. It did, however, discuss many of the issues which were of growing concern especially among the NHS trade unions, and the minority group's proposed recommendations were widely noted within the labour movement. This led directly to the battle over pay-beds in the mid-1970s, which forms the immediate background to the politics of commercial medicine today.

Barbara Castle and Pay-Beds

When Labour won the election of February 1974, its manifesto included a commitment to 'phase out private practice from the hospital service'. In April, Barbara Castle, the Social Services Secretary, set up a Working Party headed by Dr David Owen, and including representatives of the medical profession, to consider the consultants' contract.[13] In the summer, the simmering hostility of NHS unions to pay-beds blew up at London's modern Charing Cross Hospital. The BMA scuttled a compromise arranged with the hospital's consultants and the Area Health Authority. With both the BMA (and its allies) and NUPE (and its allies) threatening industrial action, Barbara Castle stepped in. It was agreed that the work of the Owen Working Party would be hurried along. Labour's manifesto for the October 1974 election again pledged to phase out pay-beds. The next month, the government announced that it would tackle the pay-beds issue in the first Parliamentary session.

The consultants on the Owen Working Party wanted their pay to be more closely related to the amount of work put in. The government favoured this in so far as it would improve the lot of full-time consultants and reward those who chose to work in unpopular regions and specialties. On the other hand, Barbara Castle was determined to retain the 2/11 'differential' established in 1955. In December 1974, the government formally proposed a new Standard Five Day Contract, with two options, both involving a commitment to ten sessions. Full-time NHS consultants would continue to enjoy the 2/11 differential. Sessions worked above ten a week would be paid. The awards system would be changed to reward commitment to the NHS and the size of the 'supplements' would be reduced by the value of the recipients' earnings from private practice. The consultants would not accept these proposals and took industrial action (which they called 'sanctions'). By March 1975, direct negotiations with the BMA were under way. Castle's position was strengthened by a Review Body recommendation of significant salary increases. The consultants lifted their 'sanctions' and Castle announced that the government had accepted the Review Body report. But the new contract had been abandoned.

On Friday 18 April, Barbara Castle wrote in her diary: 'As David [Owen] and I have agreed, this is the moment to go into the attack on pay-beds.' She announced that legislation would be introduced as soon as Parliamentary time permitted. In August, the government issued a Consultative Document on 'The Separation of Private Practice from NHS Hospitals'. Not only would pay-beds and facilities for private out-patients be withdrawn, but a licensing system for private hospitals would also be set up:

> The aim will be to ensure that the total provision for private medical care after pay-beds are phased out shall not materially exceed, either regionally or for Great Britain as a whole, that which obtained within and outside the NHS in March 1974.

In October, in an attempt to lower the temperature it was announced that a Royal Commission would be established to study the NHS. That autumn's Queen's Speech promised legislation on pay-beds and on the licensing system. With the BMA leadership again threatening disruption, Harold Wilson phoned Castle to suggest that she talk to his old friend Lord Goodman, then retained by the Independent Hospitals Group, a pressure group set up by BUPA to oppose Castle's policy. The BMA's Central Committee for Hospital Medical

Services voted to take industrial action unless the pay-beds issue was referred to the Royal Commission. Castle noted:

> NUPE is making noises about the resumption of industrial action against private patients if consultants refuse to treat NHS ones – and quite right too. Once again, I begin to feel that the only way we shall get phasing out in the end will be by the direct action of the unions.

After much to-ing and fro-ing, the 'Goodman proposals' were announced on 15 December. 1,000 pay-beds would go immediately, and a quango would be established to phase out the rest.

> The criterion for phasing out shall be the reasonable availability of reasonable alternative facilities (including accommodation, services and equipment) within a reasonable geographical distance and to which reasonable access is available to those patients and practitioners desiring to avail themselves of it.

The regulation of the private hospital sector would remain 'subject to further consultation' but any powers 'might be exercised by an independent Board'. The Board would also report to the Social Services Secretary on the feasibility of introducing 'common waiting lists'. For the present, the profession argued that any scheme could 'only operate for urgent cases'; the government however believed NHS and private patients could be 'admitted on grounds of medical priority alone'. The BMA decided to continue industrial action while ballotting its members (this was publicly condemned by Goodman). The Goodman proposals were accepted by 63 per cent of consultants – by four-fifths of the full-timers but less than half of the part-timers. Castle wrote:

> This means that I am saddled with the Goodman proposals and my hopes of modifying them are gone. Yet I am saddled with them in a situation in which it is clear that we need never have accepted this fudged and dangerous compromise, if only Harold hadn't panicked and played into Goodman's hands.

The BMA suspended its 'sanctions'.

In continuing negotiations, Castle suggested to Goodman that the Bill should give the Board powers to restrict the development of large private hospitals. In return, she would 'abandon the overall size control of the private sector outlined in my original consultative document ... (I knew I couldn't get the consultative document proposal through Cabinet anyway)'. The Cabinet agreed that the Board's authorisation would be required for private hospital developments with over 100 beds in London and 75 beds elsewhere. In March, Castle insisted that the Bill refer to 'the progressive withdrawal of accommodation and services' rather than 'the progressive reduction ...' as originally drafted. 'I could not imagine anything more likely to arouse the suspicions of our side that the Goodman proposals were a device for keeping pay-beds indefinitely.'

In April 1976 Jim Callaghan became Prime Minister and replaced Castle by David Ennals. The Health Services Bill became law in November. 1,000 pay-beds were abolished and the Health Services Board was set up with Bernard Dix (from NUPE), Ray Buckton (ASLEF), Dr Derek Stevenson, Dr Cyril Scurr and the Liberal peer Lord Wigoder in the chair. (Stevenson and Wigoder later became directors of medical insurance companies.) In May 1977, the Board published a report on common waiting lists. In May 1978, Ennals formally offered the consultants a new contract of ten sessions, 'with the possibility of extra regular sessions ... The limit on extra sessions would be five, but three for consultants who wanted to do private practice.' Full-timers would enjoy new financial benefits. The awards system would be reformed so that 'outstanding service to the NHS as well as clinical or academic excellence can be sufficient to qualify a consultant for an award'. But further disagreements prevented this contract coming into force. In December, Ennals announced the introduction of common waiting lists for urgent cases and the seriously ill. By 1979, the number of pay-beds had been reduced to 2,400 (from 4,150 in 1976). The Health Services Board had authorised twelve private hospital developments and refused one.

The pay-beds policy was a failure. Between 1976 and 1979, 42 per cent of English pay-beds were 'phased out'. The amount of private practice in NHS hospitals was only slightly reduced – indeed in those three years the number of private patients treated went down by just 3 per cent. (Admittedly, in subsequent years pay-beds would come to play a smaller role in a larger private sector.) Was failure inevitable? The momentum was set by the health service unions, as Castle acknowledged many times in her diaries. At a Cabinet meeting in July 1975, 'I made their blood curdle with warnings of the industrial action health unions would take if I wasn't allowed to legislate for the phasing out of pay-beds. (Thank God for the unions!)' Castle herself strove hard within the constraints she faced – driven in part by personal ambition:

> A fight on this issue would put me back right where I wanted to be in the NEC stakes ... It is I who have had to fight single-handed to get any licensing provisions included at all (they were never in the Manifesto or the Queen's Speech). So I want to be able to claim this unto myself for righteousness in the eyes of our own side.

The media were hostile, as was the public. A BUPA poll in April 1976 found that even among trade unionists, 42 per cent favoured keeping pay-beds compared to 25 per cent who wanted them phased out. True, the consultants' sanctions did not bite hard: 'Even David keeps agreeing they were never operative anyway.' But the BMA certainly gave obsessive, extremist leadership. It may be that Castle could not have pushed the consultants much harder without serious damage to the NHS.

Another constraint was the government's Parliamentary position. In 1974, Labour started without an overall majority. In October it won a tiny majority which was soon lost and it became dependent on the support of Liberals and Ulster Unionists. But this only strengthened the Cabinet's existing contempt for radical change. With even the soft left marginalised, Barbara Castle felt, 'I only know that if I get any control mechanism at all into the legislation it will be a miracle, given the opposition I've got in Cabinet.' In fact, that small miracle took place, at the Cabinet meeting on 25 March 1976:

Shirley [Williams] then said we would be 'attacked' for the licensing proposals. The form of control by the independent board was okay, but she was worried about the figure of 75 beds. If we discouraged the building of private hospitals we should lose a lot of foreign exchange from rich overseas patients. Denis [Healey] backed her pontifically. Harold Lever came nagging back. We really should get this matter into perspective. What did a few private hospitals matter compared with the breakdown of morale in the NHS? We must realise that the view of the profession was that we were trying to undermine private practice. Despite all this the PM nobly discharged his last obligation to me and got all my proposals through. On the figure of beds, however, I suppose it was inevitable he should show his 'neutrality' by yielding a bit. Unfortunately I played into his hands by saying I would be prepared, if it would get agreement, to agree to one hundred beds in London and fifty in the provinces. Harold seized on this to say: 'I suggest one hundred in London and seventy-five in the provinces.'

The mid-1970s would have been an excellent time to nip in the bud the growth of private medicine. But the focus was all on the pay-beds at the expense of giving proper attention to private hospitals, to private practitioners, to the sources of the demand for, as well as the supply of, private treatment.

The government should have tried to tackle private medicine as a whole. True, Castle and Owen were not simply phasing out pay-beds. Castle was concerned by the prospect of private hospital developments. She wrote in February 1975 that David Owen

gets quite tetchy at the idea of our trying to control the quantity of beds in the private hospitals that will undoubtedly spring up everywhere. He is far more reactionary about this than my officials are! I say firmly that I see no reason why I should not announce that I intend to keep the number of private beds to the levels of the pay-beds currently allowed in the NHS. I am convinced that we have got to fight like hell to prevent the building up of a vast empire of private medicine. And with not enough money to keep the NHS expanding and improving as it ought, our whole policy is in danger.

But the Consultative Document of that August was aptly entitled 'The Separation of Private Practice from NHS Hospitals'. It assumed that private hospitals would grow up to replace the pay-beds and suggested merely that the total private sector should not end up 'materially larger'. This was an exceedingly modest restriction – and one which was subsequently dropped. Owen suggested introducing what Castle described as 'an ingenious plan' for moving to ' "consolidated" waiting lists ... under which private patients would have to wait their turn with NHS patients in the medical priority queue'. But this idea was effectively abandoned (indeed the Tories under Mrs Thatcher strengthened slightly the procedures David Ennals instituted).

All concerned on the government's side sought to change the consultants' contract. But the negotiations dragged on for five years and resulted in a marginal reform of the awards system and the effective destruction of the 1955 'differential' introduced by the Conservatives. Controlling private hospital developments and changing the consultants' contract would have limited the supply of commercial medicine. But negligible attention was paid to the demand for private treatment – and without that reduced, the policy was almost bound to come unstuck. The pay-beds policy took energy away from more important battles over the contract and over the financing of the Health Service. The left called for the abolition of private medicine altogether, and this was demanded by Labour Party Conference in 1975. But with Labour already installed in government and already committed to a different policy, this was empty posturing.

In BUPA's view, Labour's policy had:

> formalised the existence and *raison d'être* of the independent health sector and far from weakening its position the legislation has proved instrumental in bringing about much needed stability, whereby consultants use independent hospital facilities, occupancy levels increase and hospitals become economically viable, future markets are assured and financial institutions are willing to invest in the private industry.

Notes

[1] Gordon Forsyth, 'The Semantics of Health Care Policy and the Inevitability of Regulation' in Gordon McLachlan and Alan Maynard (eds), *The Public/Private Mix for Health*, Nuffield Provincial Hospitals Trust, 1982.
[2] Harry Eckstein, *The English Health Service*, Harvard University Press, 1959.

This work is the source of much of the information and argument in the present chapter.
[3] Samuel Mencher, *Private Practice in Britain*, Occasional Papers in Social Administration No.24, G. Bell and Sons, 1967.
[4] Eckstein, op.cit.
[5] Ibid.
[6] Quoted in John E. Pater, *The Making of the National Health Service*, King Edward's Hospital Fund for London, 1981. This work is the source of much of the information and argument in the present chapter.
[7] Eckstein, op.cit.
[8] An observation made by Richard Titmuss, cited in ibid.
[9] Eckstein, op.cit.
[10] Quoted in Rudolf Klein, *The Politics of the National Health Service*, Longman, 1983.
[11] Pater, op.cit.
[12] *Hansard*, 30 April 1946.
[13] The final section of this chapter draws heavily on Barbara Castle, *The Castle Diaries 1974-76*, Weidenfeld and Nicholson, 1980, and also on Rudolf Klein, 'Ideology, Class and the National Health Service', *Journal of Health Politics, Policy and Law*, Vol.4 No.3, Fall 1979.

Chapter 2

Thatcherism and Commercial Medicine

It is sometimes suggested that the rapid expansion of the commercial medical sector since 1979 is the result of 'market forces' supplemented by dissatisfaction with the National Health Service. Recent expansion can be attributed as much to the highly visible hand of the government as to the 'hidden hand' of the market. The Treasury and many – perhaps most – Cabinet Ministers have been anxious to see reduced NHS spending and the introduction of policies of piecemeal privatisation. However, it is also true that individual Ministers of Health and Secretaries of State for Social Services have varied in their commitment to private medicine. Despite all the attention to cuts, the NHS has not been subject to the swingeing changes many expected. Nor has private medicine, despite its initial surge, grown at the rate expected by its most eager advocates.

Had public support for the principles of the NHS been less, none of the reasons for believing the National Health Service superior to private systems – grudgingly acknowledged by many Conservatives – would have prevailed and the government would have made radical changes in the way the services are financed, organised and delivered. The government's support for the private sector has been piecemeal, and while Ministers have looked long and hard at alternatives, drastic changes have not been implemented, nor, in the immediate future, are they likely to be.

This is not to understate the significance of the policies already adopted. Some areas of the country, like the London health districts, have been told to cut up to one-seventh of their expenditure over a ten-year period. At the same time the gap between rich and poor, the ageing of the population and the increasing reliance of the poor on state benefits, have resulted in rising ill health after the fall in the 1970s. Whatever success has been achieved in defending the NHS is offset by the growing pressures upon it.

The Thatcher government's policies towards the NHS and private medicine cannot simply be read off from its ideological assumptions. The Cabinet is divided between a pragmatic course and another involving the fundamentals of 'free market' theory.

Conservative 'Market Theory'

The far right of the Conservative Party is fundamentally opposed to the National Health Service, believing that only the 'market' can provide medical care efficiently. Since its inception in 1948 the NHS has come under its continual attack, but only since the 1960s have right-wing intellectuals have begun to present alternatives.

The most influential have been the Institute of Economic Affairs, a group of professional reactionaries inspired by the 'free market' texts of Hayek, Friedman and others. Mingling esoteric economics with Victorian morality their ideas met support only in economics and social science departments where their ideas were contrasted with 'mainstream views'. The arguments of the different right-wing writers on health are complex, not because of their sophistication (not always in evidence) but rather because they are so confused about what type of alternative system they want. For some, it is the American medical care system, for others it is a utopian free market, but what unites them all is their opposition to the basic characteristics of the NHS (good and bad). Certainly, the National Health Service was one of the main 'socialist' baddies that all virile free-marketeers, at some time in their career, had to denounce. Even Hayek came down from his high theoretical perch to say nasty things about it:

> It may seem harsh, but it is probably in the interest of all under a free system, that those with full earning capacity should be cured rapidly of a temporary and not dangerous disablement at the expense of some neglect of the aged and mortally ill. Where

systems of state medicine operate, we generally find that those who could be promptly restored to full activity have to wait long periods because all the hospital facilities are taken up by people who will never again contribute to the needs of the rest.[1]

Arthur Seldon, chief populariser of the IEA, argues that too little has been spent on maintaining the nation's health, on the ground that total expenditures on health care in the USA, which is 'mostly private', have been rising faster than in Britain. There are other defects: doctors emigrate to countries where they are less restricted, consumers feel no sense of control over the NHS (or other public services) and doctors are consulted over trifling ailments, while the lack of competition produces unaccountable bureaucracies. The best way to improve the general welfare is by 'putting welfare by stages onto the market'. Seldon is confident that the substitution of private welfare for public would create a new storehouse of wealth such that 'no new pensioner will have known poverty'. We may suppose that Hayek (calling for 'some neglect of the aged and mortally ill') was merely the more candid of the two. Nevertheless some of Seldon's criticisms do coincide with many people's experience. Patients often do feel a lack of choice within the NHS, and sometimes use services for (what doctors see as) trifling ailments. (Ironically if choice were expanded such inappropriate use could well grow.)

Sixteen years later, Seldon was arguing:

The NHS must fail to supply the British people with the best medical care they want because it prevents them from paying for services that suit their personal family requirements, circumstances and preferences.[2]

In the 1960s the IEA was hardly taken seriously, but now, with the ascendency of Thatcher, its ideas were granted some credence.

In April 1984, the Institute published *State Expenditure: A Study in Waste*, by Liverpool University's Professor Patrick Minford. This called for public expenditure cuts of £43 billion by 1990 and contained two sharp declarations of policy. First:

...the assumption will be that health services are paid for by the individual and that he buys full health insurance, structured in a normal way with near 100 per cent insurance for very serious bills.

Second: 'Selling off hospitals, though not politically easy, is a self-contained operation which, once carried out, guarantees future efficiency.'[3]

Even the *Times* took exception to Minford's scheme, arguing that private medical insurance on which his suggestions were based covered only a limited number of items, and that if services were privatised that they would become inefficient because of their captive market.[4]

The IEA was not the only 'independent' policy group to catch the attentions of Tory MPs. For several years the Adam Smith Institute has been publishing its slimmer, more impatient, attacks on all aspects of the public sector. In October 1984, for example, the Institute published a report on health and social services, part of its 'Omega Project' – 'the most complete review of the activity of government ever undertaken in Britain'.[5] This group recommends the adoption of American-style 'Health Maintenance Organisations' in place of the NHS. The authors of the report included Hugh Elwell, consultant to Private Patients Plan and other commercial medicine companies.

These perspectives are widely shared among the current breed of dry Conservaties. The IEA's *Litmus Papers* were published by the Centre for Policy Studies, created by Margaret Thatcher and Sir Keith Joseph. Seldon's work with the IEA has earned him an OBE, while Professor Minford, says the *Times*, is 'occasionally consulted by the Prime Minister'.[6] However Ministers have been careful not to endorse these views explicitly. The *Daily Telegraph* reported only that Professor Minford's paper would be studied 'closely'.[7]

In October 1983, the Bow Group – whose members have included several Cabinet Ministers – published *Beveridge and the Bow Group Generation*, which stated:

When at the Party Conference last October the Prime Minister declared that the Health Service was safe with us, a short-term political gain may have been achieved, but the election should, and could, have been won without that pledge.

The National Health Service was accused of an 'in-built tendency to expand indiscriminately'. Moreover, the NHS did not aim to achieve 'equality of treatment':

> Adequate health care, yes, but the continued existence of a private sector within and outside the NHS illustrates that in practice such equality has only ever existed in the minds of ideologically-motivated politicians.

The Bow Group's alternative was that:

> Fiscal encouragement should be given to individuals who arrange for their own health insurance and employers should be encouraged to establish mutual health funds which would be 'contracted out' in the same way that occupational pensions currently are. Hospitals and doctors would contract with the health authorities and the private sector on an item of service payment basis within a framework of overall cost control.[8]

Exactly a year earlier, the Selsdon Group had published a pamphlet alleging that the NHS was 'the most obvious failing of the welfare state' which should be 'privatised entirely':

> We would be content to see the principles of the Health Service preserved for those who are gravely ill. However, those requiring treatment for predictable and easily curable diseases would be expected to pay for their own treatment through insurance schemes.

Unlike the IEA and the ASI, the Bow and Selsdon groups define themselves as linked to the Conservative Party. Furthermore, since these were publications for general distribution we may infer that policies discussed in private were even more radical.

But while the right-wing radicals would like to plunge the knife deep into the heart of the National Health Service, those actually in charge have been somewhat more cautious. The Prime Minister's aides dismissed the infamous Think Tank suggestions as 'politically inept' while a former Health Minister, Kenneth Clarke, has questioned publicly the value of private medical insurance and says that he would like to see the private sector 'somewhat larger, not vastly larger' and that 'private provision is not necessarily more efficient or cost effective'. Former Social Services Secretary Patrick Jenkin was replaced by the 'drier' Norman Fowler. However, even he soon adopted the language of pragmatism:

> What the advocates of compulsory [medical] insurance have to show is that it is a more effective and efficient way of providing patient care at reasonable cost. I do not believe that case can be sustained.[9]

Are these the final statements a Conservative government is likely to make?

As we have argued, support for the commercialisation of health services is very widely spread in the Conservative Party. These are not simply the ideas of a 'lunatic fringe' of academics. DHSS Ministers stand against the more radical proposals and it would certainly augur a major change in their outlook for them to take on board full commercialisation. However, the radical proposals are long-term options under consideration within the Conservative Party. If other factors secure the Tories' popularity, Mrs Thatcher may decide to think again.

Health Service Cuts

Labour's representatives as well as those of the professional bodies and the unions have faced an uphill struggle against health service cuts. The government, for its part, has had an equally difficult job convincing even its own supporters that it is not randomly closing down local hospitals. There are several reasons for this dilemma, related largely to the complex nature of NHS financing.

The best account of the apparent incompatibility of Ministerial claims of NHS 'growth' with people's experience of 'cuts' has been provided by the cross-party Social Services Committee of the House of Commons. In its 1986 report on Public Expenditure, the committee points out that in 'cost' terms NHS spending grew by 19.3 per cent between 1979 and 1985.[10] However, that figure takes account only of inflation in the economy generally while the NHS has faced rises in pay

and prices which exceed that general rate. Indeed the increase
in NHS spending in 'volume' terms was just 10.5 per cent in
that period. That growth was largely accounted for by the cost
of the family practitioner services which are not controlled by
government cash limits. In the hospital sector, the growth in
expenditure in 'volume' terms was a mere 6.3 per cent.
Ministers have consistently argued that resources have been
found by improving the efficiency of the NHS and taking the
'cost improvement programmes' into account the increase in
'volume' terms in the spending on the hospital service between
1979 and 1985 was 8.8 per cent. The spending increase
between 1979 and 1980 was hardly characteristic of Mrs
Thatcher's administration. Between 1980 and 1985 the
growth in 'volume' terms of the hospital budget, even taking
efficiency measures into account, came to 5.6 per cent. While
a very small figure when set next to ministerial claims, that
still however appears to support the Thatcher government's
argument that NHS spending has grown under its care.

The next stage in the debate is the recognition that the need
for health care is not static. While still Minister for Health,
Barney Hayhoe acknowledged that the resources of the NHS
needed to grow by 2 per cent every year 'in order to meet the
pressures' of an ageing population, medical advance and
government objectives. It is these calls on NHS services which
finally bring down the official image of a prospering National
Health Service. To quote the Social Services Committee:

> The most telling way of representing the shortfall is to say that
> between 1980-81 and 1985-86 the cumulative total underfunding
> of the Hospital and Community Health Services current account
> was £1.325 billion at 1985-86 prices, after taking full account of
> the cash-releasing cost improvements.

With a General Election imminent, the public expenditure
statement of November 1986 was comparatively generous
towards the NHS, but even so represented an increase in the
hospital budget of only 1.4 per cent, and that assumed that the
inflation rate experienced by the NHS in 1987-88 would be
just 3.75 per cent.

Ministers' concern about 'overmanning' in the NHS may

have been inspired in part by the desire to encourage Health
Authorities to make use of commercial facilities.

A DHSS Circular pointed out:

> Where absolute increases in manpower are proposed they
> should be specifically and directly linked to absolute increases in
> the volume or quantity of services to be provided. But even then it
> should not be assumed that increases in directly employed staff
> are necessarily required. The private sector can make a valuable
> contribution to the development of health services.

Health Authority strategic plans now encompass the
assumption that services can be maintained only by shedding
'ancillary' jobs. In fact, no workers in the NHS are truly
'ancillary', all are mutually dependent. The sad thing for the
NHS is that when workers are pushed beyond the point of
endurance into taking industrial action, then both they and
the patients suffer – the 1982 health dispute led to an increase
in the NHS waiting list of 121,000.

Of course, industrial conflict in the NHS and growing
waiting lists provide free advertising for commercial medicine
and combined with financial restrictions form a major assault
on hospital services. As Gene Burleson of American Medical
International puts it, 'The cuts in the NHS create a demand
for private care.'[11]

Leaving these arguments aside, how has the Conservative
government treated the NHS? One important goal has been to
undermine the status of the NHS as a service provided by the
state as a right, free when needed. Ministers have opened
private hospitals and encouraged Health Authorities to make
use of their facilities. They have arranged cut-price medical
cover for civil servants and regularly consulted with the
leading lights of the private sector. The trade directory of the
American commercial hospital chains warmly applauded
such encouragements:

> Opportunities are especially bright in countries with ailing
> national health systems such as England. Government support
> for private sector build-up has been especially encouraging for the
> American companies operating there.[12]

A more direct attack on the principles of the NHS, and on patients, has been the increases in, and extension of, prescription charges and user fees. Between 1979 and 1986 the NHS prescription charge was raised from 20p to £2.20. In 1979 patients paid the full cost of routine dental care up to a maximum of £5; by 1985, patients had to pay the full cost up to £17, and in addition 40 per cent of any further costs up to a maximum payment of £115. The government also introduced hospital charges for overseas patients, although many foreigners receive free treatment under reciprocal schemes and the administrative costs of collection have probably exceeded the income generated. At the time many saw the introduction of charges for foreign patients as paving the way for a more general policy of charges for NHS users.

Health Authorities have also been encouraged to turn to charitable endeavours to raise extra money in fund drives reminiscent of pre-war 'flag days'. This lends charitable connotations to the NHS and helps erode the idea that medical treatment is a right. Besides, charities and the voluntary sector themselves need money, and NHS fund raising, if successful, could seriously impair their own services. Fund raising drives also distort health-service planning – money goes to glamorous specialities and technologies, which involve running costs drawn from local budgets.

Tired of 'consensus management' in the NHS, and wishing to stamp its authoritarian conceptions of 'leadership' and 'the right to manage' over all of society, the government has been looking for ways to introduce mainstream business practice into the National Health Service. On the advice of Roy Griffiths, Managing Director of Sainsbury's, one of the country's most profitable retail chains, a plan was adopted to appoint business people on short-term contracts into the NHS's top jobs.

Alongside this, the government has been pressurising Health Authorities to 'contract out' domestic, catering and laundry services, in an attempt to drive down wages and conditions. The proportion of domestic, catering and laundry services contracted out actually declined during the first Thatcher administration, and feverish attempts to install contractors employing workers at unacceptable rates of pay have led to strikes and allegations of falling standards.

Commercial Medicine

Turning to commercial medicine itself, the most important policy change so far extends the controversial principle which was carried forward from the voluntary hospitals before the NHS – the right of consultants to undertake private practice.

Until 1979, consultants came in four varieties: those with full-time contracts; those with maximum part-time contracts, obliged to give a more or less full commitment to the NHS but able to practise privately and paid 9/11 of the full-time salary; other 'part-time' consultants, paid according to the number of sessions worked; and 'honorary' consultants, not paid at all. Since 1980, however, full-time consultants have had the right to 'earn' up to 10 per cent of their NHS income from private practice without any deduction from their salary. Also, the 'maximum part-timers' are now paid 10/11 of the full-time salary. As a result, many consultants switched contracts. The number of maximum part-timers rose by 28 per cent in 1979-80 and the number choosing 'full-time' work rose by 7 per cent that year and by 5 per cent in 1980-81.

In the words of David Bolt, at the time the chief negotiator for the consultants:

> In many ways both of these changes were an encouragement to private practice; the whole-time consultant could now carry out private work, where previously he had been completely barred from so doing; similarly the financial loss that had been involved for the maximum part-timer in giving up the pay for two sessions was effectively halved, and this fact provided a positive encouragement to those who had previously had great doubts and anxieties as to whether they would earn enough to offset their losses.[13]

One other policy greatly encouraged the desire of consultants to undertake private work and to involve themselves more closely in private sector growth. In his 1981 Budget, the Chancellor of the Exchequer introduced the Business Start-Up Scheme (later the Business Expansion Scheme) which gave Treasury support to small investors in new companies. This has been used by consultants to invest in private clinics and has given a big boost to those consultants eager to attract City finance to their schemes.

Pay beds formed another issue of concern to consultants.

The 1974-79 Labour government was committed to phasing out private practice from NHS hospitals, although pay-beds were reduced by only 40 per cent and the number of patients treated declined hardly at all. The Conservatives have increased pay-bed numbers but pay-bed charges have also been increased, encouraging private patients to use the commercial sector. Ironically, while this has strengthened the private hospitals, it has meant higher costs for the medical insurers. Linked to the policy over pay-beds has been Conservative policy towards private hospital development. The former Labour government set up the Health Services Board to preside over the phasing out of pay-beds and to monitor and, to a strictly limited degree, control the development of private hospitals. The new Conservative government abolished the Board. Since 1980 new developments have required authorisation from the Social Services Secretary only when they would involve at least 120 beds or would take place in especially designated districts, of which there are none. As a result, no hospital developer has needed to seek authorisation since 1980. Hospital companies can therefore develop where they like, even in areas already saturated by private facilities.

The Department of the Environment has also been promoting commercial medicine. Planning restrictions have been weakened. In 1980, a DOE Circular to local planning authorities aimed 'to ensure that development is only prevented or restricted when this serves a clear planning purpose and the economic effects have been taken into account.'[14] The following year, another Circular included a Memorandum which insisted that authorities'

> decisions in respect of each application will continue to be based solely on planning considerations, regardless of whether, in their view, the proposal to develop a private nursing home or hospital would be prejudicial to the interests of the National Health Service. Nor should their decision be influenced by the fact that the proposed development is in the private sector rather than the public sector.[16]

To paraphrase, the alleged economic advantages of private hospital developments are 'planning considerations' while any arguments about their effects on local NHS services are to be disregarded.

A rather more difficult policy to implement concerns the NHS's relationship to the private sector. In 1981 a DHSS circular – drafted by Stanley Davis, General Secretary of the Registered Nursing Homes Association – encouraged Health Authorities to use commercial medical facilities. This circular stated:

> When planning the provision of NHS services (including short-term needs) health authorities should take into account the current and planned facilities available in the independent sector.[16]

This Circular also overturned the previous rule that Health Authorities were not allowed to contract with profit-making organisations.

In February 1983 an informal Circular was sent to chairs of Regional Health Authorities, claiming:

> Although the private sector of health care is comparatively small, the benefits of partnership with it are disproportionate to its size ... Independent sector capital might be used to provide expensive equipment for, say, a district general hospital on the basis of a leasing/rental agreement (or for joint use by an NHS or independent hospital). [Pay beds could be] managed for a fee by the independent sector. [Wards could be] sold to the independent sector, which would run [them] outside the NHS but would have guaranteed access to the main hospital facilities.[1]

What the Private Sector Thinks

Government support so far has been too cautious to ensure stable growth within the private sector. In consequence, development has been uneven and erratic, and there is a strong feeling within the private sector that they have been 'let down' by Ministers.

Former Health Minister Dr Gerard Vaughan openly looked forward to the private sector providing 25 per cent of medical treatment in the country. Electoral commitments, however, have stayed the government's hand. Furthermore, the indigenous private sector is mostly composed of small hospitals and commercial chains of a yet limited size. The larger groups are American, so that if the government had acted to provide even larger incentives to the private sector it would have speeded the dominance of the Americans, with possibly unfavourable electoral consequences.

What can we expect in the future? One extreme possibility remains the wholesale dismantling of the National Health Service, or at least the replacement of its tax-funding by a form of insurance. Whether either of these becomes politically feasible depends as much on the Conservatives' popularity as it does on moves within the party or on technical arguments about the alternatives to the NHS. There is certainly considerable evidence that a radical agenda for the health service is taken seriously. The Conservative government has repeatedly looked at alternatives to the inherited, comprehensive, tax-financed health system.

The 1979 Conservative Manifesto declared:

> The Royal Commission is studying the financing of health care and any examination of possible longer term changes _ for example greater reliance on the insurance principle – must await their report.

The Commission rejected the insurance option, but this did not halt the government's 'examination of possible longer term changes'. In June 1981, a working party was set up to examine ways in which the National Health Service could be privatised. Civil servants were sent to the USA, Australia, France, West Germany, Holland and Scandinavia to study their medical systems. But in July 1982 the Norman Fowler announced:

> The government has no plans to change the present system of financing largely through taxation, and will continue to review the scope for introducing more cost consciousness and consumer choice and for increasing private provision which is already expanding.

Treasury civil servants, however, are understood to have drawn up plans for the privatisation of the NHS which were discussed in a series of Cabinet Committee meetings. In September 1982, the Central Policy Review Staff (the 'Think Tank') produced a report outlining possible ways of reducing public expenditure. Two options were defined: 'partial change' including charges for visits to GPs and stays in hospital and 'comprehensive change' including replacing the NHS by an insurance-based system. This report was sent to Ministers but the 'wets' were able to stop it being discussed in Cabinet. The report was leaked to the *Economist* and led to the Prime Minister's famous pledge:

> The NHS is safe with us. The principle that adequate health care should be provided to all, regardless of ability to pay, must be the foundation of any arrangements for financing the NHS.

Note that Mrs Thatcher promised only 'adequate' health care, and she left open the possibility of different 'arrangements for financing the NHS'.

Collaboration Plans

There is growing pressure from the private sector for measures to assist its 'co-operation' with the National Health Service and help stabilise private sector growth. One of the proposals that has been doing the rounds concerns the commercial sector and NHS resource allocation. The present system of resource allocation in the NHS was established by the Labour government in 1976. The RAWP system (named after the Resource Allocation Working Party) was in many respects a progressive proposal to bring about the long-term equalisation of funding between the health regions. In practice, it has been used to starve inner-city areas of funds.

A DHSS-funded study of private medicine by the Medical Care Research Unit at the University of Sheffield showed the enormous variation from one health region to another in the extent to which elective operations – that is, those non-urgent procedures for which NHS patients would expect to wait – were carried out privately. The report argued, 'If NHS resources are to be distributed in proportion to the need for health care in each region, the allocation might have to take the size of the private sector into account.'[18] While these ideas were already current inside the DHSS and among its academic advisors, the wording and presentation of the study suggested that the Sheffield team's work was preparatory to the implementation of the policy.

The effect of this proposal would be the devastation of NHS hospital services in London and the Thames Regions – areas

which are already RAWP 'losers' and which also contain high
numbers of private hospitals and beds. Those able to to so
would feel forced to purchase private medical insurance, and
as the numbers going private increased, the National Health
Service would be cut accordingly. As a consequence the NHS
would be unable to provide universal coverage in these
Regions. The next step could be to take money away from
these regions with large numbers of nursing homes, abortion
clinics or private GP clinics and so on. The final step would be
to argue that the overall budget for the NHS should take
account of private medicine. In a Parliamentary question, the
Social Services Secretary was asked whether he had
considered 'taking account of the distribution of private
medical resources when determining RAWP allocations'. His
reply was highly ambiguous:

> We allocate additional resources on the basis of our judgement of
> the relative needs of the Regions at the relevant time and the
> principles laid down by the Resource Allocation Working Party
> are our main but not our only guide.[19]

The commercial medical sector frequently finds itself
divided on government policy. One prominent point of
division concerns the Health Services Board, set up by the
1974-79 Labour government to phase out pay-beds but
scrapped in 1980. Since then influential figures inside the
private sector, such as Oliver Rowell, General Manager of
Nuffield Hospitals, have called for its resurrection. This
indicates that the private sector has not been able to form
stable cartels, with the result that in some areas hospitals are
now in active competition for patients. Without 'guidance'
from a quango, and in lieu of the formation of a unified and
aggressive trade association of all the private hospitals, we can
expect a severe 'shake-out' in the commercial sector.

Naturally, the commercial sector is looking for ways of
reducing the costs of its operations and the costs of private
medical insurance. It is dissatisfied with the current level of
tax allowances available for private cover and has been
lobbying hard for their extension.

Hugh Elwell, an influential private sector expert, has
called for

the provision of tax-relief to health insurance premiums to those aged 65 and older ... The loss of revenue due to this tax provision is difficult to assess – projections vary from £5 million to £15 million.[20]

During the 1983 election campaign Norman Fowler said that extra tax concessions 'would be something for a future Conservative government to consider'.[21] And in November 1983, Nigel Lawson pointed out: 'There are enormous tax incentives for pensions at the present time, though not for health care or education. That is one of the things we are discussing and looking into at the moment.'[22] On the other hand, the government is opposed to the expansion of company 'perks' and it is clear that company schemes fall within this description (although BUPA disagrees).[23] On the other hand, a further proposal which has been canvassed is the extension of VAT to medical insurance on the grounds that it is a luxury service. The *Financial Times* observes, 'How can anyone seriously maintain that private health and education should be exempt from VAT, especially when good public sector substitutes exist?'

The private sector also wants drugs to be made available at NHS prices to private patients. According to Hugh Elwell,

A pledge to do this was enshrined in Conservative Party manifestos in the 1970s, but was unaccountably missing from those of the last two General Elections. This small encouragement, however, would cost little but would be a valuable means of involving family doctors in private medicine.

Although this option remains open, it seems unlikely to be acted upon in the short term. According to the former Health Minister Kenneth Clarke:

The possibility of providing prescribed medicines to private patients through the National Health Service has been raised with successive governments by representatives of the medical profession but has not been adopted because of the additional costs involved.[24]

The daily course of political life is not smooth. The Thatcher government, despite all its claims to radicalism, has not been able to implement those policies towards the NHS which would be closest to its heart. The NHS has sustained some damage – through financial stringency rather than ideological initiatives – but this has been relatively limited. The commercial sector, fed so many promises in the past, feels hamstrung. However Conservative government support for commercial medicine will continue and will, for the most part, help to counter its economic difficulties. In the longer term – that is, under a new Conservative administration dominated by 'dry' ministers – the National Health Service may well be relegated from its present role as a universal, comprehensive service to that of a 'safety net'.

Notes

[1] Quoted in Vic George and Paul Wilding, *Ideology and Social Welfare*, Routledge and Kegan Paul, 1976, p.140.

[2] A.Seldon (ed.), *The Litmus Papers: A National Health Disservice*, Centre for Policy Studies, 1980.

[3] Patrick Minford, 'State Expenditure: A Study in Waste', supplement to *Economic Affairs*, April-June 1984.

[4] *Times*, 16 April 1984.

[5] Adam Smith Institute, *The Omega File: Health and Social Service Policy*, The Institute, 1984.

[6] *Times*, 16 April 1984.

[7] *Daily Telegraph*, 16 April 1984.

[8] Michael Lingers, *Beveridge and the Bow Group Generation*, Bow Publications, 1983.

[9] *Guardian*, 13 December 1983.

[10] Fourth Report of the Social Services Committee, Session 1985-86, *Public Expenditure on the Social Services*, House of Commons paper 387, ordered to be printed 2 July 1986.

[11] Quoted in *Thinking of Going Private?*, NHS Consultants' Association/NHS Unlimited, 1984.

[12] Federation of American Hospitals and the Association of Investor-Owned Hospitals, *1983 Directory of Investor-Owned Hospitals and Hospital Management Companies*, FAH and AIOH, 1982.

[13] Quoted in *Independent Medical Care*, February 1984.

[14] Department of the Environment, Circular 22/80.

[15] Department of the Environment, Circular 2/81.

[16] DHSS, Circular HC(81)1.

[17] This circular was published in full in *The Health Services*, 3 June 1983.

[18] B.T.Williams, J.P.Nicholl, K.J.Thomas and J.Knowelden, 'Analysis of the Work of Private Hospitals in England and Wales 1981', *British Medical Journal*, 18 August 1984.

[19] Written Answer, *Hansard*, 24 July 1984.

[20] Hugh Elwell, 'NHS Lessons Norman Fowler Has Yet to Hammer Home',

Daily Telegraph, 26 October 1983.
[21] Quoted in NHS Unlimited, *Briefing 7*, 1983.
[22] Quoted in *Times*, 24 November 1983.
[23] See the Introduction by Lord Wigoder to BUPA's 1983 Annual Report.
[24] Written Answer, *Hansard*, 23 February 1984.

Chapter 3
Private Medical Insurance

Only a small and declining proportion – presently around 20 per cent – of those seeking private treatment are able to pay for it over the counter. This chapter will examine how and why the insurance market has grown despite the existence of National Health Service, how it has changed and the problems it faces.

The leading medical insurance companies have not simply provided the finance for the expansion of commercial medicine, they have nurtured and shaped it. If in time past private medicine was essentially a personal contract between a doctor and patient, today it is increasingly a business in which a financial intermediary – the insurance company – plays a growing role. The number of medical insurance customers today (they are known in the business as 'subscribers') hovers around 2 million, but this figure is more than doubled when dependents are included. The majority of customers are well-off, though increasing numbers are employees of medium-size to large companies, to whom the option of 'going private' has become a symbol of success according to market analysts. 'If there is one benefit that is seen as the prized perk after the company car', says one observer, 'it seems to be private medical insurance.'[1] But private medical insurance is more than simply a 'prized perk', more than an indicator that its holder has become one of Mrs Thatcher's chosen few. Private medical insurance and its substantial growth in the 1970s and 80s shows that the better-off groups in society are not willing to accept the limits on public services that successive governments have imposed. G. David Lock, chief of Private Patients Plan, the second largest insurance group, claims that, 'Political opinion has moved greatly in favour of self-help and away from a suffocatingly protective welfare state.'[2] The government agrees with him. To them private medical insurance is not merely an escape route from a declining NHS for themselves and their supporters, it is one of the symbols of a vigorous new capitalism, shorn of the welfare state.

It was not always so. At one point, in the mid-1940s, the forerunners of the present insurance companies were on the verge of giving up. Like the dinosaurs, they had outlived their function. Who in their right mind would want to pay for medical care when it could be obtained for free? Remarkable though it seems, the dinosaurs were able to lose a little weight, don some new clothes, and emerge resplendent as the ideal lifestyle consumer good of Thatcher's Britain. Gone is the image of dusty, spider-written ledgers. In its place, the brash new image is that of smart hospital accommodation, smiling, crinkly-faced medics, colour television and high tech equipment. The medical insurance industry is more than just a way of paying for the world of private practice, it seeks to embody and personify that world. This, as we shall see, is its foremost sales gimmick.

The Companies

Three companies provide around 90 per cent of private medical insurance in Britain. These are British United Provident Association (BUPA), Private Patients Plan (PPP) and Western Provident Association (WPA). BUPA is the largest with around 62 per cent of the market, followed by PPP with a 19 per cent share. WPA, based in the Bristol area, has 7 per cent, and the titbits are shared between a sprinkling of other 'non-profit' groups and a growing number of new market entrants, several with links to foreign multinationals, one of which, Health First, from North America, is spending heavily on promotion to expand its market share.

One of the common misconceptions about BUPA and the other provident associations concerns their 'non-profit' status. They are not charitable organisations as many people think, and as their propaganda seems to imply. In fact, they operate along strictly commercial lines. But there are crucial differences between them and the offshoots of large commercial groups who are now competing for a share of the market. For the provident associations, private medicine is not simply a business, it is a crusade. The provident associations can rightly claim to have undergone risks to re-establish private medicine in the post-war period that no investor-owned organisation would have touched. It is this missionary purpose which makes provident associations rather unusual commercial entities. Profits are important, but their primary purpose has been to conserve the privileges of medical elite and set enough aside to expand the cause of private medicine and ensure that a small section of the population could retain its privileges in the face of the equalising thrust of social democracy.

The managers of the provident associations have never needed to justify their actions to shareholders since none exist. These organisations are 'non-profit distributing', limited by guarantee and run by 'guarantors' (known as Governors) – a self-selected clique of people with connections. Company profits – 'surpluses' as they are coyly called – therefore go back to the organisation, to be used for purposes decided by the guarantors. This status gives these companies several substantial benefits. They do not have to pay corporation tax on their profits, and they can take advantage of the wonderful image of being 'non-profit' organisations, and therefore having only their 'subscribers' interests at heart.

In every important respect, however, they are ordinary insurance companies, governed by the same statutory instruments and regulations, with the same scrupulous regard to the protection of their assets.[3]

Post-War Origins

Private medical insurance existed long before Margaret Thatcher took up residence at No.10 Downing Street, although in her the supporters of private medicine found a Prime Minister who was willing to let her approval of commercial medicine be known, and more than willing to use private facilities, avoiding the NHS. Like many of her adopted class, she appears to believe that she has a public duty to use private facilities, leaving the NHS to those who cannot afford them.

The content and tone of the following statement, drawn

from BUPA's second annual report (in 1949), following the unification of the existing provident associations, imparts a strong sense of the meaning of the association to both its guarantors and subscribers:

> The Governors feel ... that they are making a not unimportant contribution to the efforts of the middle class to maintain the amenities and standards to which they have become accustomed. It is their aim not only to continue this work so long as there is a need, but to extend its scope.[4]

Medical insurance has had to emerge from its limited social and economic base as an individual act of purchase to become part of the 'private welfare state', that system of 'top hat' pensions, insurances, perks and hand-outs first described twenty years ago by socialist academic Richard Titmuss.[5]

Today's provident associations were amalgamations of previous regional hospital pre-payment schemes, and were formed by consultants, businessmen (like Lord Nuffield, sponsor of BUPA, and Sir Bernard Docker, sponsor of PPP) and the administrators of the previous provident schemes.

The origins of the provident associations lay in the shambolic patchwork of private, public and voluntary hospital services that existed before the creation of the NHS. BUPA's own beginnings can be traced back to St Thomas's Hospital, today a leading NHS teaching hospital (still with strong links to BUPA), and that institution's need to generate extra income from middle-class patients.[6]

During the war there were 37 separate provident schemes, only nine of these members of a national association. Plainly, not all could survive the organisational changes that were already occurring in hospital care. Driven perhaps by his strong sense of identification with the middle class, Lord Nuffield played the determining role in bringing about the amalgamation of these societies, mainly by acting as guarantor to individual societies, by attempting to create uniform standards and by promoting a unified scheme. The role was similar to that played by the large Rockefeller and Carnegie foundations in the reform of American medical education following the First World War.[7]

On the eve of the creation of the NHS even the stronger provident societies faced possible eclipse, as was most certainly the fate of the working-class contributory schemes. Nuffield's personal financial backing was announced at a conference of all the societies in 1946. These groups and individuals judged that the lure of snobbery and privacy would enable the provident associations to retain their most loyal customers, and with the return of a Conservative government, expand from there. The first annual report of the amalgamated British United Provident Association was rather glum in tone: 'Present conditions cannot, for various reason, be described as favourable for rapid development or expansion.' An underwriting deficit was made, and membership fell to below 34,000.[8]

The Hospital Service Plan (later Private Patients Plan) had similar origins though, with its regional base in London, it retained stronger links with the British Medical Association. PPP's first advertisements (in 1946) asked, 'Can you afford to wait for the NHS?' Another carried the by-line 'freedom from fear'. WPA, the third largest provident association, was established in 1945. Based in Bristol, it has refused merger entreaties from the larger companies. There are several other 'non-profit-making' groups. These include the Bristol Contributory Welfare Association (founded in 1935), the fourth largest after WPA, Exeter Hospital Aid Society, founded in 1927 and the Iron Trades Insurance Group, specialising only in group policies, who entered this market in 1982.

The rising prosperity of the middle class, the steady stream of press criticism of the NHS, and the improvement in surgical techniques, created encouraging growth in the mid-1950s. However, many private nursing homes were sub-standard. Furthermore, the virtual moratorium on NHS capital spending meant that NHS private rooms were hardly of the quality to which the private clientele was accustomed. Nor could insurance continue to be sold simply on its old exclusive appeal. Indeed as it grew in size this type of image made it an easy target for its critics. In general, the post-war period saw the emergence of a belief in the classlessness of contemporary society. 'Going private' was therefore projected by right-wing intellectuals and the right-wing press not as a privilege but as part of a consumerist and individualist rejection of standardisation, bureaucratisation and lack of personal choice in the NHS.

The history of BUPA is that of well connected potential patients, doctors and businessmen, doing something for their own class (or people just below their own class). It is probable that the organisation, having survived 1948, would have died in the early 1950s had it not been rescued by the new Conservative government's unwillingness to replace outdated NHS facilities or to build new hospitals. In its manifesto for the 1959 General Election, the Labour Party pointed out that the Conservatives had completed only one new hospital. Looking at it another way, BUPA could hardly have failed to succeed given the financial clamps attached to the National Health Service.

The provident associations today sell policies through direct mailing, market research, advertising, discount offers through banks (including the Co-op), clubs and professional bodies, television advertising, leaflets in Post Offices and circulars to civil servants. The promise, barely concealed behind the gloss, is that with insurance you can be sure that you will be first in the queue. Whatever else private medical insurance may represent, this message is the bottom line.

The Insured Population

Until the early 1970s the privately insured population rose steadily but not spectacularly. In 1950, BUPA, PPP and WPA had a total of 50,000 customers. By 1964 this had risen to 616,000.[9] After then growth rose sharply. The total number of customers (many policies also cover the spouse and children) rose from 1.058 million in 1977 to 1.917 million in 1982, with a slight dip in 1975 and 1976. In 1980 the numbers covered by medical insurance rose by 27.5 per cent and in 1981 by 15 per cent. By 1982, however, growth had levelled off at 3 per cent. Today, around 5 million people have some level of private medical cover. This figure excludes the 'permanent health schemes' which provide sickness benefits but do not cover private treatment.

Half of the growth in subscribers to provident associations was accounted for by company schemes. When BUPA was formed, only two such schemes existed. By June 1955 1,700 group schemes were negotiated. Five years later this figure had more than doubled, and another five years later almost doubled again. By 1977, company schemes contained 424,000 subscribers. By 1982, the figure reached 933,000. Company schemes now cover half the 'subscriber population' and, if employee-paid company schemes are added, the proportion rises to around three-quarters. As this implies, the proportion of individual subscribers has declined, from roughly 45 per cent of subscribers in 1977 to around 30 per cent today.

Subscriber growth has now fallen back from the peak years of 1979 and 1980. The smaller organisations are now picking up new members at the expense of BUPA, whose market share has shrunk by 10 per cent over the last decade.

Variations in Insurance Coverage

Since private medical insurance is a luxury good, the spread of its customers reflects the class structure. Coverage is highest in the South of England and among the middle class, and lowest in the North and among the working class.

The General Household Survey reveals that 23 per cent of 'professionals' are covered by private medical insurance, compared with only 1 per cent of the semi-skilled and unskilled.[10]. Those most likely to be insured are middle-aged professionals, of whom 28 per cent are covered. The survey also reveals large regional variations. While in the Outer Metropolitan Area of London 14 per cent of the population is insured the proportion falls to 3 per cent in Scotland and the North. Variations inside London are equally notable. The number of subscribers in some boroughs is too low to be detectable, while 13 per cent is the highest proportion recorded. The London average is estimated at 10 per cent – in the region of 700,000 people. Parts of Buckinghamshire have rates as high as 18 per cent.

What Insurance Covers

Medical insurance varies enormously in its coverage. Little cover is available for consultations with GPs, childbirth, chronic care, geriatric care, psychiatric care, 'alternative' treatment, dental or optical treatment or cosmetic treatment. There is no insurance at any price which offers fully comprehensive cover. Private medical insurance in Britain assumes that essential aspects of care are going to be supplied by the National Health Service. Unlike other types of insurance where the premium declines over time or where benefits are accumulated by the policy holder, the only inevitable characteristic of private medical insurance is its increasing cost: the average premium has doubled over the last six years. As *What Insurance* has commented: 'This means that over a lifetime [a] single man could be paying over £7,000 in premiums without ... ever needing to make a claim.'[11] Moreover, the premiums sharply increase at retirement, the point at which income falls most sharply, forcing many subscribers to give up their policies. Cheap cover may lull the customer into a sense of security but, as the Consumers Association has observed, may expose policy holders to unforeseen risks. Some hospitals outside London charge rates which exceed the insurers' 'provincial' benefit level.[12]

Types of Cover

Until the mid-1960s the provident associations were relatively small, premiums were low and renewal rates were high. However, although the companies achieved reasonable levels of surplus, administration accounted for a large proportion of their costs. Then, as now, customers and insurers were sheltered from the true costs of medical care by the National Health Service. Nevertheless as the available range of treatments widened, subscription costs rose. The insurance companies looked for ways to lower their administrative costs, and saw group policies – pioneered by the American insurance plans – as the most cost-effective route to market growth.

(a) Group Insurance

According to the Chancellor of the Exchequer, 'Perks are an inefficient and often wasteful way of rewarding effort.'[13] Certainly, the medical insurance industry tries to deny the embarrassing fact that its policies, like company cars, are largely another way of motivating and rewarding senior staff. According to Lord Wigoder of BUPA:

> Health insurance is no longer regarded as an executive perk – if it ever was – but is now widely accepted by all sections of the

community as a wise and prudent investment, promoting efficiency and good industrial relations in industry and providing peace of mind for subscribers and their families.[14]

But perk it is. As Income Data Services, which regularly survey this market, have observed:

> Most organisations in our Study started a private health insurance scheme as a 'perk' for senior management, executives or directors, or because it was considered to be a necessary benefit in order to attract the right calibre of staff.[15]

Group insurance, negotiated by senior management, could be said to contradict the claims made for private medical insurance by the intellectual right-wing, since cover is provided on the basis of job grade and has nothing to do with individual choice. But group policies generally led to younger subscribers, and the spread of group insurance – particularly to non-executive employees – provided the medical insurance companies with political ammunition against their opponents. According to BUPA's executive medical advisor David Gullick,

> ...the more that rank and file union members are transferred into potential private patients, the more difficult it will be for their leaders to pursue their vendetta against the private practice of medicine.[16]

Extending cover to the working class has brought its drawbacks too, for working-class subscribers are significantly more prone to ill health and therefore more expensive to cover.

Today, BUPA covers approximately 30,000 company groups and PPP 8,500 company groups. The medical insurers sell company policies by referring to the fostering of employee goodwill, and the rapid treatment of key staff. Medical insurance is promoted partly as providing the protection the NHS at first promised but later apparently failed to deliver. As PPP observes,

> From a management point of view, a company with a slimmed down workforce is demanding more and more from smaller staff. With long waiting lists for acute surgery, it pays management to get fast treatment in emergencies.[17]

There are three main types of company-negotiated scheme – some are wholly paid for by the employees and some wholly by the employer while 'assisted' schemes are partly paid by each. In some cases, long links have been established between employers and particular provident associations. The BBC's (employee-paid) policy with BUPA began in 1951, while Marks and Spencer have been with PPP for over 25 years. However the really substantial growth of group policies has been relatively recent, due in some measure to the imposition of wage controls in the 1970s. Companies organise and pay for the cover of senior employees to increase their loyalty and commitment. The Automobile Association introduced its scheme 'to improve the benefits package for management grades' and extended it to retired managers as 'a goodwill gesture'. The extension of goodwill to its roadside mechanics has not been thought necessary. This general picture of generosity towards senior management and stinginess towards the workers – hardly a phenomenon limited to company perks – is confirmed by Income Data Services: only five company-paid policies in their survey covered all employees, and even these contained length of service restrictions.[18]

Some organisations do have special needs which require either special health arrangements and/or special arrangements to deal with highly mobile employees. Many large companies engage nurses and doctors to supply occupational services. For some occupations – from oil-rig workers to pilots – a fast-stream approach to medical treatment may be necessary. Management consultant Dryden Gilling-Smith argues that the definition of 'key worker' should not merely embrace those who face special risks or geographical isolation:

> It may sound callous, but it may nevertheless be true to observe that the anxiety or otherwise of someone on a production line in a car factory, or employed by a local authority to empty dustbins, may have less effect on the way he does his job than the anxiety of a key member of a creative team in an advertising agency.[19]

Despite discounts of up to 50 per cent (usually 25 per cent), the take-up of employee-paid policies is very low, and the same is true even of the assisted schemes. Usually only 5-15 per cent of employees opt into these schemes, evidence that the discounts are not enough. Family cover can still cost over

£500 a year. There is good evidence that growth in this important sector has all but ended. In early 1983, Neil Jameson, Head of Marketing for BUPA, said that growth was now 'nil'.[20]

Imbucon Management Consultants have shown that the proportion of executive staff with private medical insurance rose from 30.1 per cent in 1974 to 68.9 per cent in 1984.[21] But a sample of all grades of staff by Reward Regional Surveys showed that company perks were slipping back. Furthermore, 'health insurance schemes were still being blocked by political objections from trade unions.'[22] According to Gilling-Smith, this is due to the 'pathological' refusal in the mind of the 'die-hard lefty' to accept the fact 'that one person's time is worth more than another person's time'.[23] Certainly many unions have supported the view that the more private medical insurance grows, the more the government is given the opportunity to cut back the NHS – an argument explicitly put by PPP.[24] Union opposition has been a factor, though IDS report this to be of mixed effect. In some industries, notably banking and insurance, employees have pressed employers to introduce schemes and expand benefits. By contrast, attempts by the government to induce civil servants to take up a voluntary scheme have backfired.

The chief threat to further growth is the financial condition of many British companies. In the early days of the group policy boom premiums were set low, but now insurance companies are properly assessing the costs of cover for each company group and charging accordingly (this is known as 'experience rating'). Formerly, employers found that they could limit premium increases simply by changing to another insurer. 24 per cent of the companies surveyed by the Reward organisation had changed their insurers between 1982 and 1983. However, the provident associations are finding it harder to offer cut-price rates to attract customers from their rivals. Employers are increasingly finding that private medical insurance is an uncontrollable part of their costs. The magazine *Your Business* has identified 'What the employer must ask himself in deciding about a scheme – is it an escalator he really wants his company on?'[25]

(b) Individual Cover

The high cost of serving individual subscribers and the steep increases in private medical costs have led to the relative decline of the individual policy. But insurers have not given up. Rather the onus has been on companies to create cheaper forms of cover in order to retain individuals who leave company schemes through retirement, or who were previously members of associations or clubs. PPP's Private Hospital Plan and Retirement Health Plan provide cover at a much reduced price. The Hospital Plan pays for private treatment when the customer's consultant cannot find him/her an NHS bed within six weeks. The Retirement Health Plan works on the same principle, and is open to people aged between 50 and 74. The level of cover provided by these policies may quickly become exhausted, and subscribers are warned off three central London hospitals. The scheme offers 'a unique combination of NHS and private hospital benefits' in other words, the plans advertise the benefits of treatment that is in any case provided by the NHS.

Individual policy holding has declined largely because of its costs. Despite the attraction of 'cut-price' policies for those entering retirement, there is clearly some dissatisfaction among long-term subscribers facing rising premiums. One correspondent to the *Financial Times* observed:

> There are many elderly subscribers to private health who have been paying their higher subscriptions for years, with little or no claims for benefits, and who now find it difficult to maintain the higher subscriptions in their retirement, just the time of life when they are most likely to need treatment.[26]

Marketing

Despite the peeking of the market in the early 1980s, private medical insurance has been one of the few growth areas of the economy in recent years, and this is largely due to the insurers' clever use of marketing. In 1964 BUPA spent £74,000, or 1 per cent, of its subscription income on publicity. By 1981 the Manchester Business School found 'evidence of a more expansionary, marketing-oriented strategy by the major associations'.[27] BUPA first began to use television advertising in 1979, although perhaps the use of glossy magazines has produced the most effect.

Medical insurers have recognised that the careful employment of marketing concepts can be more effective than massive advertising budgets. Marketing involves the identification of, first, the products or services to be offered; secondly, the people to whom these should be provided, and how; thirdly, the precise mix of the products; and finally how the products should be priced and offered for sale.[28]

It might not be baldly stated, but the promise of treatment ahead of NHS patients is nearly always a part of the advertisements and other publicity. As the consumer magazine *What Insurance* has observed:

> Flexibility is the word often used in the private health brochures. This is a euphemism. It means the right to jump the queue for minor operations. Whether this is good or bad depends on your political views, but this is really what the private vendors have to offer. References to convenient times naturally mean having the thing done as quickly a possible.[29]

All information which highlights the 'plight' of the NHS is therefore free advertising to medical insurers. The NHS receives criticism for the poor state of its hospitals (the responsibility of the government), for its failure to ensure that patients are adequately informed (the responsibility of the medical profession), and for the inadequacy of its preventive services (the responsibility of both government and the medical profession). Combined, these factors provide the 'atmospherics' which assist the private market.

Private medical insurance is promoted as the gateway to desirable compensations to being in hospital – privacy, 'sumptuous' accommodation, extra nursing attention and sympathetic doctors. Just as important as advertising in the media has been the direct approach to companies or individuals – through direct mailing or sales representatives. There have been frequent examples of advertisements placed within employees' pay packets, membership associations' publicity material (the AA's, for example), bank magazines, etc.

In 1981 the press and television advertising by the three largest medical insurance companies cost £1,365,000. BUPA doubled its annual advertising budget between 1979 and 1981. Currently it stands at around £2 million. Certainly, this is only a tiny fraction of the total £2.6 billion spent on television and press advertising in 1981, and less than one-tenth of the advertising budget of the biggest retailer, Tesco's. However these figures are deceptive, given the large part of the marketing effort devoted to direct selling (for company schemes), direct mailing, exhibitions (such PPP's stand at the Ideal Home Exhibition) and so on. Indeed a large portion of the administrative costs of these organisations can fairly be allotted to sales and marketing.

The Advertising Standards Authority usually allows advertisers a fairly wide latitude (it has observed, for example, that without companies being able to 'appeal to fear', no one would want to take out an insurance policy).[30] Yet the Authority has upheld a complaint against BUPA and looked hard at an advertisement from PPP. In the case of BUPA, the company falsely implied in its advertisements to employers that up to one in eight of their employees might have to go to hospital in any one year. The PPP advertisement, about which the ASA received 41 complaints, stated that 'your son could wait up to 16 weeks with appendicitis,' whereas in fact acute appendicitis would be dealt with immediately. PPP, in its defence, stated that it had not intended to denigrate the NHS, and that the advertisement had also contained the words, 'The NHS is fine if you're desperately ill.' The companies have moved on from the original tiny clientele identified by the founders of post-NHS medical insurance – namely, those who would always seek private attention at any cost. Other potential customers require clear incentives. For these, PPP's graphic representations of the NHS waiting list act as a reminder of the perils of not being covered.

While the product offered by the provident associations and the commercial insurers is basically the same, each of the companies must stress the distinctiveness of its own offerings. BUPA is building up its image as a multi-faceted health care organisation, providing hospitals, screening centres and other services as well as insurance: 'The BUPA Health Service'.

For-Profit Insurers

The provident associations resent the intrusion of the commercial insurers as much as they dislike the foreign hospital chains. BUPA's Lord Wigoder says that,

Commercial insurers, mostly from abroad, have begun to move into what they have believed was a very large and expanding market. Some are doing so by quoting what appear to be loss-making premiums unlikely to be maintained after the initial business has been secured.[31]

This was perhaps a case of pot calling kettle black: this was arguably the way BUPA itself attracted many customers during 1980, which led to the narrowing gap between revenue and outgoings that year despite a considerably enlarged pool of customers.

In fact BUPA is just as much involved in capitalism as its rivals. BUPA has 14 subsidiary companies, two of which are incorporated in Hong Kong. Despite its parentage of the Nuffield Hospitals chain, it also runs BUPA Hospitals Ltd, which is, unlike Nuffield, a for-profit enterprise, as well as medical screening centres and nursing services. Not all these subsidiaries, by any means, are particulary active or successful. But this is not the point. When the provident associations suggest that they are 'non-profit-making' in order to denigrate their rivals, they are drawing a distinction without a difference.

For their part, the new 'profit-making' insurers face a substantial handicap in attempting to attack the market share of the provident associations. The problem is not simply that the providents possess, according to a manager of Crusader Insurance (now part of the American Cigna Corporation) 'a tremendous brand image',[32] but rather that they can afford to lose some of their market share to loss-leading opponents in the knowledge that they have a good chance of regaining the custom later.

Since most of the new companies have entered the market only within the last four years, it is too early to assess their success. It is apparent that many of the company group policy buyers are showing a high level of sophistication with regard to the discounts offered by providents and commercials alike. In 1983, for example, United Biscuits purchased a company-paid scheme for senior management but arranged a voluntary scheme for other employees through Mutual of Omaha (now marketed as 'Health First'). Similarly, in the last few years, Safeway Stores has been insured with BUPA,

PPP and WPA (and returned to BUPA), switching whenever it thought it had received a better offer. Whether this proves to be a temporary phenomenon or grows in importance will be determined by whether insurers are willing to offer policies at or below their true costs to obtain new business. While the willingness of customers to switch does open up new opportunities to for-profit insurers, rapid and substantial fluctuations in trade could lead small companies into financial difficulty. They therefore have to wrest a significant market share away from the providents and maintain this over several years.

Professor Alan Maynard considers that commercial insurers have one effective weapon in their armoury which the 'non-profits' do not possess, namely their ability to 'cream' the market. In order to seize market share from a 'non-profit' company a commercial insurer

> could identify segments of (the) community who were paying in excess of their actuarial risks ... If the profit-making company then marketed a scheme whose contributions were related to actuarial characteristics of the good risks, they could 'cream' the non-profit making market ...[33]

BUPA do suggest that there is some element of cross-subsidy between insured groups, in particular that young patients subsidise older patients. However the extent of this is fairly limited. Even as early as 1955, the age limit of 65 years was reimposed (it had been temporarily abandoned in 1950) to stem the financial haemorrhage of the companies' funds and to avoid scales subject to 'constant alteration'.[34]

The new companies have had to pay dearly to obtain even a small share of the market. Some might have entered the fray because they believed that the Conservatives were going to damage the NHS so severely that the established insurance groups would not be able to keep up with the demand. On the other hand,

> should a left-wing government be elected, a prompt reversal of current trends may be feared. It is possibly this fear which has prevented any new entry into the private medical insurance market by commercial insurers. Such fears may only be overcome when a partnership between the state and private health

provision has become a *fait accompli*, and it is working well enough
to prevent a government, whatever its colour, wishing to interfere
with it. There is obviously a long way to go before this position is
reached, but should the prospect emerge of a continuing period of
stability under this or a moderate government, it is likely that
more conventional insurers will want their share of a market
which could be worth £1,000 million per annum.[35]

BUPA, PPP and WPA have good reason to be upset by the
increasing number of insurance companies nipping at their
heels. Until 1980, the provident associations operated as a
cosy oligopoly. Today the market is increasingly price
sensitive as each new company attempts to buy its way in.
Orion Insurance (Netherlands), Health First, backed by
Mutual of Omaha (USA), Allied Medical Assurance Services
(UK) and Crown Life (UK) are large companies, despite the
general decline in the world-wide insurance market.[36]

Perhaps even more worrying to the providents is the
growing trend of self-insurance. Since the summer of 1983, the
Inland Revenue has permitted employers to set up their own
independent private medical schemes by means of a trust
arrangement. This means that companies can develop their
own insurance schemes with the help of external consultants
at substantially less cost. One company which has developed
this type of policy is Allied Medical Assurance, linked with the
financial consultants MPA. The charge for their scheme is the
cost of the claims plus 5 per cent. Administrative components
of the charges set by the provident associations are four times
as high.

Industry Prospects

'The one thing worrying the private health business in Britain
is the return of a Tory government,' said a tongue-in-cheek
editorial in the London *Standard*, several weeks before the 1979
General Election.[33] They needn't have worried. The
favourable election result (from the point of view of the
Standard) coincided with the short-term boom in the medical
insurance industry. However, as an earlier chapter showed,
the Conservatives have certainly not given the companies the
support that they thought was their due. When the boom

fizzled out, many in the commerical sector blamed the government's lack of 'bottle'.

Another view is that the downturn in the insurance market had given the industry a chance to take stock of the situation. While it is hardly likely that the insurers themselves felt too pleased to see the boom come to an end, there are some valid elements in this perspective, at least in so far as it relates to companies buying cover for their employees. This 'perk' was being increasingly made available to more junior levels of management, presenting senior management with an element of the wage bill which seemed to be getting out of control.

The private medical sector is chronically unable to control its rising costs. These are indicated by stiff rises in charges – passed on to the insurers and by the worrying tendency of the benefits paid out catching up with subscription revenues. The companies' total income has of course grown considerably during the recent period, but the gap between income and benefits has been narrowing, in BUPA's case dramatically so, leading to an underwriting loss in 1981. In the following year, they were forced to raise rates mid-year by 20 per cent and a further 15 per cent six months later.

Beneath the symptom of rapidly rising premium levels is an extraordinary movement in hospitals' allocation of costs, with a growing proportion of benefits being spent on 'ancillary' costs as opposed to daily bed charges. According to Robert Graham, Chief Executive of BUPA, when the company introduced cost ceilings for certain procedures in 1984, all but three of the 180 acute hospitals marked up drug charges by up to '500 and 600 per cent'.[38] There are other reasons for the soaring inflation, some of which are endemic to medical care and some of which are linked solely to the nature of the commercial medical business. The cost problems of the NHS and the private sector are certainly not simply the same, as Alan Maynard has suggested.[39] In private practice, doctors and hospitals have so far had few incentives to keep fees and charges down, since the bills get passed directly on to the insurer. The American corporations certainly make an impressive effort to encourage their nursing staff to carry out their tasks economically, but since doctors and hospitals are reimbursed on an item-by-item basis, within insurance payment limits, and since their interest in the patient is largely financial, they have every inducement to pitch their charges at the top of the appropriate scale.

Another reason for rising treatment costs is that a declining proportion of patients are treated in subsidised NHS pay beds, and in any case the charges for these have substantially risen. Furthermore, the plain fact is that medical care is getting more and more expensive each year. Length of stay may be reduced and throughput raised, but doctors are finding more conditions that they can treat and since private patients have paid for their treatment (or have had someone else pay for them) they have no 'cost-conscious' inhibitions on claiming. (Ironically, this criticism has been lodged against the 'free' National Health Service, but this is inappropriate given the rationing mechanisms the NHS employs.)

In response, most companies have diluted the cover they offer. BUPA, in a widely noted move, introduced new restrictions on levels of reimbursement for the more expensive hospitals, causing these to charge BUPA patients supplementary fees. Later on, in order to reassure employers, it struck a deal with the hospitals to instigate a policy of voluntary effort to police rising charges, although this was not a great success. The interests of medical insurers are inextricably linked with those of the private clinics. Any difficulties that occur in one sector are almost immediately passed through to the other. Rapid growth, such as that which occurred just after the Thatcher government took office, has brought with it various problems which the industry as a whole now finds difficult to solve. The first temporary problem concerned the lack of private facilities. However this quickly gave way to overcapacity as hospital beds, planned at the outset of the boom, flooded onto the market.

Another of BUPA's responses to the cost crisis has been to create further distinctions between policy holders – only those now paying luxury prices are entitled to go to luxury hospitals. There are now separate charges for three bands of hospital, with coverage extending to the limits of each band. More recently, a PPP scheme has taken this approach a stage further, with one extra band and more detailed categorisation. Consultants' fees come to around 30 per cent of insurance costs. At present BUPA lays down maximum fee schedules, though it would like to arrange tighter limitations. Consultants have responded by consistently putting in claims for the maximum payable.

Competition is much more evident today than even five years ago. Switching from one insurer to another may lead to lower premiums, and may help the cheaper insurers, i.e. those that have the lowest administrative overheads though not the highest public profile. The dilution of existing policies may leave customers inadequately insured in the mistaken belief that what they take for granted from the NHS they will also receive from a commercial organisation.

In the USA, the fear of personal bankruptcy and a more world-weary assessment of medical insurance (whether commercial, non-profit or state) has led wary consumers to arrange insurance for treatment not normally covered – 'medigap' as this is known. In Britain, AMI's introduction of private treatment on credit was both a way of attracting new customers without insurance, and a way of helping those with insufficient insurance to pay for their services. This corporation, with 35,000 patients yearly, mostly in London, began issuing 'medical credit cards' in 1984. In 1985 it began to offer its own system of insurance directly to companies. Although the company claims not to be competing with the BUPA, these moves put them on similar terms: they are both offering insurance and running a chain of hospitals.

In the long run it is likely that this process of merger between the insurance and hospital markets will continue, with companies developing 'health maintenance organisations' along American lines, with insurance and medical care offered in one package. In the short run, the evidence suggests that more competitive market pressures are leading to the break-up of the oligopolistic market conditions that prevailed before 1982. The result of the 'war' between the insurers and hospitals over the increasing costs of private medical care remains to be seen. In any case, it is a powder keg for the industry and a lesson to any radical Conservative government which thinks the replacement of the NHS by private insurance will be easy and cheap.

Notes

[1] Fennel Betson, *Your Business*, September 1984.
[2] G. David Lock, *The Need to Control Costs* (paper given at *Financial Times* private health care conference; London 25 and 26 March 1985).
[3] Alan Maynard, 'The Private Health Care Sector in Britain' in G. McLachlan and A. Maynard (eds), *The Public/Private Mix for Health*. Nuffield Provincial Hospital Trust, 1982.
[4] BUPA Second Annual Report, 1949, quoted from A. Bryant, *A History of the British United Provident Association, 1947-1968*, BUPA, 1968. p.24.
[5] Richard Titmuss, *Income Distribution and Social Change*, Allen and Unwin, 1962.
[6] Bryant, op.cit., p.2
[7] E. Richard Brown, *Rockefeller Medicine Men*, University of California Press, 1979.
[8] Bryant, op.cit., p.21.
[9] S. Mencher, *Private Practice in Britain*, G. Bell, 1983.
[10] OPCS *General Household Survey 1983*, HMSO, 1985.
[11] *What Insurance*, January/February 1984.
[12] *Which*, June 1984.
[13] Interview in the *Times*, 24 November 1983.
[14] Introduction by Wigoder to the BUPA 1983 Annual Report.
[15] Quoted in Income Data Services, *Private Medicine Insurance*, Study 292, June 1983.
[16] *Guardian*, 1 February 1984.
[17] IDS, op.cit.
[18] Income Data Services, *Private Health Insurance*, Study 317, July 1984.
[19] Dryden Gilling-Smith, *The Role of Private Health Care in the Total Remuneration Package*, (paper given at *Financial Times* private health care conference 25 and 26 March 1985).
[20] *Guardian*, 1 February 1983.
[21] *Financial Times*, 11 October 1984.
[22] *Guardian*, 24 April 1984.
[23] Gilling-Smith, op.cit.
[24] Private Patients Plan, Report and Accounts 1983.
[25] *Your Business*, October 1984.
[26] Letter from J. Stark, *Financial Times*, 25 February 1983.
[27] University of Manchester, Centre for Business Research, *The UK Private Health Insurance Market*, 1981.
[28] G. Rayner, 'The Advent of Marketing in Health Care', *Health and Social Service Journal*, 26 April 1984.
[29] *What Insurance*, January/February 1984.
[30] Advertising Standards Authority, *ASA Case Report 90*, 13 October 1982.
[31] BUPA Annual Report 1982.
[32] L.M. Edmans, 'Private Medical Insurance: Potential for Growth with Decline in NHS', *General Policy Market*, Vol.79, 1980, pp.614-8.
[33] Maynard, op.cit., p.135.
[34] Bryant, op.cit., p.35.
[35] Edmans, op.cit., p.16.
[36] Eric Short, 'Loss Hit Insurance Operators Hope for Happier New York',

Financial Times, 21 January 1985.

[37] *Evening Standard*, 19 February 1979.

[38] Quoted in *Financial Times*, 22 January 1986.

[39] Alan Maynard, 'Private Practice, Answer or Irrelevance?' *British Medical Journal*, 16 June 1984, pp.1849-1851.

Chapter 4

Private Hospitals: An American Invasion?

The transformation of private hospital care in the last decade to fifteen years has been truly radical. For one thing, the total demand for private treatment, as measured by the numbers enrolled with medical insurance schemes, massively increased in the late 1970s and early 1980s. Then, this demand was met in new ways. The relative importance of private clinics and of NHS pay-beds has switched, to the detriment of the latter. Meanwhile, the clinics have fundamentally changed in nature, becoming far more commercial and capitalist in financial structure, marketing strategy and purpose. This is primarily due to the influence of US corporations which have entered the market.

The Years of Peace

Aneurin Bevan preserved the pay-beds when the voluntary hospitals were integrated into the NHS, hoping thereby to forestall the development of a 'rash of nursing homes'. But the demand for private treatment subsequently fell short of the facilities made available, and in the first twenty years of the National Health Service the number of pay-beds fell gradually from 6,647 in 1949 to 4,350 in 1969. In that period, the average occupancy of these beds rose from under 50 to 60 per cent. The number of pay-beds then rose to 4,640, only to fall back again to 4,125 by 1976. Meanwhile, the occupancy rate fell to 52 per cent in 1973 and 41 per cent in 1976. The number of private patients treated in NHS hospitals went up from 70,962 in 1955 to 120,274 in 1972. By 1976, the annual figure had fallen to 94,323.[1]

The explanation for the sudden decline in the mid-1970s

lies, of course, in the attacks then being made on private practice by the political and industrial wings of the labour movement. Barbara Castle managed to 'phase out' 40 per cent of the pay-beds but, given their low occupancy, this did not in itself create any major bottle-neck in the availability of private care. However, its effect was to shift private practice out of the NHS. As David Bolt, former leader of the consultants' negotiating body, explains:

> We put a fair amount of pressure on consultants to move towards facilities outside the NHS. Even after the change of government in 1979 we used to impress on consultants that they now had a five year 'breathing space' which they should use since, if at the end of that time the opposition were to come to power, there would be very little notice before all NHS facilities were closed to private patients. As a result there has been a very striking development in terms of provision of private facilities over the period.[2]

While in the early 1970s, around three out of every four private patients were treated in the NHS, the reverse is now the case.

Bevan 'disclaimed' a total of 277 private hospitals and nursing homes when creating the NHS, although some of those were not functional even then. Many others closed subsequently, unable to compete with the facilities offered to private patients by the NHS. But at least two dozen of the disclaimed clinics are still open today and performing surgery, including such famous names as the Manor House Hospital (run by the trade union-linked Industrial Orthopaedic Society), the Royal Masonic Hospital (founded in 1933), the Italian Hospital (1884), the Harley Street Clinic (1834) and King Edward VII's Hospital for Officers (1889). Many of these institutions had (and have) a closely defined clientele and were not primarily intended for the ordinary private patient enrolled with BUPA or one of the other medical insurance schemes. Others were run by religious foundations.

BUPA became concerned by the falling provision of private treatment outside the NHS and in 1957 established a charity to buy up clinics which would otherwise close and to develop its own where appropriate. Two years later, at the suggestion of Lord Nuffield (who had, almost single-handedly, created BUPA), this charity was named the Nuffield Nursing Homes

Trust. By 1966, in the words of Oliver Rowell, the chain's general manager, Nuffield had taken over

> small private hospitals in Bath, Bournemouth, Bristol, Edinburgh, Hull, London and Oxford and – even more exciting – had built purpose-designed NNHT hospitals in Birmingham, Exeter, London, Shrewsbury and Woking.[3]

Nuffield's developments were financed by loans and gifts from BUPA and PPP and by local appeals to consultants, businesses and potential private patients. The chain can also be said to be partly financed by the state, as charitable status halves its rates and frees it altogether from corporation tax. A recent brochure explains:

> The greater part of Nuffield Hospitals' charitable income comes from payments made under deed of covenant both from individual and company donors. It also receives gifts of single donations, shares, property, legacies and gifts in kind. A gift of capital to Nuffield Hospitals is not liable to Capital Transfer Tax. Because Nuffield Hospitals is a charity it can reclaim from the Inland Revenue the tax already paid on covenanted gifts, thereby significantly increasing the value of each payment.
> Higher rate tax-payers have an extra incentive to help. Income tax relief is allowed on the gross value of covenanted payments subject to certain limitations. Covenants by limited liability companies can be set against Corporation Tax liability.[4]

One way or another, there were 21 Nuffield clinics by 1973 with 668 beds, treating 24,711 in-patients while by 1978 there were 29 clinics, 953 beds and 39,015 in-patients.[5] Nuffield's advantages and its success seemed clear. However, the chain was not well prepared for what was to come.

The American Invasion

Ten years after the opening of their first British store on London's Haymarket, McDonald's hamburgers, with UK sales of £165 million, opened store number 165. Perhaps even this corporation, the largest fast-food outlet in North America, was surprised at the level of success of its British offshoot, for there must have been some doubts as to whether its rather bland, but competitively-priced, products would be to the taste of a nation weaned on fish and chips. However, the competition already in the market was a positive example. The Wimpy chain, which had introduced the British to burgers, had grown rapidly but had settled down to variable standards. McDonald's diagnosed a 'quality gap' in the fast-food market and, stressing the uniformity of their products, went to fill it.

Much of the experience behind the expansion of corporate medicine in the USA had been drawn from precisely this type of service industry, so the experience a corporation like McDonald's had in adapting to the British market helps us understand how the American hospital chains adapted to Britain. It so happens that in contrast to the purveyors of fast food, the hospital chains had to adapt their style of operation considerably. McDonald's experience – both in Europe and the USA – had been that the public demanded bright, airy and clean stores. The food had to be hot and had to be fresh. The most profitable lines were the side orders and these had to be a selling point. It is argued that McDonald's stress on strict quality control, bulk purchasing, spartan financial control, and the fostering of team spirit among its young workforce ('We take blood out of their veins and put in ketchup') backed up giving people what they wanted with an organisation to match.

While McDonald's was able to reproduce its approach in Britain, the hospital corporations would have courted disaster if they had followed suit. In the USA, the hospital chains really do run along 'fast-food' lines. Hospital corporations underline their commitment to this approach through rigid standardisation and bulk purchasing. Why couldn't this method work in the British market? First of all, standard-isation in Britain, 'turnstile medicine', is evocative of the NHS. This approach might be successful in the USA (except that many Americans dislike the rigidity of corporate hospitals) but in Britain and Europe it would have been disastrous. In Britain, commercial medicine strenuously avoids any approach that smacks of the impersonal. Furthermore, at least at first, there was very little real experience in Britain of running hospitals on fully commercial lines – until the early 1980s, the majority of non-NHS hospitals were still 'charities'. Obviously McDonald's could charge market rates for its burgers, but in health care the competition – the NHS and the charity hospitals – charged either nothing (in the case of the former) or rates which did not secure profits. The private nursing homes had not been money-spinners – the chief beneficiaries of private practice were the doctors themselves. However, just as in the USA in the mid-1960s when medicine became vastly profitable (and hence created a gap for the chains to fill) so also the growth of new markets in Britain, and especially in London in the early 1970s, gave the corporations an opportunity not to be missed. But the nature of the opportunity had to be precisely diagnosed.

After their initial surveys of the British market, the American companies realised that it was not in their interest to enter into price competition with existing providers. They therefore had to find a slot in the market where they could charge prices which represented the full costs of production plus a return on their investments. Naturally this meant the luxury end of the market and the attempt to attract patients for whom the cost of treatment was a secondary consideration. The main market they set their sights on initially was the foreign 'import' market. Britain was a better base than America for its exploitation.

London was the initial base for the American companies operating in the UK, and functions also as their European and Middle Eastern centre of operations. American Medical International was the first to set up in Britain through its link to, and eventual purchase of, the Harley Street Clinic in 1970. AMI was followed in 1976 by the Humana Corporation, with its purchase of the prestigious Wellington Hospital.

In the 1970s these hospitals were almost exclusively for the rich, in particular the foreign rich. The Wellington became famous as the Harrods of medical care. Indeed Humana still advertises the Wellington as the 'five star hospital'. AMI struck a special deal with British Airways for flying in patients. In many cases the arrangements were made direct through foreign embassies.

The companies also used their London offices as recruiting stations for their management contracts in the Gulf states. There were a number of reasons for this. The first relates to public school and Oxbridge education of many members of the Gulf oligarchies. The British were a known quantity, and

British medical treatment highly favoured. The other obvious source of English-speaking medical staff presented some difficulties. The Americans demanded higher salaries, partly because they were used to them back home, but also because Americans are taxed on their world-wide income, so a short-term position overseas is not that lucrative. Not every company with Middle East management contracts and British recruiting offices took up the opportunity to develop hospitals in Britain. One of these was the Whittaker Corporation of Arlington, Virginia (which in 1983 had six hospitals operational in the Middle East). Whittaker's recruiting drive in 1982 attempted to attract 1,000 NHS staff, in addition to the 650 it had already recruited.

It was precisely this kind of opportunism for which the hospital chains (indeed all types of capitalist organisation) have become famous. Their policy was to adapt what knowledge they could to this vastly different situation and make up the rest as they went along. As an executive of one of the American corporations has explained, it is important not to extrapolate from how such companies operate in the USA to how they run in Britain. With regard to medical staff, for example, the companies were used to dealing with quite young physicians anxious to maximise their incomes to pay off vast loans incurred in medical school. In Britain, private hospital doctors were almost exclusively consultants, and they were on the whole older and more experienced. Furthermore, the level of private work they were willing to undertake was on the whole limited, and often restricted to weekends or evenings. Logically, therefore, each private hospital needed to attract as many consultants as possible.

The social class and age of the patients attracted to the hospital chains in the USA is considerably different from their usual type of customer in Britain. In the USA, half of the patients treated by the corporate chains are in fact public patients, the majority with Medicare, the federal insurance plan for the elderly. In Britain, the first corporation hospitals, like the grand London hotels, were international centres for the well-heeled, with all the attendant problems that flowed from the mixing of the intimate aspects of medicine with cultural variety, requiring interpreters, special diets and knowledge of protocol.

In some respects, the hospital companies suffered fewer government restrictions than in the USA. While the town planning process was slow and cumbersome, and exploited by hostile Labour councils, the government (especially after the abolition of the Health Services Board) washed its hands of the need to 'plan' (in effect restrict) the commercial sector. The contrast with the USA could not have been stronger at least until Reagan's election. Extensive information on proposed hospitals have been required by state and federal planning authorities. New facilities have been required to obtain a 'certificate of need'. Furthermore, some American states created ordinances especially designed to block the chains (just as in some discreet upper-class communities zoning laws were used to keep out McDonald's). These measures did limit the geographical spread of the hospital corporations but perhaps only marginally affected their growth. In Britain, if an investment company really wants to risk millions of pounds in developing a new facility where there are twenty others, the government's response has been 'that is not our problem'.

The ample rewards derived from treating foreign patients in the 1970s had to be set against the political risks. Even the British-owned part of private medicine felt itself under threat during the 1970s and no Labour government would be likely to welcome foreign profit-making concerns. Initially therefore – despite later claims that they were in Britain 'for the long haul' – the American companies were interested in recouping maximum short-term financial benefits. The election of the Thatcher government changed everything. From being viewed with suspicion, the companies now felt that they were being welcomed with open arms.

There are eight US groups with hospitals in Britain or in the process of developing hospitals. These are AMI, HCA, Humana, Charter, Community Psychiatric Centres, National Medical Enterprises, Universal Health Services and Corporation. The California Nu-Med based health maintenance organisation, FHP, has also announced its intention of entering the British market. Each of these companies has a distinct perception of the British market. Some, like Humana, run hospitals only in London. The size of each group's investment reflects how it sees future prospects. Each company is examining the blend of services it must generate to maximise revenues (and therefore profits); similarly each company attempts to project a distinct impression of itself to attract customers.

The US corporations have a number of distinct advantages over their British competitors. They can take a longer-term view of the market, and assess current financial flows accordingly. Access to Wall Street gives them an enormous financial advantage. Furthermore, they are used to competition from other multi-hospital systems and, although they recruit managers from both the NHS and their UK competitors, they are not restricted by the narrowness of the British approach. The American companies are able to 'think big', and 'act big' too.

The accountancy methods of these enterprises are crucial to their financial success. Unlike charitable hospitals, they aim to make a profit and they have to pay corporation tax and full rates. Even though they may be able to show efficiency advantages next to hospitals not run in 'chains' they are still forced to have higher charges to survive. This is largely why the American corporations have been accused of overcharging by British insurers and foreign customers. BUPA's Chair, Lord Wigoder, may have been referring to the American chains in his company's 1981 Annual Report: 'The profit motive can lead to excessive charges, not always for beds, but sometimes for drugs and other services.' BUPA's General Manager for Marketing Operations, Derek Allan, is concerned to fight against 'what had been happening in the States where the bed charge was only a part of the hospital bill which would perhaps include as much again in terms of other services or charges'.

As the largest hospital management company in Britain, and the third largest in the USA, AMI's market presence is significant. The company also has the highest profile in Britain, due to its early entry, large advertising budget (estimated at £500,000 p.a.) and the enthusiasm with which its representatives seek the spotlight. Though the company does what it can to hide its US origins (it always refers to itself as simply AMI and all its staff, bar its chief officer, are British) as far as general business policy goes, it is American to its fingertips. According to one company statement, it is the purpose of AMI to pursue 'opportunities in other countries for the delivery of American-style health care tailored to local customs and needs'.

The company has clearly benefited from being here first. This decision has been credited to Royce Deiner, former Chief Executive Officer, who argues:

> In every country where we have studied national health programs (and I think we have studied them all) we have found that those programs have created their own problems as populations grew. The national health system became strained and overburdened as citizens developed a higher sense of entitlement to more advanced health care. The way to relieve that strain is to encourage the emergence of a strong private sector health system. Certainly a very good example of such a situation is the United Kingdom.

AMI has built up an enviable market 'presence' in commercial medicine, surpassed only by the insurers themselves. It has intelligently and assiduously cultivated an up-market image, and despite some set-backs (even American companies make mistakes) has arrived at the comfortable position of market leader over both its 'non-profit' and commercial rivals.

AMI entered the British market through the purchase of the elderly (though gracious) Harley Street Clinic. It was certainly not the company's style to use so ancient a building, but at the time image mattered at least as much as practicality. The owner of the clinic was Dr Stanley Balfour-Lynn, who as part of the deal with AMI, became chairman of its European subsidiary and the British mouthpiece for the company. Again, this was a matter of convenience, since Balfour-Lynn hardly fitted in with the American management philosophy.

Other hospitals followed. In 1977, the Princess Grace Hospital was given a royal seal of approval by its namesake, former Hollywood actress Grace Kelly (like AMI, also hailing from Beverly Hills, California). Together with its existing 'sister' hospital, the company boasted that the hospital performed 'more major open-heart surgery than any other hospital in Britain'.

Despite the overall decline in the number of patients from overseas, a high proportion of AMI's surgical workload remains foreign in origin. The company's ability to carry out complex surgery does indicate that despite the private sector's preference for mundane, low-risk surgery, most of their facilities have the ability to do something rather more.

The return of a Conservative government in 1979, combined with well publicised rumblings of dissatisfaction with the high charges levied on foreign patients, indicated to the company that they had every reason to move 'down market', both to draw in British patients to fill the beds left unoccupied by departing foreigners and also to take advantage of the expected boom.

The newer 'community hospitals' were created to spread the company's experience and prestige to the provinces. One of the first of these to open (in April 1980) was the Princess Margaret Hospital in Windsor. This was followed by the 100-bed Clementine Churchill Hospital in Harrow and the Alexandra Hospital, just outside Manchester. The following year, the small Chiltern Hospital in Great Missenden in Buckinghamshire opened its doors, followed by the Chaucer Hospital in Canterbury and the Priory Hospital in Edgbaston.

Like their parents in the USA, companies like AMI make bold claims about their 'efficiency'. Vice-President Jim Barker has claimed that AMI kidney transplants run £2,000 to £3,000 cheaper than those performed by the NHS.[6] The company also points to its management award for the speedy construction of the Manchester clinic. AMI executives, along with the rest of the commercial sector, also like to claim that they 'may' be more efficient because their throughput of patients is faster than the NHS (though not as fast as NHS pay-beds). One reason is that AMI staff are certainly more conscious of the cost of resources as each department has its own budget and a target performance rate. An AMI nurse has explained how those sections which had been most effective at reducing costs were 'rewarded' with champagne prizes.[6]

This experience is echoed by the Director of Nursing for the Alexandra Hospital:

Financial awareness is not something that nurses bring with them when they come into the hospital. But it's an area in which we have to do some work, both in terms of formal and informal training, in order to give them an appreciation of the matter. It is quite a lengthy process if one is to do this in a way which will not antagonise the nurse, because all of us within the profession would very easily be antagonised if we were being asked to put business before the patients.[7]

As yet, AMI's UK units do not offer courses in 'stress reduction' or 'dual administrative and clinical career ladders'. However eagerness evidently pays off – those who buy the company ethic do apparently go places.[7]

If the transition from NHS nursing to AMI nursing requires some adoption of American-style nursing attitudes, the day-to-day management of AMI hospitals exudes the latest trends in American managerialism. The US parent began its own programme to train administrators in 1977.

At present the majority of the managers of its British hospitals are NHS-trained, and are bound to remain so for the foreseeable future. However methods are applied similar to those set down in Beverly Hills. AMI's British chief explains: 'The company provides the maximum centralisation of direction with the maximum delegation of decision making.' In practice this means a method of 'management by objectives'. According to Burleson:

> Budgets are negotiated, not imposed from above, and when agreed they become a firm commitment on the part of the management team. The performance of each level of management is measured by results against budget ... The hospital director ... is responsible for all the employees of the hospital. He is the managing director and is responsible for providing a high standard of service as well as ensuring the financial viability of the facility.

The larger organisational tasks, including finance, computing, legal services, training and marketing are handled from head office.

AMI's collision with the insurers explains its development of alternative schemes to finance private patients in its hospitals. In the summer of 1984, AMI announced the launch of its 'AMICARD'. AMICARD was not, as the brochure on the scheme explained, medical insurance:

If you do have medical insurance, you will find AMICARD credit is a useful way of supplementing your cover, subject to your credit rating, particularly in areas not covered by current health insurance, for example, maternity care.

The card was intended to meet those bills not covered by BUPA, and which might turn patients away from AMI hospitals, and to tap into new markets – treatments not covered at all by medical insurance.

But the credit card is basically a way of extending the individual's budget, and not a way of covering risk. Hence it was inevitable that if AMI was to present a serious challenge to BUPA, it would have to develop its own insurance or prepayment scheme. This was announced in December 1984, to start by the following summer. The scheme was not intended to put AMI in the role of a competitor with the insurance companies, so it was said, because the company would only deal directly with employers requiring cover. In fact, company schemes are the lifeblood of private medical insurance, and if this strategy were a success it would spark off something of a trade war.

It might be said that AMI probably had no desire to enter into the insurance business; it would have preferred to stick to running hospitals and compete for patients whose insurance covered the full costs of treatment. Certainly, the chances of making money from private medical insurance were slim, and by 1984 meagre. Behind the plan was AMI's attempt to create its own pool of private patients as had been achieved by BUPA. AMI's involvement with insurance also shows the company's depth of commitment to the British market.

Despite their evident dexterity and skill in adapting to British market conditions and their now dominant position in the market, it is important to remember that AMI Hospitals Ltd, placed beside the NHS, is miniscule. World-wide, AMI has 40,000 employees, but its British operations add up to around the half the size of an average NHS District Health Authority. In the field of elective surgery, however, AMI plays a role disproportionate to its size.

The Hospital Corporation of America is the biggest commercial hospital chain in the world, and a company with a mission: 'to attain international leadership in the health care field'. According to the company:

The sun never sets on the HCA operation. As night falls in Nashville, the sun shines brightly in Sydney, and the steady pulsebeat of around-the-clock activity at 350 hospitals continues around the world.

Britain, therefore, is just one outpost in this imperial quest. But, according to Robert Crosby, HCA's executive Vice-President, 'we try to maintain a low profile when we enter a country because we don't want it to appear that here is a big American company coming to take over the health care system.'

HCA's style of entry into the British market was dictated by the fact that Humana and AMI had already arrived. 'The company's goal is definitely to be "number one" in the United Kingdom,' Art Ouelette, Managing Director of the UK subsidiary, told company directors in 1983: 'not necessarily the largest, but most assuredly the best.' Their rivals – American and British – had already saturated the London market, bringing the response from HCA that 'they did not want to add' to the overbedding. HCA's delayed entrance to the UK was due also to the company's caution. They did not fully understand Britain and certainly wanted to build only where the local market was viable. 'One of the things we recognised in our survey and analysis was that there were specific geographic centres that lacked what we define as adequate private acute care hospital services,' Ouelette told the industry's trade magazine. It was initially decided by the corporation's British subsidiary (then going under the name of Hospital Corporation International) that the optimal size for its UK hospitals would be around 80 beds: large enough to make the self-provision of pathology services feasible and to ensure reasonable occupancy figures. However, not everything went according to plan.

The company initially decided to start from scratch with a newly-built hospital in Southampton, sneezing distance away from the new Southampton General Hospital. The new private facility would act more or less as the Southampton General's private wing. In a rather twee flourish the Corporation decided to give the clinic a name which reflected the upper-class health faddism of the past – Chalybeate Hospital – the name meaning 'water containing iron and sulphur', reflecting a time when Southampton was famous for its spa.

As one local community physician wrote at the time, the company's marketing was slick:

> The company has striven to smooth the way for its proposal, using public relations consultants to put its case. Presentations of the proposal, complete with hospitality, have been given to doctors at an expensive Southampton hotel and allotment holders who would be displaced by the development are being found new sites, where, instead of carrying water as they do now, they would have individual water supplies and fenced plots.[8]

Such thoughtful provision on the part of a corporation with revenues then exceeding \$3.5 billion might have suggested that HCA was, after all, a 'people-oriented' organisation, to use Art Ouelette's words. However, even the allotment holders – not, one supposes, likely to enjoy BUPA cover – must have wondered about the company's apparent largesse. Certainly, aside from the public relations exercises, very few people, including the local health authority and the Community Health Council, were consulted about the 'need' for a private hospital in Southampton. The company claimed that it would bring fresh employment to the area, and that when fully operational the hospital would employ 119 medical and nursing staff and 85 others. Yet the question asked by SCOTCH – Southampton Citizens Opposed to Chalybeate Hospital – was 'Where would those staff come from?'.

Although Chalybeate Hospital eventually became operational, the company had come out of the affair badly. It had spent time and money attempting to sweeten the local community, but it had attracted a lot of adverse publicity. For future development, therefore, it decided to change tack.

The opportunity presented itself in the form of a chain of small hospitals facing some financial difficulty. Seltahart Holdings were mid-way through their programme of constructing a total of six hospitals. Two were up and running, and another was set to open. HCA acquired the company in May 1982 for £14 million. Although the purchase of these small hospitals, averaging around 40 beds each, was HCA's way of testing the market, the move was viewed as important enough for Dr Thomas F. Frist Sr to take time off

from the supervision of his chain of 368 hospitals, to visit one
of them: the Parkway Hospital in Solihull, Birmingham. The
first thing Dr Frist checked was that the rooms were attractive
and the beds soft.

The company cannot today be satisfied with its poor
visibility in the British market-place. Posh private medicine is
associated with Humana's Wellington and AMI's London
hospitals. 40-bed hospitals are hardly going to be regional
centres, and at least two of the hospitals have had to pay the
local NHS for pathology services. As Art Ouelette remarked:
'It is rather difficult to justify putting a full service pathology
department into a 36-bed hospital.' Maybe because of this,
the Corporation has been looking for a gap in the market
where it could really make its mark. The company
investigated the option of creating a 76-bed hospital in
Edinburgh, but was pipped at the post by a consortium
including BUPA. It looked into the feasibility of building a
clinic in Hampstead on the site of a hospice, and it set up a
market research study to define the need for private beds in
the psychiatric sector.

The Corporation is noted for its intelligence, and its caution
is probably justified. In 1982 a company representative stated
that three to five years would have to elapse before there was a
return on its investment. The company has yet to decide
whether to stick or make a higher bid.

Humana Inc., on the other hand, had decided by 1982 that
it had all the cards that it wanted to play. For the last few
years in the USA the company has pursued a policy of limiting
hospital acquisitions and diversifying into other areas – most
prominently its rather less than successful 'emergency
centres'.

Humana's hospitals are renowned for their cost consciousness, in practice meaning tight staffing standards. In Britain,
Humana set out to sell the Wellington as the prestige
hospital/hotel *par excellence*. Ironically, however, this is the
image they had inherited from the hospital's previous owners.

The result is that the Humana Hospital Wellington (all
Humana hospitals are prefixed with the Corporation's name)
is one of the largest commercial hospitals in Britain, with a
total of 230 in-patient beds, but it will remain the company's
solitary commitment to British commercial medicine.

With the exception of the new market entrants, the remaining US hospital chains are psychiatric care specialists. Charter Medical, says one of the company's advertisements, 'has become an international leader in psychiatric hospitals because it understands the issues that impact quality of care in today's dynamic health care market place'. The emphasis of psychiatric care, says the company, 'has shifted away from large, remote, state institutions toward modern, freestanding, private facilities in the community'. This was the formula that provided the company with a threefold growth in beds between 1979 and 1985. In the USA, the federal and state government policies on de-institutionalisation, and the growing tendency to transform family problems like child disobedience into medical terms like 'maladjustment', provided a huge boost for the private psychiatric industry.

Private psychiatric clinics are viewed quite favourably as a business enterprise because compared to surgical hospitals, they have low capital costs, little need for costly ancillary services and low staffing requirements. It is also relatively easy to position them in a favourable market 'niche'.

Charter Medical's British units are extremely 'well positioned' from geographical, clinical and marketing angles. It runs two clinics in London, the Charter Clinic Chelsea, with 45 beds, and the newer Charter Clinic Hampstead with 33 beds. Charter's bread and butter is its 'stress-related' treatment programmes for companies, and they have taken on quite prestigious experts in the field of alcoholism and stress management as medical directors.

Community Psychiatric Centres' operation in Britain is larger in scale, with three hospitals in London and Birmingham and a total of 280 beds. CPC has another string to its bow – kidney dialysis centres. In 1983, CPC owned or managed 49 kidney dialysis centres in the USA, dealing with 1,770 patients. With reduced reimbursement rates in the USA, the business is less profitable than it was (even so the federal government pays centres $127 for every treatment).[9] However, CPC plans to expand this business, and has used its psychiatric hospitals to develop the trade here. So far one contract has been won for a period of seven years to deliver services in Wales treating 28 patients per week, at a treatment fee of £77.50 (providing a potential income of £2,170 weekly).[10]

In 1985, three more US medical care corporations entered the British scene: National Medical Enterprises, Universal Health Care Services and Nu-Med Inc. NME purchased most of the British assets of United Medical Enterprises.

By 1986 the mood of the market had changed, as opportunities for expansion had all but dried up. Nevertheless, the Americans had arrived.

The Resistance Forces

The American corporations, of course, were not alone in recognising the opportunities opened up by the growth of medical insurance, Barbara Castle's attacks on NHS pay-beds and Margaret Thatcher's hostility to public services and public expenditure. Other companies were formed to develop private clinics. But they soon found that, along with the existing charitable nursing homes, the issue became not how best to exploit this market but rather how to fight off the American invasion.

The NHS pay-beds are the odd man out in all this. The number of authorisations has been increased, but beds authorised for private use can also be used for NHS patients, so low occupancy by private patients is not a problem for Health Authorities in the way that it is for private clinics. The government has continuously increased the pay-bed charges making treatment in NHS hospitals less attractive to private patients but thereby also giving Health Authority Treasurers more reason to push their DHAs into greater involvement in private care. Health Authorities have responded by upgrading their private facilities, but this means that pay-bed authorisations are more likely to refer to specific identifiable beds, in which NHS patients are less likely to be put, thereby posing potential problems of low occupancy.

But these problems are little next to those faced by the middle-aged clinics, the relics of the days before the invasion. The religious foundations have sometimes proved unable or unwilling to compete in the new commercial market. Between 1979 and 1985, four religious hospitals closed or stopped treating acute patients and the proportion of private hospital beds found in religious clinics dropped from 28.5 to 17.5 per cent.[11] In Edinburgh, the Little Company of Mary decided to close St Raphael's Nursing Home when BUPA moved into town. Sister Ignatius, the Provincial Superior, explained: 'We want to provide a service which we would like to feel is more individual but we cannot compete with firms which have limitless amounts of money to pour into its places.'[12] By contrast, the Sisters of the Daughters of the Cross of Liège decided to enter the world of commerce. In 1975, AMI took over the management of the Sisters' St Anthony's Hospital in Cheam, Surrey, and it was transformed into a successful international centre for open-heart surgery. The Sisters clearly gained confidence with their experience and the contract with AMI ended in March 1984.

Nuffield is having its troubles in the new climate, and lost its position as market leader to AMI in late 1984. From 1982 to 1984, the occupancy of the Nuffield clinics dropped from 74.9 to 70.0 per cent. The chain's surplus plummetted from £2,593,708 in 1982 through £912,595 the following year to just £326,052 in 1984: this latter sum was described by the charity's chair as 'not enough to provide a safety margin compatible with financial prudence'. The data on patients treated which had previously been set out in Nuffield's annual reports did not appear in the 1984 publication. Nuffield's response has been in part a £30 million development programme, extending and upgrading its clinics to win back customers impressed by the technical standards of some commercial hospitals. The charity's first marketing director was appointed, a new logo was adopted and a new name too: the Nuffield Nursing Homes Trust became Nuffield Hospitals. A video tape was prepared featuring BBC television presenter Frank Bough along with 'improved brochures for individual hospitals'. Oliver Rowell, the general manager, has also led campaigns for the restoration of the Health Services Board to control private hospital development, for the formation of a single trade association for the private sector and for more responsible behaviour from the 'wallet-motivated' consultants. He kicks himself for opportunities missed:

We were over-conscious of the need 15-20 years ago to keep the cost of private treatment right down. As a result we did not allow ourselves the chance to develop in-house capital. I wonder if we were not running scared ... We might have risked increasing the charges and built more hospitals ... if by the mid-1970s we had 51 hospitals, and not 21, we probably would have kept all these American concerns out of the country. I am really criticising myself on this. We left the way open.

However, Rowell is no doubt correct that Nuffield

will definitely survive. We don't have shareholders or dividends to pay. You might see us shutting down a hospital or two in areas of high competition, but it would be totally wrong to throw in the sponge or start spending millions on marketing to win the day.[13]

Nuffield may not have benefited from BUPA's decision to set up its own chain of private hospitals, perhaps out of frustration at Nuffield's caution, perhaps to promote the image of an all-round BUPA Health Service. The official rationale, though, is simply: 'We started building because there was an obvious need to do so. We took the view that if nobody else was going to fill the gap, it was incumbent on us to do so. The situation has now changed.'[14] By 1985, BUPA owned or managed ten clinics and that was 'the end of our first big thrust in hospital building'. BUPA claims its hospitals 'contributed substantially to our surplus' in 1984, in which year 'some 27,000 patients were seen and 24,000 operations performed'. BUPA Hospitals Ltd is now experimenting in new fields, such as the development of a home for the frail elderly in Milton Keynes (where the care provided is not covered by BUPA insurance policies) and the first management contract with an NHS unit, the nuclear magnetic resonance service provided at the National Hospital for Nervous Diseases in central London. But a planned joint project with the NHS in Oxford fell apart in some confusion. BUPA is also considering the development of tiny, 20-bed clinics: 'It is our view that in time what is going to happen is that there will be private centres of excellence with satellite hospitals around.'[15]

BUPA Hospitals is in fact a for-profit company but it has no doubt benefited from its parent's name, its detailed knowledge of medical insurance cover across the country and its large financial assets. Some of the more obviously commercial companies have found the going less easy. One, United Medical Enterprises, has withdrawn from the market altogether.

UME's tale has ironies for politicians of both major parties. The company was, after all, founded by Labour's National Enterprise Board, through the merger of the Allied Medical Group and Umedco. The NEB took a two-thirds share in UME and ruled that its component companies should no longer operate in the British private medical sector. Instead, UME operated as a hospital developer, manager and supplier, primarily in the Middle East, but boasting experience of 27 countries in all. A brochure explained:

> UME starts with the extra strength and flexibility that stems from the skills developed with Britain's Department of Health and Social Security and from the knowledge bank that exists within its personnel.

The election of Mrs Thatcher's government gave UME new ambitions, as it was now permitted to enter the British market. The company's original goal was impressive: a chain of twelve well equipped hospitals. To quote UME's Managing Director:

> UME proposes that each Independent High Technology Hospital will be developed in close proximity to a major teaching hospital, will offer full resident medical officer cover and will also offer facilities on a contract basis to the NHS. Such hospitals (which will be jointly owned by UME and Institutional Investors and run by UME) will generally provide facilities of around 100 beds (subject to local demand) and will offer a higher level of care, backed up by the latest advances in medical technology, than is presently available in the independent sector.

But the achievement was more modest. UME bought the site of the NHS London Jewish Hospital in Stepney Green, but the project was strongly opposed at the town-planning stage and then ran into financial problems. In January 1981, the company announced plans to develop a major private hospital for children in Great Portland Street. The development was subsequently taken over by the Hospital Capital Corporation, with the aid of oil-rich finance, and was eventually sold to AMI. UME's plans for Milton Keynes and for the site of Battersea General Hospital came to nought. Then in June 1983, as part of the government's programme of privatisation, UME was sold off to the London and Northern Group, a conglomerate involved in civil engineering, house building and oil-rig servicing. Finally, in January 1985, UME's British operations were sold off to American corporations: National Medical Enterprises (no relation) paid £9.95 million for a hospital recently opened near Maidstone, a development in Halifax, sites in Bristol and Cheshire and two hospital management contracts; Universal Health Services bought the London Jewish site for £1.5 million. UME itself was not sold off and continues to operate in other countries.

Perhaps the most consistently impressive British hospital developer in the UK, apart from BUPA, is the Community Hospitals group. This company was formed by MJH Nightingale (now Granville and Co.), a small merchant bank. Its goal was to develop ten to twelve clinics, financed by investments from City institutions and made feasible by the support of local consortia of consultants. Consultants with a busy private practice are expected to invest £5,000 in the local clinic while others are expected to invest £1,000. While this is a valuable token of commitment, the money raised thereby does not make a major contribution to development costs and creates 'internal contradictions' for Community Hospitals. As Alan Hird, one of company's directors, has said:

> There is a problem area between local doctors and the way a central institution thinks. The local consultants are only interested in their hospital. But it is not their hospital, it is their patients'. And there will always be the dilemma of whether to pay a dividend or buy a new piece of equipment which may save lives.[15]

By the end of 1984, Sir Peter Thompson, who chairs Community Hospitals, was able to report:

> Some £10 million has been invested in seven hospitals, which had a combined capital cost of £24 million. Of these, three were still in build at 30 June 1984 (Surrey, Mount Stuart and Caldaire) – two opened in 1983 (Bolton and Peterborough), and two are now in their second year of full operation (West Yorkshire and Hertfordshire). No dividends have yet been paid by any of the

operating hospitals. It is hoped that dividends will be paid next year by the hospital which opened first (West Yorkshire), since it will have absorbed its start-up costs from profits earned in its first two years.[16]

In 1984, the company recorded a consolidated loss of £244,000 and Sir Peter explained:

The start up phase of any new company is always the most difficult for investors, particularly when the period of gestation from investment to dividend flow is as long as four years in an individual hospital. With new hospitals being started at the rate of two or three a year, it will take a further two or three years at least to make Community Hospitals the planned ten hospital group with all the underlying hospitals in profit. In these circumstances, the 'development' period is indeed extended.

Clearly, while the company's development programme has been impressive – forged, incidentally, by recruits from AMI and HCA – only time will tell whether Community Hospitals will become a stable, profitable enterprise.

A handful of companies with a smaller investment in the development of private hospitals should also be mentioned. In June 1981, Mathercourt Securities created the London Private Health Group which bought the Garden Clinic in Hendon, North London and a share of the Ridgeway Hospital in Swindon. Lord Constantine reported in his 1983 Chairman's Statement:

There are three other hospital projects which are at an advanced stage of investigation by your Group, whilst preliminary enquiries and discussions involve another two potential health care schemes.

In early 1984, the company reached a major financial agreement in principle with the Australian Paul Ramsay Group only to find 20 per cent of the hospital company's shares being bought by Medic International Ltd and allies. Negotiations with the Australian company ended, the London Private Health Group bought Medic, was renamed Health Care Services 'and it was decided that the company would not proceed with new hospital projects for the time being'.[17] Subsequently, three of the company's directors resigned and £50,000 was paid in compensation.

Similarly, the Fleming Mercantile Investment Trust set up a subsidiary, Sloane Independent Hospitals, to exploit the perceived opportunities, but these clinics were later sold to AMI. The Hospital Capital Corporation sold its Park Hospital near Nottingham to AMI along with the Portland Hospital for Women and Children, while a project in Worcester was taken over by HCA.

Peter Townsend and Ken Turnbull set up Seltahart Holdings in 1975 and, with the builders YJ Lovell, started to develop a chain of six small provincial hospitals, subsequently sold to HCA. Messrs Townsend and Turnbull have now established Nationwide Hospitals and embarked on the development of another half-dozen hospitals with around 20 beds each, as part of 'continuing care programmes', also involving nursing homes and sheltered housing.

Perhaps the most interesting recent British entrant is Grand Metropolitan, the huge multinational, which in 1984 achieved a pre-tax profit of £334 million (or nearly ten times Nuffield's turnover) on a turnover of £5,075 million. Ranked ninth in the 'Financial Times 500', Grand Metropolitan has interests in food, brewing, tobacco, day care centres, public services contracting and hotels. The conglomerate is experimenting with health care services, as shown by its acquisition for $124 million of Quality Care Inc. in January 1985. This provides services for convalescent and infirm Americans in their homes in 193 different locations. This was followed soon thereafter by Grand Metropolitan's announcement that it would be buying Pearle Health Services, the largest American retailer of eye-care products, for $386 million. At the end of 1985 Pearle had almost 1,300 company owned and franchised offices in the USA, UK, the Netherlands, Belgium, Canada, Mexico and Puerto Rico. In the USA, the company has made exploratory investments in 'retail dentistry' – chains of dental shops and 'immediate health care', primary care centres, known to American physicians as 'Doc in a Box'. In the UK, GM Health Care now owns hospitals in Worthing, Bath, Basingstoke and Droitwich with a total of 150 beds. These clinics, it should be stressed, are at present of no great significance to Grand Metropolitan. But if the future shape of private medicine is determined by the developers' ability to throw money around, then Grand Metroplitan is the only

British company with the brute force to stand up to AMI and HCA.

Conclusion

In the last decade, then, private hospital provision has been transformed in character as well as size. Leaving aside the special case of NHS pay-beds, the traditional sectors – the religious clinics and the Nuffield Hospitals chain, for example – have been in relative, when not absolute, decline. A host of new for-profit chains have entered the market, saturating demand in some areas. City finance has been attracted to the sector and building companies and consortia of consultants have also invested in developments, the latter's involvement raising awkward issues of potentially conflicting interests. The most successful and dynamic hospital chains have been the Amereican corporations, especially AMI and HCA. The former remains bullish, while the latter has become more cautious. Small British chains – such as Seltahart, Sloane, UME and the Hospital Capital Corporation – have sold their clinics to the invading forces. Others, especially BUPA and Community Hospitals, have developed with some success, although their long-term prospects cannot be wholly secure.

In the long run, a US take-over of the private hospital business would be a mixed blessing to the private patients and insurers. In one sense, the American corporations justly boast of their cost-consciousness. But more generally, as Oliver Rowell warns,

> There are newcomers to the UK who, possessing only experience gained in other countries, seem blind to the perpetual danger of private treatment committing suicide by pricing itself beyond the reach of the consumer.[18]

In July 1985, Lord Wigoder expressed his concern about 'the arrival from abroad of highly profit-motivated groups building on a substantial scale. The pressures from their shareholders must lead to an increase in charges, and they are setting out to dominate the market'.[19]

The transformation has not been a matter of ownership alone. The new hospitals tend to be somewhat larger and better-equipped than in the past, and the traditional sector has been upgrading its facilities wherever possible. (But it remains the case that only a handful of private clinics can boast the facilities of a run-of-the-mill NHS District General Hospital and no 'full service' private hospital yet exists.) With the end of the medical insurance boom in 1981, the developers have been surveying new fields of operation. Many clinics now offer health screening facilities. The companies are gingerly moving into the care of the elderly and chains of nursing homes and sheltered housing units are now being developed. The American corporations like Charter and CPC, but also AMI and HCA, are involved in the development of clinics offering short-term psychiatric care for alcoholics, drug addicts and patients suffering nervous breakdowns. AMI has also entered the field of private general practice. Meanwhile, management contracting has developed within the private sector, with BUPA, AMI and National Medical Enterprises (in UME's shoes), leading the way. (But Nuffield Nursing Homes Management Ltd ceased to trade in February 1983.)

The companies are also keen to develop links with the NHS, to counteract over-capacity by treating NHS patients and to manage NHS hospitals. This opens the prospect of an American invasion of the public health care sector as well as the private.

Notes

[1] Michael Lee, *Private and National Health Services*, Policy Studies Institute, 1978.

[2] *Independent Medical Care*, February/March 1984.

[3] O.J. Rowell, 'The Best of Both Worlds', *Hospital and Health Services Review*, September 1983.

[4] *A Healthier Attitude to Private Medical Care*, Nuffield Hospitals, n.d.

[5] *Report and Accounts 1983*, Nuffield Hospitals, 1984.

[6] *Health and Social Services Journal*, 24 October 1984.

[7] *Independent Medical Care*, December 1983.

[8] John Ashton, 'Kentucky Fried Hospital', *Times Health Supplement*, 4 December 1981.

[9] *Modern Healthcare*, 15 May 1984.

[10] Tony Heath, 'Health Care Firms Win NHS Kidney Unit Contracts', *Guardian*, 4 January 1985.

[11] *Financial Times*, 13 February 1985.

[12] Quoted in NHS Unlimited, *Private Hospitals and Their Owners*, Memorandum 1, edition 3, 1984.

[13] *Financial Times*, 13 February 1985.

14 Quoted in NHS Unlimited, op.cit.
15 Ibid.
16 *Report and Accounts 30 June 1984*, Community Hospitals plc.
17 *Annual Report 1984*, The London Private Health Group plc.
18 *Hospitals and Health Services Review*, September 1983.
19 *Newcastle Journal*, 11 July 1985.

PART TWO
THE PRIVATE LIFE OF THE NHS

Chapter 5

Public Versus Private:
The Historic Compromise

The National Health Service has never been a monolithic, state-run system of medical care. Some on the left have believed that it represents an island of socialism in capitalist society, while extreme right-wingers have seen it as evidence of growing totalitarianism and the death of freedom. Neither view is correct.

Since July 1948, the National Health Service has relied upon a working partnership between public and private organisations. The terms of the partnership have been negotiable, but the balance of power between the partners has remained undisturbed. The regulation of nursing homes might be reformed, but the homes remained private property. Hospitals might accept charitable income, but they did not lose their public status by doing so. In health care, as in the national economy, the mixed economy flourished. The mixed economy that made up the NHS differed from the usual because public institutions dominated private ones – or, at least, they appeared to do so. This appearance of public superiority is the source of illusions on both left and right. The reality has always been much more complex, and many important political debates around health care have concentrated on the public sector's reliance on private provision. Typical of these debates are the BMA's Family Doctor's Charter of 1966,[1] the surveys of provision for the

elderly infirm,[2] the implementation of the 1967 Abortion Act
and the regulation of the pharmaceutical industry.

The left finds it difficult fully to grasp the politics of health
even though the creation of the NHS is Labour's greatest
success story. Two factors explain this paradox. The NHS has
not evolved in a unified way, but in a series of separate, though
interrelated, steps. Ideological commitment – to the NHS as
the jewel in Labour's crown – prevented the left from seeing
the creation for what it really was: a heterogeneous range of
interests and activities combined together by government
intervention. Believing the health service to be a single
institution – 'The NHS' – socialists forgot that it was based on
public-private collaboration.

The dependence of public health services on private
provision has not followed a single pattern across the whole
industry. On the contrary, the loose nature of NHS
organisation has allowed different partnership arrangements
to emerge, each with its own impact on the quantity and
quality of service provided, and each with its particular
interest-groups. As the market has shaped aspects of health
care, so the market's traditional opponents have responded,
but only according to each aspect's appearance. Drug
company profits have been criticised, and the prescribing
habits of doctors attacked, but no effective understanding of
the disease-oriented medical philosophy that underpins both
prescribing and pharmaceutical production has reached
trades unions or political organisations opposed to the market.

One commentator's observation that no Marxist analysis of
health care exists reflects both the multifaceted evolution of
the NHS and the weakness of contemporary Marxist thinking
about the state.[3] A comprehensive assessment has not
emerged, partly because of the sectional biases that confuse
class interests with trade union thinking, party advantage or
sociological concern, but also because the historical
dependence of public health care on private provision has
always been a taboo subject for many socialists.

The left's taboo has become the right's advantage. The
reality of state-run health care is that pharmaceutical
production, the whole of general practice, dentistry,
ophthalmic services and high-street pharmacy, the bulk of
postgraduate medical education (including virtually all

journals), the hospital supply industries, most organised residential provision for the elderly infirm, and about half of the legal abortion services are outside the state's direct control. 'Socialised medicine' is rightly applauded for its virtues, and organised labour can take some credit for the formation of the NHS. But there is more to health care than a state-financed hospital network, and many reasons why the medical profession subscribes to state medicine. Failure to recognise the true extent of the public-private mix in health reveals how widely the professional definition of a health service has been accepted. Not only does 'Medicine' substitute itself for 'Health', but 'Hospitals' for 'Community' and 'Cure' for 'Prevention'. While many in the labour movement do talk critically of the NHS as a 'National Sickness Service', these criticisms have not been taken further. The three examples of public-private collaboration discussed in this section do not exhaust the scope of the mixed economy of health care. They are the major areas of the mix in services, apart from private medicine itself. Aspects of health service activity affecting fewer people, either as users or providers, but still involving both public and private institutions, include the care of the elderly infirm and the provision of abortion services. Since 1984, the long-term care of the elderly infirm has devolved onto NHS hospitals, local authority residential homes, institutions run by charities and profit-making private nursing homes. As NHS finance was concentrated on acute care, the private sector became a useful reserve of long-stay beds. One source estimated that more than 40 per cent of the 28,000 beds in private nursing homes in the late 1970s were occupied by NHS patients, and attracted NHS subsidies.[4] In the early 1980s the flow of money from the social security system into private homes became a major concern of even Mrs Thatcher's government.

Abortion services have been more or less equally provided by the NHS and private institutions, since the 1967 Abortion Act.[5] In areas where pressure from women's organisations for NHS, i.e. free, abortion services (especially day-care abortion) has motivated otherwise reluctant Health Authorities, contracts with charitable organisations like the Pregnancy Advisory Service (PAS) have substituted for the development of in-house facilities.[6] For the women concerned this substitution has real advantages. They no longer have to pay the (not inconsiderable) fees of the charitable abortion service, nor the higher charges of profit-seeking private gynaecologists; the NHS picks up the bill for them. The precedent that they are endorsing, of clinical services being contracted out to private suppliers, is not their first concern. It may become so if the effects of private provision on the quality and character of medical care follow the trends demonstrated by independent contractor services, the drugs industry and medical technology. Fortunately, this has not yet happened; if anything the abortion charities have to date set the standards for expertise and a caring approach.

Like other nationalised industries, the National Health Service acts as a stable support for private enterprise. It provides a large market, allows private interests easy access to decision making in health care from the level of budget-allocation to that of the doctor-patient relationship, and offers subsidies to secure a predictable level of service. In that sense, profit-seeking industries may be seen as parasitic on the health service, for their primary objective – maximum profit – can become an influence on the nature of medical care, displacing an objective that is all too vulnerable: the satisfaction of people's medical needs.

Nevertheless, the charge of parasitism is only partially valid. Given the priorities of organised labour since 1948, the public-private mix in health care stands as a valid approach to the provision of comprehensive services to the whole population. Exceptions may occur, as in the growth of private medicine in the late 1960s and early 1970s. Then the anger of the left at blatant abuse of power (by consultants) for the pursuit of privilege (of both doctors and patients) prompted political action. No such action has grown around the equally scandalous inequalities and class injustices perpetrated by commercial pressures within general practice, dentistry, drug promotion or unplanned technological experimentation. Most of the left, most of the time, has in effect accepted the NHS as an organiser of private enterprise, from the self-employed, single-handed pharmacist through the chain-store opticians, to the multi-nationals of the pharmaceutical trade. That fact supports the private sector's claim to be symbiotic with the NHS, in a relationship of mutual advantage.

Thatcherism

The 1979 Conservative government aimed to shift the balance within the public-private mix in health care. Expanded private provision was seen as a source of relief to the Exchequer, burdened by the rising costs of the NHS. Differing views of the ideal balance existed within the Conservative Party then, as they do today. The most pragmatic within the party anticipated relatively minor changes, and acted as a useful shield for Margaret Thatcher when, in 1983, she was forced to calm Tory party fears and the voters' anxieties by saying that she had 'no more intention of dismantling the NHS than she had of dismantling Britain's defences'. Drier Conservatives favoured radical monetarist proposals for replacement of the present health service with some system of individual health insurance. This option is not simply an eccentric preoccupation of the Adam Smith Institute.[7] 'Think Tank' reports in the same vein gained some support within the Cabinet, and the DHSS was instructed to investigate the feasibility of insurance systems.[8]

This spectrum of Conservative opinion and expectation has prevented Thatcher's Cabinet from pursuing any consistent privatisation policy within the NHS, except in the limited areas of laundry, cleaning and catering. Thus, rapid success in shifting responsibility for health care spending onto private budgets has eluded the government. Even the 'boom' area of private medical services has failed to stop rising public spending. The private sector has encountered its own problems of supply and demand.

The independent contractor services are dominated by small business mentality and skills, and at first glance appear ripe for monetarist experiments. Yet the evolution of general practice since 1979 has, if anything, been in the opposite direction, with increased professional pressure for more resources, and a dispute over contracted-out deputising services that embarrassed the government. Pharmacists have had to supervise a 1100% increase in prescription charges without being able to notice a decrease in NHS spending on drugs or in public demand for medicines. Opticians have become the victims of a deregulation move aimed to allow commercial, non-professional, interests to supply glasses, and the option of buying NHS glasses was abolished for most of the population before being axed altogether.

The pharmaceutical industry has had a bad press during Thatcher's administration. Successive drug scandals have pushed pharmaceutical monopolies into the headlines and profitable pills off the prescriptions. Over-pricing has made generic prescribing (prescribing by chemical name, not trade name) and generic substitution (chemists substituting cheaper versions of one drug for expensive, branded versions) live issues. Ministers have acknowledged the need to reduce drug prices, a nervous industry has agreed to negotiations to cut profits in the hope of averting further controls, and Treasury pressure has forced the DHSS ministers into an embarrassing U-turn on limited drug lists.

Sometimes it is difficult to see how badly the Conservatives cope with health politics, for the endless succession of closures and counter-campaigns preoccupy socialist thinking, and tinge it with gloom as unstoppable changes overcome resistance. Yet a detailed look at how the Thatcher government has handled problems, and attempted to work out its strategy and tactics, reveals weaknesses which could be more effectively exploited by the left.

The radical right is trapped by traditions and by the complex structure and overlapping interests within the health service under present conditions. Conservatism can no more sweep away its enemies and the many obstacles to a free market economy than the left can abolish the power of the privileged and impose economic planning. The Conservatives have to revert to a long march through the institutions and practices created, in part at least, by the labour movement and the Labour Party. Despite their experience and assets, they are finding the journey difficult.

Traditional allies, in medicine, move against them. Outside pressures force Tories to constrain the profit levels of the pharmaceutical industry, intervening against all Thatcherite reason in private industry's affairs. Conservative MPs rebel against the withdrawal of NHS optical goods, whilst deregulation of optical services gambles with the profitability of manufacturing industry. The more political twisting and turning the Tories must do, the slower practices and relationships change within health care. Advocates of planning for health, and critics of the market's capacity to provide equitable and effective medical services, have more need and more opportunities within health politics to challenge the assumptions and initiatives of contemporary conservatism.

Notes

[1] *A Charter for the Family Doctor Service*, discussed succinctly in R. Klein, *The Politics of the NHS*, Longman, 1983.

[2] See, for example, P.Townsend, *The Last Refuge*, Routledge and Kegan Paul, 1964.

[3] See Chapter 7 of C.Ham, *Health Policy in Britain*, Macmillan, 1982.

[4] *Observer*, 8 July 1979.

[5] For a background to the 1967 Abortion Act see V.Greenwood and J. Young, *Abortion in Demand*, Pluto, 1976.

[6] *Hansard*, 25 November 1983.

[7] The Adam Smith Institute is the modern expression of traditional far right views that favour hotel charges for hospital care, charges for consultations with doctors and more competition within health care.

[8] The DHSS review of insurance funding for health care began in 1980, but its findings were never made public.

Chapter 6
The Contracting Professions

The nationalisation of the hospitals in 1948 rescued the voluntary and private hospitals from a future of economic distress, and many of the municipal hospitals from stagnation. A similar rescue operation removed the uncertainties of the market for the new front-line of the NHS, the community-based services of general practice, dentistry, ophthalmics and pharmacy, but without full nationalisation.

Doctors, dentists, pharmacists and opticians became independent contractors to the new health service. They obtained public funding, and no longer had to compete for customers, but they retained their freedom from control by the NHS administration. These independent contractor professions are now guaranteed a basic income that is related to workload and open to supplementation through extra activity. They represent the largest component of public-private collaboration within the NHS.[1]

That does not mean that these professional groups are part of the private sector. Far from it. They rely on state subsidies to stabilise incomes and pay for facilities, and in that sense are more like clients than entrepreneurs. However, they are not employees, subject to discipline and direction, and cannot demand standard employees' rights to good working conditions, appropriate training and adequate resources to do the job. Like entrepreneurs, they must provide for themselves – and their main market is the NHS, not the population.

Independent contractors are flexible. They could convert into state employees by simple modifications of contracts and payments. And they could return to the private sector, if the population could offer more than the Treasury will allow. Their connection with the NHS is a piece of history, frozen in the class relationships of post-war Britain. A reforming

Labour government organised a class of tradesmen and aspiring professionals into a state service, on behalf of the working people, but without enforcing public accountability on them. Since 1948 the professions and the state have argued about how much support, and how little control, was needed to keep services running.

Yet, paradoxically, the independent contractor services may be as progressive and socialist as the more centrally directed hospital network, despite their market origins. Countries with flourishing private health care have tended to lose their generalist community health workers, in favour of specialists sallying out from their hospital bases into private practices in the community. A divided health service, with a generalist layer acting as a filter before a central specialist core, is not unique to Britain; the European state socialist bloc has similar systems, and its value is being rediscovered in capitalist economies stretched by rising health care spending (the USA and Sweden are good examples).[2] Perhaps the explanation of the paradox lies in the relative powerlessness of the European left. Only Britain was able to establish a Welfare State and National Health Service in spite of a war-ruined economy. Richer countries, like Sweden, created health services as part of their economic growth, whilst the socialist bloc made its health services out of the post-war conflicts between classes. Britain's working class was strong enough, after 1945, to make itself felt without making itself master.

Like the health service itself, independent contractors are a heterogeneous group of professional workers, stretching across a commercial spectrum from near-salaried (general practitioners) to largely market-based (opticians). Each group demonstrates the consequences of public and private collaboration in health care, in different ways and to different extents. The features of each professional group allow us to anticipate the impact on health care of further shifts of balance between public and commercial services.

General Practice

General practitioners are shopkeepers. They still wait for customers to call in, even though GPs have had nothing to sell since 1948. Individuals must decide that they are, or will be, ill, and become that particular sort of customer, a 'patient'. Some general practitioners do approach *all* 'their' patients, to offer specific services to individuals who are not ill (like immunisation against german measles, or cervical smear tests), but this is not mainstream work, is uncommon enough to be talked and written about regularly, and anyway often gets delegated to 'lower' professionals, like nurses.[3] The heart of general practice medicine is the face-to-face contact of doctor and patient, tradesperson and customer.

The family doctor's contract with the NHS (through the Family Practitioner Committees) reflects this market relationship. The GP is bound to provide services, on request, to his/her patient, although s/he may give the job to a (shop) assistant, if s/he is serving someone else. S/he will be paid a subsidy for each customer s/he accepts as a patient, and will get bonuses for particular services provided: night-time visits, contraceptive advice, maternity care, immunisation and cervical smear tests. The original subsidy is unrelated to his/her work, and a 'good' patient is one who never visits the doctor, but for whom the doctor is paid. The next best is a woman who only visits the doctor for maternity care, contraceptive advice and the immunisation of her children, for she is a real money-spinner.

This piece-work system of payment was strengthened by the Family Doctor's Charter (1966), which systematised piece-work fees, bonuses and direct grants into a system of remuneration so complicated that it occupies a small volume (ironically called 'The Red Book') that all GPs have, but few seem to understand fully. This system finances each GP (through a salary element), rewards seniority (but without testing wisdom), pays fees for patients (capitation) and for work (fees for item of service), encourages re-education (but without insisting upon it), promotes group practice (without specifying collective or collaborative work), underwrites the cost of buildings, and pays the bulk of ancillary staff wages (without dictating wage-levels). An administrative machinery, within Family Practitioner Committees, transforms claims and costs into fees and reimbursements, whilst specialist accountants decipher The Red Book and devise new tactics for increasing practice income. Medical politics, and negotiations between GP representatives and the DHSS about money, focus on the intricacies of private dependence on public wealth, and the scope for private evasion of public responsibility.

Whilst the independent-contractor GP will grasp the taxpayer's money as willingly as might a German or French peasant, s/he will not accept responsibility to taxpayers or to the elected representatives of the taxpayers, or to the appointed officials of government. Independence is sacrosanct, once the money is handed over, and 'responsibility' is owed only to the individual customer, the patient. The unequal relationship between the doctor and the patient does not dent the professional argument, which pretends that we are 'free to choose' our doctors, as if illness and the fear of illness were equivalent to desires for consumer durables. In reality, few shop around for medical bargains, and those that do must often enter the fully commercial sector to satisfy their wants.

The combination of market relationships and state funding has many advantages, and therefore is viable despite its internal contradictions. Doctors get a good financial deal without the stresses of competition, and with an individualised system of accountability biased in the professional's favour. The state gets a stable medical service, with a more-or-less contented workforce. It does not have to build health centres for all doctors, but only a few as token centres of excellence that presuppose a persistent periphery of less-than-excellence. It does not have to pay union rates for ancillary staff wages, but only a proportion of wage-rates 'negotiated' in the paternalist warmth of family medicine. It does not even have to pay for all the piece-work done, because the paperwork of claiming is an early victim of the rushed, seven-minute-long consultation.

Public-private collaboration in general practice may benefit its organisers, but it has mixed effects for consumers. The distribution, uptake and use of GP services varies according to the class composition of the population.[4] The lists of GPs in predominantly working-class areas tend to be longer than those of their peers in 'better' areas, and working-class populations have higher rates of illness, disability and premature death from almost all causes. Whilst working-class patients may visit their GP more frequently than professional and managerial workers, they seem less likely to benefit from

long consultations, detailed explanations and full investigation of their complaints.[5] The class differences in the provision
of services have many causes, but the demand-orientation of
GPs is one of them. The best response is given to the best –
that is, most articulate, well organised, comprehensive –
demand, which in turn is most likely to come from people
whose education, understanding and confidence most closely
match the doctor's. The cleaner who complains only of
'dizziness' or 'weakness' poses a formidable diagnostic
problem to a doctor who may be bewildered (and even
frightened) by class, race and sex differences. The teacher
whose growing tiredness, poor concentration and worsening
irritability prompt an admission of 'anxiety' or 'depression'
may be talking the doctor's language, and have done half the
work too. The latter patient is favoured over the former, and
the 'good neighbourhood' dominated by orderly and relatively
affluent people is sought out in preference to tower-block
estates and peaks of local unemployment. Since the doctor is
not goal-directed, but simply patient-oriented, s/he cannot be
blamed for wanting patients who are 'good' in all senses – not
quarrelsome, easy to understand, and simple to serve. If GPs
were paid on results, or for achieving specific goals, then areas
with high-illness rates might become more attractive, because
they could be more lucrative. Fortunately for general
practitioners, a medical consensus on 'success' in treatment is
rare, and then often short-lived, so no practical system of
rewarding success has yet emerged to reverse the bias created
by the independent contractor's fixation with demand.

Patient-centred medicine may be better than a specialist
obsession with organs or diseases located, as if by chance, in
individual human beings, but it is nothing new. The market
origins of general practice include the whole person, and the
supposedly scientific depersonalisation of medical care is a
more recent change, associated in Britain with state-run
hospital medicine. The evidence that patient-centred medicine is enough to meet the health needs of Britain's
population is scanty. Half the diabetics in Britain are
unknown to the NHS. Half of those with blood pressure high
enough to threaten their future health are also unknown to the
medical services, including their patient-oriented general
practitioners. Half of those known will not be on any

medication, and only half of those being treated, will be adequately treated.[6] This 'rule of halves' probably applies to all the major health problems in this country: asthma, arthritis, epilepsy, bronchitis, and so on. There are many obstacles that prevent this mass of unmet need from being met by medical services, but the first of them is the blindness of professionals who cannot lift their eyes from their customer's expectant faces.

For all the proclaimed autonomy of general practitioners from NHS control, no significant shift away from public to private provision of service has occurred within general practice since 1979. On the contrary, such changes as there were reinforced earlier ideas about the value of public services in primary care, and even promoted concepts of planning and accountability within family practitioner services. Before Thatcher's first electoral victory the BMA had failed to gain support for a new policy in general practice, involving an extension of fee payments for items of service.[7] The BMA's hope was that more activities – taking blood pressure, or syringing ears, for example – could attract fees. The more the workload of the GP could be itemised, the more the payments system would be sensitive to the actual work of the doctor. Such a productivity deal would also have an added advantage of flexibility, since itemised work converts easily into an itemised account. From the payee's viewpoint, the source of payment is less relevant than the fact of payment. Whilst the NHS pays for the items of service, general practitioners benefit from public provision. Should the NHS succumb to Thatcherism (or worse) the same itemised accounts could be presented to the insurance companies that filled the gap, or even to the patients themselves.

Nevertheless, the profession rejected the idea, and the BMA's draft policy sank so far out of sight that five years later there was no evidence of any *new* policy for general practice, merely a restatement of the cost-effectiveness of funding general practitioner services through the NHS.[8] Fees for items of service were not disclaimed because of an ideological shift to the left: the Medical Practitioners Union produced counter-policies in 1979,[9] and went on to press arguments about planning, resource-provision and accountability in 1984,[10] but at no point has it constituted more than a vocal minority of doctors. The BMA plan was cold-shouldered by the mainstream of general practice, partly because of the obvious administrative complexity of claiming, checking and paying such fees, and partly because the present payment system's bias towards a salary element imposes no demands on personal workload. Productivity deals that make individuals work harder for the same rewards are unlikely to become popular.

Whilst the BMA adopted a centrist position and distanced itself from the more ambitious hopes of the Conservatives, general practice was scrutinised and solutions offered for its weaknesses, particularly in the cities. The Acheson report on primary care in London suggested 150 ways in which general practice, community nursing services and the hospitals could work better, and in harmony.[11] The Black Report identified class inequalities in health and health care as the major problem facing the NHS and the welfare state, and proposed community-based initiatives to improve health services in the most disadvantaged areas.[12] Professional debate included arguments about the failure of independent contractor services to distribute themselves according to need,[13] and about the need to replace this independence with salaried status for general practitioners.[14] Preventive medicine became an important theme for the Royal College of General Practitioners,[15] even if the College could not avoid defending its profession with reports that were kind to urban doctors,[16] and that explained apparent inequality as natural differences.[17] The political climate within medicine did not shift towards either the financial obsessions of the private sector, or the competition-consciousness of the market economists. On the contrary, the ideas of a previous period persisted and gained significance: planning, correcting inequalities, integrating services, meeting needs.

The unexpected resistance to Thatcherism within medicine spread to other issues, until the DHSS and the BMA came to blows over the unlikely subject of deputising services in general practice. In early 1984 the then Health Minister, Kenneth Clarke, issued a draft circular outlining plans to restrict GPs' access to commercial deputising services.[18] He did so under pressure from the media, after the quality press and television had unearthed scandals involving commercial deputising, and after Tory MPs like Christopher Hawkins had jumped on the bandwagon. The Conservative press applauded Clarke's initiative. The *Daily Express* headlined the story 'Doctor Who?' and followed this with 'Why a stranger turns up when you call out your doctor'. The *Mail on Sunday* lectured: 'Doctors have had their own way for far too long ... now Mrs Thatcher prepares her own prescription.' In reply the BMA organised large angry meetings of GPs in the urban centres where commercial deputising services operate, using its financial association with the largest service, 'Air Call', to promote joint platforms of professional and commercial interests.[19]

The noise of battle drowned the sounds of hasty compromises and tactical retreats. The government had probably anticipated problems over doctors' pay when the Review Body report was due to appear, in April. With the BMA talking of a 17 per cent increase, and the government thinking of only a 5 per cent increase for doctors, the idea of a pre-emptive strike against the BMA made sense. If the profession could be bruised before April, and public hostility to undeserving doctors built up, the coming pay argument might be easier for the government to settle.

The Conservatives also wanted to teach the BMA a lesson. Professional organisations have a 'moderate' slot in Conservative consciousness, and BMA protests at hospital closures and staffing cuts offended Tory sensibilities. Rejection of Home Office doctrine on medical planning for nuclear war was a further insult added to the injury inflicted by the report on health service financing.[20] By February 1984 enough Conservatives were irritated by the BMA's outspokenness for a brawl to be sparked off by a minor incident.

There may have been other considerations. Repeated DHSS claims to be spending more than ever before on the NHS did not appear to square with ward and hospital closures and rising professional unemployment. Conservative propaganda and the daily experiences of health service workers and users told very different stories, and the government may have guessed that belief in the safety of the NHS in Tory hands was shaky, even in loyal areas. In that situation an attack on 'bad medicine', in the shape of the hurried and impersonal visits of GP deputies, might restore a little credibility. Even if it did not, the issue needed attention before the opposition parties exploited it to attack the government's record yet again.

With this mixture of motives and justifications in the background the Health Minister announced his plans, and began discussions with the medical profession's representatives.

They had plenty to talk about. So many uncomfortable issues appeared from the deputising story that the scandals that started the media bandwagon became minor nuisances, and able negotiators had to keep their options open and become very flexible indeed to avoid further embarrassment. Clarke's initiative could have backfired on the Conservatives. Commercial deputising services are a form of private medicine. General practitioners using them are contracting out their work to unknown doctors, without any real control over the quality of the service given by their deputies. Since the Conservatives had great hopes for contracting out medical services, promoting a private nursing home boom with ample state subsidies and measuring up non-urgent surgery and family planning for the same treatment, the last thing the Ministers needed was too much discussion about the failings of commercial medicine. The more that 'abuse' of deputising services is studied, the more obvious such failings become. Overriding political objectives required the DHSS and the BMA to find some way of judging commercial services to be fundamentally sound, and therefore available to general practitioners.

The GPs had an interest in such a solution, for an attempt to control their use of deputising services could set a precedent for other controls that might, in the end, destroy their independent contractor status completely. The more the DHSS controls GPs' activity, the nearer the doctors are to being state employees. The general practitioners would have to account for themselves, to their employer, for what they did, and did not do, in general practice. The thought appals the BMA, and worries the DHSS as well. Whilst control over general practitioners has its attractions, the prospect of a new breed of salaried GPs clamouring for more health centres, more staff and better equipment has no appeal to Health Ministers struggling with the Treasury and the Cabinet to retain their present share of public spending. Both sides could agree to a solution that changed little in practice, but reflected well on all parties. Kenneth Clarke was able to introduce limited controls that might modify GPs' use of deputising services without seriously limiting them, whilst the BMA acted responsibly to put its own house in order.[21] Justice was seen to be done, even when it had not been done at all, and the government was able to split the Review Body's proposed pay award (of nearly 7 per cent) into two parts with barely a murmur of protest from the profession.[22]

Although the government could not win an outright victory against the BMA on deputising services, it did not reduce its pressure on the medical profession. In 1984 plans for a limited drugs list were announced and pushed through against both BMA and drug company opposition. Medical pressure failed to prevent government erosion of clinical freedom and the Conservatives were able to demonstrate their dominance over a union as powerful as the BMA. The full significance of this success is not yet clear, three years later.

Publication of *Primary Health Care*, the government's green paper on the reform of family practitioner services, was postponed from the autumn of 1984 until April 1986, making the profession's organisations increasingly anxious about Conservative intentions and their own lack of any special relationship with a Tory-controlled DHSS. To influence this green paper the GPs' national negotiating body, the General Medical Services Committee, published its own hopes for a transfer of some hospital functions (like minor surgery) to general practice. *Primary Health Care* turned out to be far less radical than press leaks had predicted, maybe in part because of the imminence of the next General Election. The government proposed to alter GPs' remuneration with the introduction of a 'good practice allowance' which would be most unlikely to narrow, indeed could well widen, the gap between the standards of care experienced by middle-class and working-class patients. The government also suggested that competition amongst GPs would be encouraged by increasing the proportion of their pay which was directly related to the number of patients on their list. Despite moves to improve the range of information available to patients, the danger remained that encouraging GPs to lengthen their lists would lead to even shorter consultations and even less attention to preventive services. The Cumberlege Report on community nursing services, issued at the same time, stressed the importance of a planned approach to provision. Some of its major recommendations – like considering the amalgamation of Family Practitioner Committees and District Health Authorities and also the possibility of a salaried family doctor service – were rejected out of hand by the government in *Primary Health Care*.

Dentistry

The way in which dentists are paid has an obvious impact on the nature of the dental service, for two reasons. Piece-work payment is the norm, and dentists do not have a continuing commitment to their customers.

Piece-work payments require a sound judgement of supply and demand. If demand and supply are both high, payments can be set at low levels. If supply is low, and demand high, piece-work rates can be increased to stimulate the suppliers. Dental fees, paid in return for claims submitted by dental surgeons to the Dental Estimates Board, and determined by negotiation between professionals and the DHSS, should follow market rules. In practice, they cannot do so, since the state's funding of the independent contractors is designed to stabilise the market and limit public expenditure.

Dentistry in the NHS got off to a bad start. Both the demand and need for dental repair, and the working capacity of dentists, were underestimated. Piece-work rates were set at too high a value, dentists demonstrated their speed and stamina, and fees claimed exceeded the Health Ministry's limit. Attempts to reduce the fees for items of service provoked the 'rate wars' of the 1950s, and began the erosion of NHS dentistry.[23]

Poorly-funded piece-work payment encourages quantity, rather than quality, production. In the first years of the NHS this emphasis may have been excusable, given the back-log of unmet need inherited from inter-war poverty. By the 1970s, however, dentistry had shifted away from simple tooth extraction towards more complex dental repair, and quality of work became a significant issue. As fees for repair work were renegotiated, increasing numbers of procedures were done, and increasing numbers of people had to return to their dentists for repairs to the original repair work! The table shows the rising trend in crown filling, and refixing, between 1970 and 1975.[24]

	1970	1971	1972	1973	1974	1975
Crown procedures	415,130	461,930	511,500	624,800	739,050	862,370
Crowns refixed or recemented		49,760	60,160	78,550	91,830	112,790	134,830

Did the increase in fees in 1972 allow dentists to work profitably on those needing crowns, so demonstrating the extent of unmet need? Or did the higher fee encourage dentists to perform crown procedures on those who did not really need them? Whatever the answer, the re repair rates rose significantly from 12 per cent in 1970 to 15.6 per cent in 1975, suggesting that practice did *not* make perfect.

Dental activity seems related to the dentist's judgement of the levels of fees. Low piece-work rates for the treatment of primary teeth in children in 1973 coexisted with advanced tooth decay in 20 per cent of five-year-olds and 35 per cent of eight-year-olds who attended dentists regularly. Whilst half the adult population with teeth probably needed treatment for gum disease in the mid-1970s, only 151,360 courses of such low-paid treatment were completed in 1975. The housebound suffered the same fate. Uninviting fees for home visits helped keep home visiting low – at under 15,000 in 1975.

Since government incomes policies have been the norm since the Second World War, independent contractors like dentists have been caught between a cost-conscious state and a profit-seeking market. The privately-owned dental laboratories supplying NHS dentists with dentures and crowns increased their charges faster than the NHS increased its fees to dentists in the late 1960s, so that procedures with a large laboratory component became unprofitable. Since dentists have no obligation to provide unprofitable treatment under the NHS, patients were charged directly for such complex work.[25] Widespread leakage into private practice and confusion over the boundaries of NHS and private dentistry were the consequences of selective withdrawal of dentists from NHS work, and the cause of the complaint that NHS dentistry was hard to find.[26]

Charges to patients certainly have a deleterious effect. One study suggested that 24 per cent of those with no natural teeth, and 6 per cent of those with some natural teeth, found dental charges a barrier to regular dental care.[27]

Piece-work payment seems to have a greater negative impact on dentistry than it does in general practice, in which the bulk of professional income comes from basic salary and capitation. Capitation payments (annual payments for each registered patient) promote a long-term responsibility towards the individual by the professional, and therefore differ enormously from the short-term contract to restore 'dental fitness' agreed between dentist and customer. Lack of responsibility to the individual consumer has effects on the availability of NHS dentistry. Urgent dental treatment may not be available because it may be outside any pre-existing contract to restore dental fitness. The provision of emergency dental services then becomes a moral rather than contractual obligation for the dentist. Preventive dentistry, particularly with children, also suffers for lack of long-term contractual commitment by dentists to a defined population. The Royal Commission for the NHS (1976-79) argued in its report that the implementation of a preventive dental programme depended on finding a new method of paying dentists for the work they will need to do. The government's 1986 green paper on *Primary Health Care* proposed to extend a pilot scheme under which dentists were paid a capitation fee for child patients. Piece-work payment is too crude a reward for work, when work is long-term and preventive rather than restorative.

Optical Services

The only part of the NHS that has proved to be highly vulnerable to commercialisation are the General Ophthalmic Services (GOS) administered by the Family Practitioner Committees. To date, no one has picketed outside opticians' shops or FPC offices against privatisation. Trade unions do not educate their members about the consequences of hiving off part of the NHS optical service, and the media have been blind to the issue.

This can be explained by reference to the strong commercial element in the GOS, with its increasingly glossy high-street emporia, its growing chain-store organisation and its long history of charges to NHS customers. In a way, the GOS has never seemed to be part of the NHS at all, even though the NHS obviously subsidised it. Further commercialisation seems so likely that interest in it, let alone opposition to it, is hard to sustain. When the local hospital is closing, who cares if the government is promising cheaper private frames, even if at the expense of the NHS service?

This conclusion reflects the left's weakness in health politics, for the GOS has been a perfect model of the mixed economy within the NHS, and the Conservatives have chosen to abandon it. Between 1952 and 1973 the real cost to the NHS of the general ophthalmic services did not change. During that time the number of sight tests performed rose from 8 to 14.5 per 100,000 people, and the numbers of spectacles supplied rose from 7.5 to 9.5 per 100,000 people. The number of opticians declined from 18.2 to 13.8 for every 100,000 members of the population, implying a substantial rise in productivity.[28] Prescription of glasses did not rise as fast as sight testing, probably because charges for NHS lenses acted as a real deterrent to consumers. Privately purchased frames became increasingly popular for those that could afford glasses at all, accounting for 54 per cent of frames supplied in 1970.[29] Although those on lowest incomes were not getting adequate services whilst the better-off had access to luxury goods, that was not peculiar to the GOS, but appeared in many parts of the health service.

A significant change occurred in 1975. The real cost of the GOS rose substantially and stayed at a high level until 1982. The total number of opticians also rose, approaching 16.6 per 100,000 population in 1982, and NHS frames became more popular again, taking 41 per cent of the total sales.[30] Rising costs of private frames, the falling of NHS charges in real terms, and the provision of more stylish NHS frames may have contributed to this NHS revival, even though there was no sustained increase in the number of glasses supplied. Sight testing increased to 17.5 per 100,000 people, and reimbursement to opticians enhanced their incomes. The net

effect was a 39 per cent rise in the costs of the GOS (at
constant prices) between 1975 and 1982, which failed to
respond to increases in charges. If charges to service users
made the GOS into a model of the mixed economy until 1975,
something had weakened this regulator in the 1980s.

When the Conservatives inherited this situation, they tried
the traditional remedy of increasing charges in 1982 before
opting for a market solution in 1983. The market solution
involved withdrawal of public subsidy from two aspects of the
GOS. The supply of subsidised NHS spectacles was first
limited to children and those on social security and
subsequently withdrawn altogether. And the dispensing of
optical prescriptions would no longer be an opticians'
monopoly. Commercial organisations could produce glasses
according to an optician's prescription, and the customers
could wander (or, perhaps, fumble) from supplier to supplier
seeking bargains. The ensuing competition would have many
benefits, at least for the government. Prices of private lenses
and frames would fall, and the NHS would spend much less
on supplying 'unnecessary' frames and lenses. The fastest
growing group amongst opticians, the dispensing opticians
(who do not prescribe glasses, but only provide them to
colleagues' prescriptions), would be cut down to size by
commercial competitors, and another decline in the profession
might follow, further cutting NHS costs. Instead of being a
model of the mixed economy in health, optical services would
vindicate monetarism.

There are grounds for doubting whether the change will do
more than demonstrate monetarism's multiple negative
features. The government made the mistake of acting too
quickly, and without proper consultation, in including its
plans for deregulation of spectacle dispensing and the
abolition of NHS services for all but the statutory poor and
children in the Health and Social Services Bill of 1983. The
Secretary of State had announced the government's desire for
a thorough review of ophthalmic services in 1982, and
proposed the terms of reference of such a review to the relevant
professional bodies in February 1983. However, in January
1983 the Office of Fair Trading published a report critical of
the optical services, and in particular of the high prices of
privately-provided glasses. The government must have been

very impressed by the OFT's arguments against the opticians' monopoly, but no change was made in the terms of reference of the planned review. The abandonment of the idea of a wholesale review, in favour of an attack upon the GOS, occurred with the presentation of the new Bill in the winter of 1983. It appeared that the Conservatives had changed tactic for reasons of political dogma, and without consulting the professionals.

This caused intense anger amongst the opticians, who were keyed up for political debate through their preparations for the planned review. Working in part through the Federation of Optical Corporate Bodies and in part through the BMA, the professionals mobilised a wide body of supporters, from Community Health Councils, the police, motoring associations and Family Practitioner Committees.[31] The Parliamentary Labour Party argued consistently against the optical section of the new Bill, and even hawkish Tory MP Jill Knight spoke against the government's plans to abolish NHS services.[32] The government made devious use of the media. The eleven lines referring to optical services in the DHSS press release failed to mention the proposed attack on NHS services. An attached 'summary of main proposals' started with: 'The government proposes to take action in two areas – abolishing the rules preventing opticians from advertising and curtailing the present monopoly granted to opticians and doctors on the supply of glasses.' Only later did the summary admit that: 'The Bill will also end the general provision of glasses under the NHS.'[33] The press faithfully reflected the DHSS's distorted presentation. The *Daily Telegraph* headline ran: 'Price cut for glasses after monopoly ends'. The *Daily Mail* announced: 'Fowler's new look. Government breaks opticians' monopoly'. Neither paper mentioned the ending of the NHS supply, but the *Daily Express* did mention the health service under its headline: 'Spectacles go cut price – £5 a pair as monopoly ends'.

The *Express*'s estimate is wide of the mark. In the winter of 1983 NHS frames cost from £2.05 to £13.05, whilst single-vision NHS lenses cost between £4.00 and £8.85. Bifocal lenses on the NHS ran from £9.20 to £15.50. Old style single-vision glasses bought privately cost on average £43, whilst bifocals cost £57.[34] All NHS frames were sold at cost price, but the lenses were subsidised by up to £5 a pair; this cost the NHS about £17 million p.a. Abolition of this subsidy forced about 3 million people currently opting for NHS spectacles into the private market, and the government argued that this enforced expansion of the consumer population would allow commercial prices to fall.

This was a big gamble. The growth in the private market may not be as great as the Conservatives hope, and the commercial suppliers need to make their profits repay their investment. The volume of sales will be crucial, for established UK producers of spectacles rely upon the large (and expanding) NHS purchase of relatively low-cost glasses giving them enough return to allow small-scale production of more complex spectacles. If volume sales of single lenses and frames disappear through the withdrawal of the NHS service, or through flooding of the market with imported, loss-leader products, the cost of more complex glasses will rise, not fall, whilst the producers cut back on both production and their workforces. Instead of the market solving all problems, it will create them for those with deficient eyesight. The only winner will be the Exchequer, freed from a burdensome subsidy.

Pharmacy

The pharmacist working in the chemist's shop is paid by the NHS for each prescription provided. To earn a living deemed adequate for a professional, the pharmacist must either sell a wide range of non-medical goods, or dispense a very large number of prescriptions, or both. If financial success depends on cosmetics, photographic processing and herbal remedies, then time and energy must be devoted to that side of the business. If a large throughput of prescriptions is a major source of income, contact with patients becomes brief and the pharmacist becomes an over-qualified dispenser. Neither role easily permits the pharmacist to use knowledge gained in a three-year undergraduate training and often developed through postgraduate work. Vital functions like advising patients on drug use, drug interactions and adverse effects are minimised, whilst one in twenty hospital admissions are allegedly due to drug side effects.[35] The opportunity to educate doctors, whose knowledge of therapeutics is usually limited, is lost through lack of contact and limited time (as well as a degree of hostility and suspicion). Yet the pharmaceutical companies spend enough on promotion for each GP to have a university lecturer in therapeutics working with him/her for one month each year.[36]

The pharmacist's contract with the NHS is comparable to that of other independent contractor professions, and produces similar problems. It also has special features, with immediate implications for pharmacists and long-term ones for the whole health service.

The pharmacist's contract, largely unchanged since 1948, primarily rewards the rapid supply of medications and appliances, with little reference to the information given to individual consumers or other activity taken to protect the public. It contains no obligation to undertake postgraduate education, and sets no limit to the number of prescriptions that can be prescribed under the supervision of a single pharmacist, thereby ignoring the issue of public protection from powerful medicines. Low levels of NHS payment for prescription work make counter sales of proprietary goods essential. The contract seems to conspire against the professional's knowledge and time with the public.[37]

The contract also introduces a third party, the business owner, since the agreement exists between the Family Practitioner Committee and this business owner, who may or may not be a pharmacist. The intervening business owner limits the influence of the DHSS, acting through the FPC, on the activity of pharmacists. The immediate influence on the pharmacist comes from the business owner, who must be more concerned with profitability than with narrower professional issues like providing detailed information to individuals about drug use and drug hazards.

Pharmacy as a trade is undergoing a small revival, and at first sight appears to fit in with the Tory ideal of burgeoning small enterprises meeting people's needs. The number of dispensaries in Britain began to increase in 1981, after a decade of rapid decline. However, this increase has been concentrated in the South East, especially in the North-West and North-East Thames Regions. Areas like East Anglia, Merseyside, Yorkshire and the North West have continued to lose dispensaries as an increasing proportion of the nation's wealth has accumulated in the Home Counties. The number of dispensing contractors per 100,000 population has risen in the main growth areas, around London, but has stayed static or fallen in every other part of Britain.[38] The shift of dispensaries has not been towards areas like Northern Ireland or Wales, where doctors prescribe a lot more medicines than the national average, and where profitability seems assured. The loss of dispensaries in these areas has continued, as it has (although less dramatically) in East Anglia, where prescribing is the lowest in the country.[39] The congregation of new dispensaries in the most affluent areas conforms to the small business character of high street chemists, whose income depends on meeting *wants* through over-the-counter sales as much as on meeting *needs* through the supply of prescribed medicines.

The recent recovery in pharmacy's fortunes must have an effect on future public spending on health care, since FPS pharmacy services have been able to keep pace with NHS growth, and so contribute to the increase in NHS costs, for over thirty years.[40] There are two medical justifications for the need for growing expenditure on pharmacy services. One argues that lengthened life-spans permit more illness needing treatment, and the other that developing medical knowledge allows more effective treatment of existing disorders. Both arguments may need qualification: a longer life may postpone illnesses not accumulate more of them; and increasing 'medical' ability to deal with existing ill health does not need to rely entirely, or even largely, on more potent and more expensive medicines.

Any hopes that the drugs bill will fall because punitive prescription charges reduce consumption have long since left the DHSS. The Tory faithful may still believe in an ignorant public that wants 'a pill for every ill', but that public is either more determined and smarter than the government, or it is not the main cause of rising demand for medicines. The number of prescriptions dispensed continued to rise after 1979 despite annual increases in prescription charges, taking them from 20p per item in May 1979 to £2.20 in 1986. The proportion of prescriptions dispensed free also rose, from 65 per cent in 1979 to 73 per cent in 1984 (this figure does not include the 5 per cent of prescriptions given to holders of pre-payment certificates ('season tickets')). The ageing of the population, together with the rapidly growing numbers of unemployed entitled to free prescriptions, accounted for most of the increase.[41]

The consequences of an increasingly medicated elderly population may add to NHS costs through drug-induced illness. Even if they do not, there is no reduction in drug spending foreseeable through increased charges, since the elderly 'high spenders' avoid all charges. All that the government can hope to achieve is a stable or slowly rising income to the NHS from prescription charges levied on the relatively well. If prescription charges can be seen as an important part of NHS income, then the NHS may gain from increased consumption of medicines, and the government's only real option is to *reduce* the range of exemptions if it wants to increase the cash flow into the NHS from the public. This would be an extra tax levied on the ill, and would not be popular with the public nor with the pharmacists who would have to collect such a tax. Since income from *all* charges to patients (not just prescription charges) constituted just over 3 per cent of the NHS budget in 1986-87 it seems unlikely that this government really believes in prescription charges as a positive economic force.[42] Nor can it use charges as barriers to consumption. The only remaining justification for charging for prescribed medicines is that it encourages the idea that medical care needs to be paid for at the time of use, and discourages the memory that such services have been pre-paid, through general taxation.

The Conservatives therefore face multiple dilemmas. Only 27 per cent of prescriptions are paid for, and there seems no easy way to increase that proportion. The government cannot afford to reduce drug consumption directly because that would reduce drug company sales and threaten pharmacists' livelihoods. The move to shift some medicines once available only on prescription into the category only available over-the-counter (or on private prescription) has pleased pharmacists, who can expand their trade and their role as advisors on medication. Whether the reduced availability of 'free' NHS medicines will be offset by an increase in over-the-counter sales of the same products is a question that must worry the pharmaceutical industry. It seems unlikely that doctors will welcome their reduced role *vis-à-vis* pharmacists. 'Wet' Conservatives could cope with these dilemmas, and muddle through with compromises that would probably make the problems more complex, but for someone else, later on. Monetarists, on the other hand, have little room for manoeuvre, there being no real market in medicine consumption, but many state-subsidised business people unwilling to lose their protected incomes. The Green Paper of April 1986 made few concrete suggestions for change.

Should the DHSS want to implement a public education programme about drug hazards, using pharmacists as its outlet, it would have to argue its case with the Treasury before it went to the profession. Whilst NHS fees were low, and educational work unpaid, pharmacy business owners would insist on profitable work before desirable professional activity. In the large chain chemists commercial sales and NHS work done by salaried pharmacists may be separable; in the single shop, where the pharmacist is the business-owner, they are not. The contract's commercial bias conspires against more than professional use of time – it now attacks the small-business basis of pharmacy itself.

If the conflict between pharmacy as a profession and the chemist's shop as a business is resolved by employing salaried pharmacists in chain stores, why should not the same be done for dentists? The lower are NHS fees for dentistry, the greater becomes the lure of private practice, and the temptation for large-scale business enterprise.

Notes

[1] There are, for example, nearly 30,000 general practitioners who employ at least as many other staff, and who claim to deal with 90 per cent of all episodes of illness that are presented to the NHS.

[2] See Robert J. Maxwell, *Health and Wealth: An International Study of Health Care Spending*, Lexington Books, 1981, and B.Abel-Smith, *Cost Containment in Health Care*, Bedford Square Press, 1984.

[3] These are the concerns of the leading force in general practice, the Royal College of General Practitioners, which promotes professional improvement and high standards in medical care.

[4] See Chapter 4 of P.Townsend and N.Davidson, *Inequalities in Health*, Penguin, 1982.

[5] Ibid.

[6] J.T.Hart, 'A new kind of doctor', *Journal of the Royal Society of Medicine*, 1981, 74:871.

[7] The BMA proposed an extension to the system of claiming fees for items of service done by GPs, but met with a frosty response from the profession because of the complexity and bureaucratic inefficiency that further claims for payment would create.

[8] General Medical Services Committee, *General Practice – a British Success*, 1984.

[9] Medical Practitioners' Union, *A New Policy for General Practice*, 1979.

[10] Medical Practitioners' Union, *A New Charter for General Practice*, 1984.

[11] *Primary Care in Inner London* (The Acheson Report), 1981.

[12] Townsend and Davidson, op.cit.

[13] P.L.Knox, 'The Intra-urban Ecology of Primary Medical Care: Patterns of Accessibility and Their Policy Implications', *Environment and Planning*, 1978, A10, pp.415-35.

[14] J.Robson, 'Paying General Practitioners. Salaried Service – a Basis for the Future?', *British Medical Journal*, 1981, 283 (6301), pp.1225-7.

[15] *Promoting Prevention*, Royal College of General Practitioners, Occasional Paper 22.

[16] 'Inner Cities', RCGP, Occasional Paper 19.

[17] 'Social Class and Health Status – Inequality or Difference?', RCGP Occasional Paper 25.

[18] Deputising services are either commercially owned organisations employing doctors on a piece-work basis, or local doctors' co-operatives. The commercial organisations are mostly city-based. See NHS Unlimited, *Briefing* No.8, 1983.

[19] The BMA has a close relationship with the major commercial deputising service, Air Call, and the two organisations sponsored joint meetings for GPs to oppose the government's actions.

[20] BMA, *The Medical Effects of Nuclear War*, 1983.

[21] A compromise agreement was reached by which Family Practitioner Committees would monitor use of deputising services more closely. For some GPs this has meant an increase in out-of-hours workload, whilst for others there has been no apparent change.

[22] Between 1980 and 1985 doctors' incomes lagged behind inflation by 2 per cent (5 per cent for GPs), *BMA News Review*, July 1985.

[23] *Report of the Royal Commission on the National Health Service*, HMSO, 1979.

[24] Radical Statistics Health Group, *In Defence of the NHS*, 1979, p.14.

[25] *Report of the Royal Commission on the NHS*, HMSO, 1979, 9:13.

[26] Ibid., 9:12.

[27] Ibid., 9:24.

[28] Office of Health Economics, *Compendium of Health Statistics*, 1984, 4:73.

[29] Ibid., 4:72.

[30] Ibid., 4:73.

[31] The Federation of Optical Corporate Bodies claimed in its 'Insight' briefings that it had support for its opposition to government plans from community health councils, automobile organisations, senior police officers and Family Practitioner Committees.

[32] *Hansard*, 2 May 1984.

[33] See NHS Unlimited, *Briefing* No.11, 1984.

[34] 'Deregulation', *Medicine in Society*, 1984, 10:1-2, p.49.

[35] J.Shulman, 'Prevention of Adverse Drug Reactions', *Update,* 18 October 1983.

[36] B. Abel-Smith, *Value for Money in Health Services*, Heinemann, 1976, p.83.

[37] A.D.J.Balon and J.Shulman, 'Proposals for a New Contract', *Pharmaceutical Journal*, 28 January 1984.

[38] Office of Health Economics, *Compendium of Health Statistics*, 1984, 4:37.

[39] Ibid., 4:39.

[40] Ibid., 4:46.

[41] Ibid., 4:43.

[42] Table 3.14 of HM Treasury, *The Government's Expenditure Plans 1986-87 to 1988-89*, Cmnd 9702, 1986.

Chapter 7

The Supply Side:
Drugs and High Technology

The Pharmaceutical Industry

The growth of the UK pharmaceutical market has been supported by public money. Public investment has occurred indirectly, rather than through direct grants, loans or ownership. The mechanics of indirect state subsidy have evolved in phases, each requiring close collaboration between private enterprise and public institutions like universities, hospitals and state-funded research departments. Such collaboration has occurred throughout the advanced capitalist economies, where private financing of academic research stimulated the pharmaceutical revolution, before giving way to state regulation of drug marketing, and commercial domination of professional education.

Pump-Priming

Research and development of new drugs, particularly in the immediate post-war years, occurred in academic insititutions primed with industrial funds. Of the early antibiotics, chloramphenicol, streptomycin, neomycin and Bacitracin were first isolated at various US universities. Oral polio vaccine was developed at Pittsburg University. The local anaesthetic agent xylocaine and the anti-TB value of PAS (para-aminosalicyllic acid) were developed at Swedish academic institutions.

Private investment was certainly a pump-primer at the beginning of the 'pharmaceutical revolution', but government money bought the pump and kept it running. The best early example of state co-ordination of private drug production is the mass marketing of penicillin. In 1941 the US Office of

Scientific Research and Development started to study the large-scale production of penicillin, and supported research programmes in several different drug companies. The yield was poor, and the breakthrough in mass production techniques came from a government department itself, the Northern Regional Laboratory of the Department of Agriculture. This department obtained a patent for its process, but made it available to any interested producer, without charge. Assorted private companies had been funded by the state, produced little in return, and were rewarded with production-techniques developed at state expense. The state, in turn, obtained mass production of an essential drug without its producer being able to charge excess prices by virtue of patent monopoly.

Shift of Power
In the next forty years of the pharmaceutical revolution, the balance between private and public powers over drug production, distribution and consumption shifted in favour of profit-seeking industries. The drug industry has developed control over postgraduate medical education, sponsoring academic conferences, research programmes and educational events, as well as funding (through advertising) dozens of medical journals and newspapers in each capitalist country. Although the industry, as a whole, cannot dictate the exact development of medicine, it can certainly keep it on the right (pharmaceutical) lines. The partnership between professionals and pharmaceutical companies is one aspect of the industrial domination of socialised medicine, and provides the mechanism for profitable control of drug distribution and consumption. Production itself is state-funded, in the UK, by a much less publicised mechanism, the Pharmaceutical Price Regulation Scheme (PPRS). This is an agreement between the DHSS and pharmaceutical producers that sets a fixed level of profit on drug sales to the NHS, whilst allowing for variation in individual drug prices. The PPRS is the primary, or hidden, form of public regulation of private drug production, and it works to the advantage of the industry. Other, much more public, forms of regulation, like controls on advertising or the activity of the Committee on Safety of

Medicines (CSM) are secondary controls that work against the industry's direct interest. The political relationship between the state and private industry varies through adjustments in the balance between primary and secondary regulation. Tighter advertising controls, for example, can be the public and private price paid by the industry for continued, favourable trade guarantees with the DHSS.

Prescribing

The industry's influence over drug use depends more on its manipulation of doctors (and other health workers) than on a direct approach to consumers. The medical profession has the prescription pads, and has consistently opposed encroachments on its right to prescribe whatever its members see fit. This 'clinical freedom' works to the financial advantage of drug companies, who reciprocate by paying careful attention to professionals' attitudes, knowledge, stomachs and appetites for money. When clinical freedom was eroded by the introduction of restricted lists of available drugs in hospitals the industry became defensive, but not inactive. Where clinical freedom still ruled, amongst Britain's 28,000 GPs, the representatives still performed their daily face-to-face education of doctors in the virtues of the latest product, whilst postmen staggered under the weight of unsolicited advertising.

The effort was worthwhile. There appears to be a close relationship between prescribing habits and drug advertising with exceptional drugs that are hardly advertised but widely prescribed because they either dominate the field, or are the only marketed examples of that particular drug-type.[1] This promotion of drugs by the industry has produced a dramatic increase in UK drug usage. In 1959, 236 million prescriptions were issued – about five per person – at the cost of just over £81 million. By 1977, six and a half prescriptions were issued per person, totalling 351 million, at a cost of £665 million. The net ingredient costs of all prescriptions rose tenfold between 1959 and 1977, from £52 million to £520 million.[2] Whilst international comparisons suggest that the NHS has been able to limit drug price rises, there is also evidence that drug prices are increased to pay for mass marketing rather than for research and development.[3] Our price limitation could be a consequence of both the dependence of professionals on the pharmaceutical industry, and the efficient social provision of services that has replaced the more costly market approach to health care.

Drug promotion shapes medicine, directly and openly. The pharmaceutical industry promotes chemical solutions to personal and social problems, and legitimises medical responses to non-medical circumstances, through its blatant advertising. The general practitioners faced with ill, unhappy, uneasy, hopeless and poor patients have an average of seven minutes per consultation for them, and are under pressure to do something decisive that will at least appear to help the problem, if only by softening painful symptoms. Mood-altering drugs accounted for nearly a fifth of prescriptions in the mid-1970s, and formed the largest single group of drugs prescribed in terms of both number and cost. Between 1961 and 1971 there was an increase in prescriptions for mood-altering drugs of nearly 50 per cent, plus a smaller increase in the number given on each prescription. By 1971, doctors were signing prescriptions for about 60 million mood-altering tablets and capsules each week.

Yet none of these antidotes to depression and anxiety were carefully tested, through randomised controlled trials, before their mass distribution.[4] In part, the failure to test mood-altering drugs arises because 'anxiety' and 'depression' are ill defined disorders, and the impact on them of medicines is hard to measure. The lack of scientific clarity did not deter the drug producers, however, who needed no more convincing evidence of 'need' and 'effectiveness' than the rising sales graph. By their use of these drugs, doctors clearly demonstrated to their patients a way of coping with a wide range of complaints produced by unpleasant situations. Prescribing influences people's understanding and expectations, which in turn shape future demand. Expectation, demand, drugs and even diagnoses then begin to follow fashions. Bromides, then barbiturates and amphetamines, and now tranquillisers and anti-depressants, are given for neurasthenia, nervous debility or the more modern diseases, anxiety and depression.

Mood-altering drugs are the most obvious, but not the only, example of the impact of drugs on medical practice. Antibiotics are prescribed as much on a fashion basis as on a strictly scientific one. Even highly specialised treatments, like drug therapy for cancer, can be seen, in retrospect, as interesting fashions in medicine.[5]

Drug-induced Disease

Like all revolutions, the pharmaceutical revolution has its casualties. In 1937 elixir of sulphanilamide, made by a small American company, was marketed without any testing at all, and killed at least 93 people (including the company chemist, who committed suicide) before it was withdrawn. Since then dangerous pharmaceutical products have hit the headlines with regularity, despite successive attempts at regulatory legislation designed to control drug production, testing and marketing. Thalidomide was a sedative with so few side-effects, according to its manufacturers, that it could be safely sold in West German supermarkets. Its ability to damage the unborn, causing gross deformities of the limbs, prompted the formation of the Committee on Safety of Drugs in Britain (later reorganised as the Committee on Safety of Medicines).

Since Thalidomide a series of medicines have been withdrawn from general use after public alarm about their adverse effects: Practolol, Atromid-S, Opren, Zomax, Surgam and Butazolidine. None produced injury on the scale of Thalidomide, although all had fatalities linked with their use. In a sense, their choice as victims of heightened public awareness of drug hazards was arbitrary. The group of drugs known as beta-blockers used for treating heart disease all produced irreversible side-effects of damage to the eye and the abdominal cavity linings, but only Practolol, whose side effects are stronger, has been withdrawn. Opren is not the only anti-arthritic agent to upset liver and kidney function, but it was the least established and the most commonly implicated. Butazolidine had been prescribed for twenty years before its well-known ability to depress bone-marrow activity (and therefore blood cell formation) became a public issue, pushing it off the list of drugs prescribed by general practitioners.[6]

In the early 1970s, at the peak of the drug boom, it was estimated that 10 per cent of consumers of medication experienced side-effects, that between 3 and 5 per cent of hospital admissions were caused by drug side-effects, and that another 10 per cent of admissions were due to deliberate drug overdoses.[7] A standard response to the problem of a patient who is clearly ill, but without obvious cause, is to withhold medication; the relief of symptoms through drug withdrawal can be dramatic, particularly in the elderly.

As the casualties mounted, so did the restrictive legislation requiring increasing evidence of drug safety (even if not usefulness). The industry's response has been to complain at the obstacles placed in the way of drug marketing, and the price paid by those needing new medications for their illnesses. Members of the medical profession have been willing to join the chorus. A discussion at the end of a seminar on drug treatment in cardiovascular disease, published by the Association of the British Pharmaceutical Industry in 1973, contains the following exchange.

> *Mr Smith (Southampton)*: 'My impression is that European and North American countries do not accept beta-blocking agents nearly so readily as we do at the moment. Is it Dr Pritchard's opinion that the rest of the world will follow us or will we continue to be rather an isolated island of treatment?'
> *Dr Pritchard*: 'There is some truth in what you say, but I think that the rest of the world will follow eventually. The Americans have difficulty in the shape of the Food and Drugs Administration, it seems that they do not like beta-blockers at all. The poor American public – and they have my sympathy as they are being partly denied a useful remedy – are not even officially allowed to have beta-blockers for the treatment of angina. They are solely on the market for arythmias. Of course plenty of patients in effect receive a beta-blocker for angina, but officially it is given to prevent an arythmias that might develop!'
> *Mr Smith*: 'Will it occur in Germany, France and Italy where there is also resistance?'
> *Dr Pritchard*: 'I think most certainly. There has been a lot of emotion about depressing the heart, but this is subsiding now …'[8]

Testing for drug safety is a problem, but it is largely a problem of the industry's own making. In the case of Thalidomide, the techniques for proving that it did *not* cause mutations in unborn babies were not developed, whilst the drug was, and the market was wide open.[9]

Research into drug production has outstripped research into drug effects, in the rush to increase market-shares and maximise short-term profit. In the same way, research, itself heavily reliant on drug industry support, concentrates on clinical studies – the pursuit of disease and cure – rather than on operational problems – the effectiveness of treatments, and the ways of improving the service given.

Enter Mrs Thatcher
Margaret Thatcher's first administration inherited a high level of public concern about the drugs industry. An article in the *Daily Telegraph* of 27 November 1979 set the tone for years of argument:

> Millions of pounds annually are added needlessly to the NHS drugs bill by mass prescribing of expensive brand named tablets which are all available more cheaply under other names.
> Thirteen brand leaders among the most widely prescribed drugs and also available in cheaper form, added at least £25 million unnecessarily to the 1978 drug bill of £723 million.
> Of these thirteen brands, five cost twice as much as their unbranded equivalents, three cost 4, 6 and 10 times more respectively than their equivalents, while the remaining five cost between 78 and 140 per cent more.

The themes of excessive prescribing and over-pricing were pursued in press and Parliament until the government was forced to act against the drug industry, in the winter of 1982-83. Both the industry and the government also had to explain and respond to a series of drug scandals that added greater weight to media concern about the pharmaceutical industry's ethics and competence. Despite Thatcherism, it has been a worrying time for the drug manufacturers.

The initial response from the Conservatives was to commission a review of effective prescribing by an informal working group chaired by Dr P.R. Greenfield, Principal Medical Officer to the DHSS. This working group, staffed by leading medical politicians and senior DHSS officers, produced its report in February 1982.[10] The Greenfield report then became part of the public row about the drug companies, for it was not published for a year, until the House of Commons Public Accounts Committee had commented unfavourably on over-pricing of medicines, and the first and worst of the drug scandals had broken – the Opren affair.

The Greenfield report made a number of proposals to enhance the effectiveness of drug prescribing, and rejected one significant idea – the reduction of the number of drugs prescribable, through the production of a 'limited list' – because the working group was not convinced of its practicality. The main suggestion, or rather the one that most disturbed the industry, was that pharmacists could prescribe the cheapest equivalent to any brand-named drug unless specifically countermanded by the prescribing doctor. This idea, allowing generic (unbranded) versions to be substituted for branded products was seen by the Association of British Pharmaceutical Industry (ABPI) as likely to 'result in major economic losses to the country and serious progressive damage to the research-based industry'.[11]

The ABPI had prepared a thorough defence against generic substitution months before the Greenfield report had appeared, according to ABPI minutes for October 1982 accidentally sent to Mike Thomas MP, then SDP health spokesperson, by junior health minister, Geoffrey Finsberg.[12] One Dr Fryer of Ciba-Geigy reported that ABPI medical and scientific committees had already approached influential doctors and went on to say:

> It was hoped that the medical profession would be fully consulted on the matter before changes were introduced and efforts had been made to get the industry's point of view over to those who might be consulted. A meeting had been held the previous week with clinical pharmacologists to present a balanced picture of the matter.

The ABPI decided to maintain a £20,000 contingency fund for public relations purposes, to be used at the discretion of its president.

The industry's public campaign against generic substitution was not needed. The government did not implement the Greenfield report's proposal, perhaps because a behind-the-scenes campaign by the drug manufacturers reached receptive points within the DHSS and the Cabinet. In any event, the Conservatives were under pressure to resolve a more difficult problem – the allegation of over-pricing. The

Greenfield report had put the government on the defensive, the Opren scandal had bruised the drugs industry, and the Conservatives were committed to restraining public expenditure. Sir Kenneth Stowe, DHSS Permanent Secretary, argued before the House of Commons Public Accounts Committee in 1982 that the drug companies could not be exempted from the search for greater efficiency, and that their return on capital had been rising. The Public Accounts Committee advocated a reduction in the return on capital allowed under the PPRS from 25 to 17 per cent, and highlighted the issue of 'transfer pricing' – the importation by UK-based subsidiaries of foreign multinationals of raw materials held by those multinationals at artificially high prices, to disguise the real level of profits made in the UK.[13]

The government responded by freezing drug prices and announcing cuts in allowed profit targets and in promotional spending. In March 1984 it announced further plans to cut drug costs, including increased importation of cheaper medicines from the EEC ('parallel importing' that evades the PPRS arrangements), reductions in the profit margins allowed to drug wholesalers, and action on transfer pricing, based on an unpublished report from the accountants Binder Hamlyn.[14]

In August 1983 a 2.5 per cent cut was imposed, with a freeze on drug prices effective until April 1984. In December 1983 the maximum allowed return on capital was reduced from 25 to 21 per cent, again with effect from April 1984, and the amount of promotional expenditure offset against profits was reduced from 8 to 7 per cent of turnover. Health Minister, Kenneth Clarke said, in the House of Commons, in December 1983:

> The charges will mean that the price freeze on drugs – introduced in August as part of the £25 million savings agreed then – will continue, with few exceptions, through 1984-85 and beyond. Furthermore, the price freeze will be at the level established by the 2.5 per cent cut in August.

The savings to the NHS were estimated at £65 million in 1984, and £100 million per year thereafter.

There was a brief period in which prices were frozen, and the NHS saved money. From August to October 1983 the average cost of ingredients per prescription fell by 20p, from

£3.66 to £3.46. Costs began to rise after October, and by
January 1984 the average ingredient cost per prescription had
reached £3.51; the total cost of prescription ingredients in
January 1984 was 9 per cent above the level of the previous year.
In April 1984 prices started to rise again, as the DHSS began to
award extra money (in the form of permitted price rises) to
companies that, presumably, pleaded falling profit margins.
The permitted price increases ranged from 5 per cent across the
product range (Sandoz) to 20-29 per cent on two products only
(Kirby-Warwick). A possible explanation for the industry's
capacity to thaw the government's freeze is that drug company
financial managers can easily persuade the small staff of the
DHSS price monitoring unit that each firm's case is sound and
just.[15] The Conservatives were unable to maintain restrictions
on drug company profits. In October 1986 a new deal covering
65 companies revised the PPRS and reversed most of the
profit curbs imposed in earlier years. The ABPI had argued
that on sales to the NHS the industry had fallen below the
profitability of manufacturing industry as a whole, and the
DHSS agreed.

If the industry could avoid control, it could not escape from
criticism and public disgrace. Whatever its profits, its standing
has been badly damaged by the series of drug scandals that
filled tabloids from 1982 onwards. In August 1982 the new
drug Opren was withdrawn from the market, dramatically
suspended from use by order of the DHSS, after 61 deaths had
been associated with its use and over 3,500 reports of adverse
reactions had been filed against it.[16] Opren, designed for the
treatment of arthritis, rapidly gained a large slice of the UK
market for anti-arthritic medicines, being prescribed for
700,000 people between its launch in October 1980 and its
withdrawal from use.[17] This rapid success was due to its lavish
promotion in the lay press as well as in the professional media.
An editorial in the *British Medical Journal* said:

> Opren was introduced with massive publicity on radio and in
> newspapers, encouraging patients to believe it was a major
> advance in treatment, and to ask their doctors to prescribe it with
> obvious success … this extensive marketing … makes no sense on
> medical grounds because of the potential danger that side effects,
> which are too rare to appear in clinical trials, could affect large
> numbers of patients before being recognised.[18]

Although this comment is very much the wisdom of hindsight, its appearance demonstrates the growing isolation of the drugs industry. A major medical journal, dependent on drug advertising, was prepared to censure one of its sponsors. The chair of the ABPI criticised companies that indulged in promotional excesses, whilst a Pfizer spokesman told an ABPI meeting in October 1982 that talks had taken place with the editors of the *BMJ* and the *Lancet* about reports of adverse reactions, and that more meetings would be needed. A representative of Squibbs Pharmaceuticals said at the same meeting that: 'It was not possible to suppress reports, but the way in which things were reported was important.' A representative of Eli Lilly, the manufacturers of Opren, said: 'the treatment of the Opren situation in certain publications had been less than satisfactory.'[19]

The industry survived this difficult period by a combination of tactics. Acceptance of the principle of a profit and price freeze allowed it to escape from further restrictions that would constrain prescribing. The PPRS is so biased in the industry's favour that no price freeze imposed by a Conservative government – or perhaps by a government of any party – is more than a temporary solution. Prescribing, on the other hand, is much more vulnerable to intervention by any government prepared to erode clinical freedom. That Thatcher's government is prepared to sacrifice this medical sacred cow was demonstrated by the limited drugs list introduced in April 1985. Any encroachment, however minor, on prescribing and the doctor's right to choose medication regardless of price (or rationale) sets a precedent that future governments might use, and must be opposed by the industry and by the BMA. Self-criticism of 'promotion excesses' provides evidence of the industry's sensitivity, awareness and willingness to change, whilst the industry's negotiators can apply pressure in private to silence critics and fix favourable terms with the DHSS. The limited drug list represents a reduction in the industry's power to dominate the DHSS, but not a substantial change in relationships.

The significance of the uncomfortable years after 1979 lies in the energetic manoeuvring of the pharmaceutical industry, and the government's obligation to curtail the industry's profiteering, albeit reluctantly. If Conservatives committed to private enterprise and profit maximisation as the motor of progress can force a powerful industry to defend itself, what could happen if the drug companies faced a government with genuinely hostile intentions?

The Medical Supply Industries

Modern medicine is still notable for the unscientific application of knowledge. Medical technology, when applied to large numbers of people, can change many things: individual and collective knowledge, the status and influence of those applying the technology and the profits of those producing it. Meeting needs, as measured in successful outcomes for patients, is certainly not the only factor in deciding on application of new techniques, and in practice may be only a minor consideration. Other 'needs' at stake include desires for knowledge, status and profit, and all of these may be easier to satisfy than the most important medical need, the positive outcome for the patient. Producers and users of medical technology therefore form a natural alliance.

Outside the drugs industry, the relationships between producers and users of medical technology are unstructured and variable. This is now a problem. National Health Service administrators complain about the lack of policy towards purchasing equipment for the NHS.[20] And producers cannot guarantee a stable home market for their products, from which to promote exports. Would EMI, the UK-based manufacturer of computerised tomography scanners, have missed dominating world scanner sales if home markets had been ensured? The absence of an equivalent to the PPRS for the medical supply companies may become more of an issue as markets enlarge and research and development costs soar.

The economics of production may dictate different methods of public and private collaboration, when supply industries are compared with the drug firms, but they have similar effects on the nature of medical practice. A few recent applications of new technology demonstrate how medicine can take the shape of drama, magic, protection or knowledge, to the advantage of profit. They are coronary care, body imaging with X-rays and scanners, obstetric technology and laboratory automation, respectively.

Coronary Care – Medicine as Drama

Heart disease is one of the modern epidemics that have
replaced infectious diseases as a major threat to health and life.
Medicine's response has been traditional rather than
innovatory. Since preventive approaches are not well
researched, and would require a systematic approach by
underfunded community health services notorious for their
disorderly distribution and uneven quality, prevention has
taken second place. 'Cure', based on the existing hospital
network, requires a simple extension of present medical
practices, plus new diagnostic and curative technology. The
Coronary Care Unit was born from this marriage. The
industries supplying the oscilloscopes, ECG machines,
defibrillators, cardiac catheters, cannulae, drip sets and
necessary drugs were keen to help the newborn grow. The
scientists were proud parents, too, and spent hours deciphering
the ECG tapes, watching monitor screens and taking decisive,
often dramatic, action. Cardiology became a prestigious
sub-discipline within medicine, cardiac surgeons became folk
heroes, and a new range of specialist nurses began to fill the
CCU's and escape handmaiden work on general wards.

The new cure was years old and widely practised before
scepticism became official. Survival rates were unimpressive in
some units; cardiac arrest teams that galloped with trolley-
loads of technology to heart-attack victims within hospital
wards and departments seemed particularly unlucky. Studies
began to suggest that survival prospects were often as good for
those who stayed at home as for those who went into coronary
care units. Anxieties were voiced about the effect on the
damaged heart of a terrified ill person of a bumpy ambulance
ride into an alarming ward of gadgetry, drama and tension.
The real value of the technology and science became apparent
after its widespread introduction, not after more cautious
testing. Trial and error demonstrated that when heart attacks
were complicated by potentially dangerous changes in heart
rhythm, intensive care and decisive action were effective and
necessary. If that had been learned in a consciously planned
experiment, coronary care would not have expanded as it did,
and many would not have been treated inappropriately, and
possibly dangerously, for the sake of medical experience.

Body-Imaging – Medicine as Magic

Magic remains a potent force in medicine, and technology provides the symbols and proofs of this magic. The fact that machines can see inside the body is perhaps the most magical of all medical practices. The perplexed and distressed person demanding an X-ray (or, nowadays, a scan) wants his or her disorder spotted and named, and later hunted down. X-rays and scans can pick out the origins of headache or stomach pain, nausea or weight loss, more often in the sufferer's imagination than in reality. The image of a hidden geography of the body corresponds to the simplest anatomical understanding of ourselves. Ideas of function, of ceaseless change, of a turbulent and self-repairing organism barely register in the world of X-ray screens and scanner pictures. There *must* be *something* there to cause the problem, and somebody, somehow, must be able to find it.

The scanner, first used by neurologists and neurosurgeons in the early 1970s, has become a magic eye into the whole body. Like all effective magic, scanners have a high material and emotional price. Costing £500,000 to install, and £100,000 a year to use and maintain, they are an expensive symbol of power. Emotionally, they stimulate people into great efforts. Consultants struggle for resources, trading unfilled nursing posts or building refurbishment for the new machinery. Charitable citizens make sponsored parachute jumps, walk huge distances or dance until they drop, to raise money for new scanners. At least one man has died for this cause, and rumour has it that anonymous donations to local scanner appeals may come from the manufacturer itself.[21]

There is no doubt that scanners are valuable diagnostic instruments. Used circumspectly, they can reveal anatomical disorders that might otherwise go undetected, or that might need more dangerous, unpleasant and inefficient investigation techniques to be revealed.[22] The extent to which they save lives, or materially improve the quality of remaining life, is another matter. An early American review of routine CT scanning in a combined neurology-neurosurgery unit showed no change in the mortality or morbidity of people admitted, but did demonstrate that they experienced fewer invasive (and therefore hazardous) investigations, albeit at greater cost overall.[23]

Similar studies from London, Liverpool and Glasgow have

revealed the same lack of improved outcome following head injury when scanning has been used routinely. However, there is some evidence that *selective* and *early* use of head scanning reduces the death rate from complications by allowing earlier curative surgery.[24]

The same seems to be true of body scanning for cancer. Routine use reveals few treatable malignancies that could not have been found in other ways, whilst selective use yielded results that looked better for the people involved.[25] It seems that attempting to introduce technology on a widespread, almost indiscriminate scale gives limited results (from the users' perspective) whilst reducing or concealing the limited clinical skills of physicians and surgeons. The rational answer is to make clinical skills decisive, so that potential beneficiaries of technology can be selected from the mass of those unlikely to be helped, but this is of no use to industries needing high volume sales *now*.

Obstetric Technology – Medicine as Protection

During the 1970s, thousands of pregnant women became the unwitting subjects of a nation-wide trial of 'active obstetric management'. Induction and acceleration of labour, monitoring of foetal heartbeats and uterine contractions, ultrasound scanning in early pregnancy and tests of placental function nearer term, came to dominate maternity care. A new range of technological aids appeared, were bought, run and replaced, to reduce the risks of pregnancy and, in particular, the death rates amongst the newborn (perinatal mortality).

The effects were not as intended. Whilst the perinatal mortality rate fell during the decade, other factors seemed as important as, if not more significant than, the new technology.[26] Some analyses of data suggested that the new approach created risks, instead of reducing them, although this was hotly disputed.[27] More and more babies were delivered by forceps, or by caesarian section, and increasing numbers of them found their way into special care baby units, for observation by paediatricians worried by instrumental deliveries. By the end of the decade, it looked as if the advantages of active management (if any) were outweighed by the disadvantages.[28] The real indications for active obstetric management were then discovered, through the same trial and error process noted in coronary care units. A minority of pregnant women, identified as being at high risk, could gain significant advantages from the selective application of technology. Most did not benefit from the application of that kind of science, but did need and value more time for discussion, more advice and explanation, and more personal contacts with midwives. In the better maternity units, induction rates began to fall.

Laboratory Automation

The investigative sciences – chemical and physical pathology, haematology, bacteriology and virology – grew to significance with the National Health Service. Initially the investigative techniques were labour-intensive, and growing demand outstripped the ability of medical specialists to respond. New professionals – medical laboratory technicians – were created, in large numbers.

Demand for investigations of body tissue and fluids has increased inexorably. By the 1970s new technology allowed problems of increasing complexity to be solved by machine. Tests once done manually, alone or in small batches, by expensively trained technicians, became minor tasks for multi-channel autoanalysers. The more the capacity to provide, at speed, apparently objective information, the more that information seemed desirable. The more it was demanded, the more technological capacity was needed. Hospital laboratories registered throughput increases of between 100 and 250 per cent over a decade, without any concomitant staff increases. Skilled technicians slowly turned into machine-minders, overseeing this spiral of supply and demand. The volume of skilled technical work beyond automation became sufficiently small for medical specialists to regain their earlier function, and a conflict has slowly developed between doctors and technicians over their respective roles.

Like so much of the frantic activity in the NHS, this surge in investigation seems necessary. There is little doubt that laboratory investigations are useful in coping with some medical problems and essential in a minority of cases. There is little doubt, either, that 'investigation' can be an end in itself, instead of a means to an end. When in doubt, investigate! If the doctor is puzzled by the symptoms, look for everything possible in blood and urine. If action is needed, to reassure the anxious, or postpone the decision-making, or simply shorten the consultations and so end the clinic, investigations are a godsend. Blood tests (or X-rays) can have the same role as prescriptions, substituting for the time needed to think, listen, examine and explain.

Will the relationship between the supply industries and the NHS change? As yet no equivalent of the PPRS exists for the supply industry. On the contrary, the absence of an effective purchasing authority or policy for the NHS is notable. Perhaps the explanation is that the supply industries experience lower risks on capital, lower development costs, easier promotion and less competition than the drugs industry. But the development of some structured purchasing arrangement seems a possibility. The economic pressures for greater organisation of commercial relationships will come because of the crisis in NHS financing, as much as through industrial needs. With Health Authorities cutting first planned growth, then existing services, economies in supply purchases must follow restrictions on drug prescribing. If secondary regulation of the acquisition and use of technology increases and is rationalised, the supply industry must work for better primary regulation – a working relationship with health professionals and the health service that guarantees some degree of future economic stability. At the moment extra funding for the health service may seem to be the answer, so that commercial interests and the NHS will combine to endorse the sponsored sports, jumble sales and raffles of voluntary organisations. That may be a lifeline for most private suppliers (even though it did not save EMI) provided that decision making about most purchases occurs at local level. If, however, an effective national NHS purchasing authority is established as one element of secondary regulation of spending on new technology, bulk sellers will want to secure favourable, long-term contracts with the health service, even at the cost of voluntary price regulation.

Notes

1 R.Dajda, 'Drug Advertising and Prescribing', *Journal of the Royal College of General Practitioners*, 1978, 28:194.
2 Office of Health Economics, *Compendium of Health Statistics, 1984*, 4:45.
3 *Report of the Royal Commission on the NHS*, HMSO, 1979, 7:36.
4 P.A.Parish, 'The Family Doctor's Role in Psychotropic Drug Use', in *The Price of Tranquillity*, MIND occasional paper 1975.
5 See, for example, K.Sikora, 'Counting the Cost of Chemotherapy', *World Medicine*, 21 May 1984.
6 See J.Shulman, 'The Opren Affair – Scandal or Tragedy?' *Medicine in Society*, 1983, 9:1.
7 J.Shulman, 'Prevention of Adverse Drug Reactions', *Update*, 18 October 1983.
8 Association of British Pharmaceutical Industries, *Medicine in the Seventies*, 1973, p.25.
9 *New Scientist*, 25 May 1974.
10 Report of the Informal Working Group on Effective Prescribing, DHSS, 1983.
11 The claim that research would be jeopardised by profit cuts was repeated by both industry and trades unions when the limited list was introduced: for example of co-operation between industry and unions on this theme, see the autumn 1984 issue of ASTMS *Health Care*.
12 *Medicine in Society*, 9:3, p.38.
13 *Dispensing of Drugs in the National Health Service*, 29th Report of the Public Accounts Committee, 1983-4, HC 551.
14 *Hansard*, 8 December 1983.
15 Andrew Veitch, 'How the Drug Companies Thawed Out a Price Freeze', *Guardian*, 18 July 1985.
16 Shulman, op.cit.
17 *Pharmaceutical Journal*, 14 August 1982.
18 *British Medical Journal*, editorial, 14 August 1982.
19 *Medicine in Society*, 1983, 9:3, p.38.
20 See Alex Campbell, 'A Hard Slog for the Supply Council', *Health and Social Services Journal*, 29 March 1984.
21 Colin Thunhurst, *It Makes you Sick*, Pluto Press, 1983, pp.43-7.
22 R.G.Evans, 'Computed Tomography – A Controversy Revisited', *New England Journal of Medicine*, 1984, 3-10 (18) pp.1183-5.
23 H.Fineberg, 'Evaluation of Computed Tomography: Achievement and Challenge' *American Journal of Roentgenology*, 1978, 131, pp.1-4.
24 Bryan Jennett, *High Technology Medicine – Benefits and Burdens*, OUP, 1986.
25 E.Husband, 'Role of the CT Scanner in the Management of Cancer', *British Medical Journal*, 1985, 290,pp.527-9.
26 M.Tew, 'Understanding Intranatal Care Through Mortality Statistics' in L.Zander and G.Chamberlain (eds), *Pregnancy Care for the 1980s*, Royal Society of Medicine, 1984.
27 M.Tew, 'The Safest Place of Birth – Further Evidence', *Lancet*, 1979, i 1388-90, ii 523.
28 See S.Kitzinger and J.Davis, *The Place of Birth*, OUP, 1978.

Chapter 8

Compulsory Competitive Tendering

A central tenet of contemporary Conservatism is that trade unionism is unduly strong in the public sector. The 'inefficiency' attributed to public services often refers to the perceived potential for increasing the exploitation of working people. Certainly, it is this line of argument – although not stated explicitly by the Ministers primarily responsible – which lies behind the government's policy of privatising the domestic, laundry and catering services of the NHS. That the workers involved are already at the bottom of the employment heap is, for Thatcherites, no reason whatsoever why they should not be pushed down further.

The Development of the Government's Policy

The development of the Thatcher government's policy has been muddled. The 1979-83 administration achieved nothing by continually reiterating the supposed cost-effectiveness of contracting out. The individual Health Authorities would not give the policy the priority the government thought it demanded. Only since the election of June 1983 have Ministers discovered the necessary strength and self-confidence. The opposition has been well organised too, and the sheer weight of reality has reduced the potency of the policy. But at least for one of the 'ancillary' services – domestic services – the impact on the unions and the workers they represent has been severe.

In April 1981, the then Health Minister, Dr Gerard Vaughan, wrote to the chairs of the Area and Regional Health Authorities. Vaughan reminded them of the government's belief in contracting out and chided those Health Authorities which had 'not responded constructively to approaches from

153

commercial companies, notably from the cleaning industry'.
Vaughan wrote that privatisation was particularly to be
welcomed in

> domestic and laundry services, maintenance of buildings and
> vehicles, security services and transport services ... I would urge
> any Authority which is contemplating large scale expenditure on
> a laundry to consider the commercial alternatives before
> deciding.[1]

Health Authorities were not impressed and so the following
May a draft DHSS Circular was drawn up, including model
contracts for the 'ancillary' services and a list of the companies
seeking to benefit from privatisation.[2] However, this Circular
was withdrawn amid confusion. A long industrial dispute with
the NHS workers was taking place at the time. Going ahead
would have strengthened the unions' resolve, while privatisation would be that bit easier if the unions' will had
already been broken by defeat.

So 1982 became another wasted year in the pursuit of
privatisation. Then, with the NHS dispute over, another draft
Circular to Health Authorities was released in February 1983.
There were three reasons why this draft was seen as more
effective than previous Ministerial exhortation. First, year by
year the DHSS was increasing its hold over the Health
Authorities, by packing them with Thatcherite loyalists and
by strengthening the Regions' effective powers of 'review' over
the Districts. Secondly, the government announced that the
VAT position of contracted-out services would be changed.
Previously, Health Authorities had had to pay VAT when
they used private companies, but not on services provided
'in-house' – except in so far as these services made use of
supplies from the private sector. In future, however, Health
Authorities would be refunded the value of this VAT. This
change followed strong pressure from the hard-line privatisers
on the government's back benches and in the Conservative
Party outside Parliament. The third change was the most
dramatic and the most impressive. The 1946 Fair Wages
Resolution of the House of Commons had ensured that, when
public authorities relied upon private contractors, the
companies did not undercut (and thereby undermine) the
agreed remuneration for the relevant public sector jobs. The

government announced that this Resolution would be repealed.

The Health Authorities' reaction to the draft Circular was not encouraging for the government. But that June the Conservatives won their landslide victory, a victory won despite the public's loyalty to the National Health Service and belief that it was safest in Labour's hands. Safely back in power, the Tories became far more aggressive. Norman Fowler announced that Health Authorities were to cut their staffing – the first time such a demand had been made since the 1950s. This was a direct incentive to privatise as services provided by contractors did not count towards the 'manpower' totals. Then, in September, came the formal DIISS Circular on contracting out.[3] Evidently, the Minister had learned from the Health Authorities' comments on the draft Circular – not that the government should tread more cautiously, but rather that privatisation would have to be forced on the DHAs. So the formal Circular insisted that Health Authorities submit to the Regions (and ultimately to the DHSS) programmes of competitive tendering for their 'ancillary' services: private companies must be invited to put in bids and tenders could also be submitted by the DHAs on the basis of keeping in-house terms.

Some Health Authorities, shocked by the revocation of the Fair Wages Resolution (FWR), decided to insist that private contractors honour the nationally agreed Whitley pay and benefits. The government responded by issuing another Circular making clear its displeasure. In fact, the Minister's hard line ran against the perceived self-interest of the contract companies. The cleaning firms' trade association agreed to respect 'stipulated and recommended pay rates'. The established firms feared that they would be undercut by cowboy outfits and believed that revoking the FWR would foment opposition and ultimately prove counter-productive. David Evans of Brengreen accused Norman Fowler of 'astonishing political ineptitude'; the leading ideologue of NHS privatisation, Michael Forsyth MP, thought the Social Services Secretary was 'giving unnecessary political ammunition to opponents'.[4] Mike Davis, chair of the Health Care Services Section of the Contract Cleaning and Maintenance Association insisted:

We wish to compete against in-house domestic service
departments on terms of efficiency and productivity – not at the
expense of lower staff wage rates. To underpay is detrimental to
achieving good productivity and will, we believe, ultimately
reduce standards.[5]

To date, the government has remained unimpressed.

The government later became concerned at the progress of
the competitive tendering programme and the goal posts were
once again moved to favour the private contractors in a letter
sent to the regional chairs in January 1986. Health Authorities
were told to consult with the Regions before cancelling any
private contracts. If no tenders were attracted for a particular
service the Health Authority should look again at its tender
conditions. The letter read:

HC(83)18 provided that tenders should always be sought for
laundry services when capital investment of £1/2 million or more
is being examined. In future this requirement should apply
whenever investment of £1/4 million or more is being examined.

What Is the Case for Privatisation?

Privatisation and antipathy to public services are at the core of
Thatcherism. Competitive tendering for the provision of
particular services such as refuse collection had already
become the 'in thing' for certain Tory local authorities. But
two documents in particular led to compulsory competitive
tendering in the NHS. *Reservicing Health* was published in 1982
by the far-right Adam Smith Institute and written by Michael
Forsyth (before he became an MP), whose public relations
firm is consulted by the contract giant Pritchards.[6] *A Study of
Potential Savings in the Provision of Domestic Services in the NHS
(England)* was a report produced by a working party set up by
Sir Geoffrey Finsberg MP, then a Minister at the DHSS.[7]
Forsyth's pamphlet was highly influential on the right while
the working party's conclusions were cited by Ministers as
justification for their policy. Reading these documents makes
it clear how limited was the evidence for privatisation.

Forsyth starts with a general look at the 'Shortcomings of
NHS Finance'. He argues that we spend less on health
services than other countries because the market is unable to

operate. Also, we spend 'comparatively less on advanced technology equipment for the very ill'. Forsyth regards this as a criticism of the NHS, and his explanation of these alleged drawbacks is that: 'At its bluntest, "the many" have more voting power than "the few".' So Forsyth calls for a 'Re-allocation of NHS Spending'. He points out that in 1980-81 £3546 million of hospital expenditure went on direct patient care, while 'an astonishing £2000 million' went on other running costs, £950 million of that on various 'ancillary' services. The fourteen Health Regions spend varying amounts on these services:

South-East Thames RHA manages to employ 37 per cent more ancillary staff per 100,000 population than does East Anglia RHA ... Such wide variations in so major a budget item indicate two things. Firstly, *the mechanism for quality control and monitoring the efficiency of the service is clearly inadequate;* and secondly, *there is scope for huge savings to be made* in these items, with consequent re-allocation of resources to the areas of more critical need. (Forsyth's emphasis)

This could be achieved by the use of private companies. US hospitals spend less on housekeeping services and portering and rely heavily on 'specialist contractors', as do hospitals in other countries. Administrative problems and burdens fall on the contractors, which

can insist on higher performance from their managers ... and have a very good industrial relations performance to their credit also ... there is certainly no evidence that labour is bought more cheaply or misused ... the workforce ... gain a higher status job, more secure in its opportunities for advancement, with higher rates and better benefits and working conditions.

When using contractors,

detailed specifications are necessary ... The manpower formerly spent in the minutiae of administration can now be spent in watching closely the achievement levels of contract service.

In conclusion, Forsyth suggests that a 10 per cent saving in the NHS 'hotel and general budget could support, each year, the purchase of 52,500 kidney machines, or 490 whole body

scanners, or 51,000 extra nurses, or 17,600 extra doctors, or
740,000 King's Fund beds'.

Forsyth's arguments are highly questionable. His medical
priorities are not widely shared. The *Hospital and Health Services
Review*, the journal of the Institute of Health Service
Administrators, thought Forsyth's list of ways to use a 10 per
cent saving 'increases doubts about whether the author knew
what the NHS needs, and makes one feel that any waste on
hotel services is comparatively harmless'.[8] In any case, the
first section of the pamphlet – attributing the alleged
inadequacies of the NHS to its basic structure – is inconsistent
with the rest, where his solution is not structural change but
an extension of contracting out. Forsyth points out that
Health Regions do not all employ the same number of
'ancillary' staff per head of the population. As the *Hospital and
Health Services Review* commented: 'On reflection it is not so
surprising given their different revenues and, even more, the
differences in bed numbers. Ancillary staff serve beds, not
populations.' Forsyth simply ignores all the possible
explanations of Regional differences except variable efficiency.
Having failed to prove there is a problem, Forsyth provides the
solution: 'specialist contractors'. That sounds common sense
– but how many companies can have the experience of
hospital cleaning, catering and laundry that the NHS has
acquired over the years? So evidence of the efficiency of
contractors is surely called for. Forsyth openly admits that
UK cost comparisons are 'difficult', and turns to international
evidence: hospitals in America and elsewhere are more heavily
reliant on private contractors. But even if it is the case that the
British contract out relatively little, this is not in itself evidence
that we are wrong and the others are right. Otherwise, we are
offered generalities, some of them absurd, such as Forsyth's
rosy picture of the prospects faced by the companies' workers.

The report by the DHSS working party is far more factual
and cautious. It is concerned only with the 'domestic' service
in NHS hospitals, but emphasises that there is no clear
definition of this: it can extend to a 'fully developed hotel
service with the exception of catering'. This looseness of
definition would explain much of the variation in costs: 'The
provision of 'nursing support' and 'extended nursing support'
could add 40 per cent and 60 per cent respectively to the cost of

a "basic cleaning" service.' Other factors are important too, such as 'floor area, usage and surface finishes'. The working party then considers 'Contract Experience in the NHS' and suggests:

> It is believed that some of the problems which lead to the abandonment of contract cleaning may, in part, have arisen from the failure of hospital management to monitor performance adequately against an inadequately detailed specification.

The working party sets out 'Evidence from the Literature' on refuse collection in the USA and UK, nursing homes in the USA, electric power companies in the USA and airlines in Australia. The working party concludes 'savings of 10-20 per cent in some cases would not be at variance with the apparent experience in other fields'. Five military hospitals had contracted out their domestic services and reported savings of between 22 and 62 per cent. At the working party's request, the Ministry of Defence produced new costings showing savings 'ranging from a break-even point in one case to between 20 and 48 per cent in the others'. This was due only in part to greater efficiency:

> The main factors underlying the savings are:
> – reduction of overstaffing at some hospitals
> – an effective lowering of pay rates
> – changes in National Insurance and Superannuation arrangements
> – efficiency gains.

Moreover, the differences between military and NHS hospitals mean that in the latter: 'it might be reasonable to predict savings ranging up to 20 per cent in some cases'. The working party then compares the costs recorded by NHS hospitals using contract companies and those with in-house services:

> The average cost per bed day under direct labour, at £2.70, is somewhat lower than under contractual arrangements (£3.00), but given the wide spread of costs the difference between the averages must be regarded as well within any margins of measurement error.

Only sixteen contract-cleaned hospitals had been identified, which casts 'further doubt on the extent to which we can generalise from these hospitals to the NHS as a whole'. The working party turns briefly to the private sector, saying that Nuffield and AMI hospitals

> use directly employed labour to provide their domestic services. Of those [hospitals] who are independent of the groups mentioned above, one large unit and several smaller ones use contractors.

The large hospital had saved 10 per cent by contracting out, partly because, 'The hospital was able to avoid responsibility for making redundancy payments owing to a technical error by a government official.' In conclusion, the working party suggests that 'sample or pilot tendering exercises could be undertaken', and points out that the available information is 'clearly inadequate for the purpose of measuring the efficiency of such services'. The report's final paragraph reads:

> Finally, we believe that taking into account the MOD [military] experience, the evidence from other fields, limited results of the NHS costs survey and the large private hospital, there may well be savings to be made in the provision of domestic services in the NHS. Such savings, which might derive either from contracting out or from improved efficiency in domestic service departments, might range from nil, in the case of the most efficient service unit, up to possibly 20 per cent in some cases. We might speculate that in hospitals where savings are possible the average saving might be of the order of 10 per cent.

The above summary should make it clear that the working party's report is serious, closely argued and very detailed. Its conclusions are cautious, predicting savings 'up to possibly 20 per cent in some cases'. Nevertheless, the evidence produced does not really allow conclusions of even that evasive nature. Consider the facts they 'take into account' at the end: savings related to US refuse collection and Australian airlines (ignoring the studies of American electric power stations), the NHS costs survey (which definitely did not show that private contractors were cheaper) and one private hospital. Remember also that the costs survey covered sixteen NHS hospitals cleaned privately and the working party doubts whether 'we can generalise from these hospitals to the NHS as a whole', and then proceeds to generalise from four *military* hospitals and one *private* hospital. Three other points are worth stressing: the working party clearly sees that savings at the military hospitals were largely made by companies effectively paying out less in wages and in taxes; they call for 'pilot tendering'; and their study does not look at the efficiency of NHS laundry or catering services. In justifying his policy by reference to this report, Norman Fowler was being more than a little disingenuous. But to a large degree, the working party had dug its own grave.

The Health Service View of Privatisation

The development of NHS services, however, is not solely a matter of politicians and their motivations. It is also worth considering the views of the National Health Service itself, as expressed by the relevant professional associations and by Health Authorities.

In listening to the views of NHS administrators, we should certainly bear in mind their interests: managers in the 'ancillary' services find their jobs threatened and self-esteem challenged by competitive tendering; and the widespread privatisation of 'ancillary' services would encourage right-wing politicians to extend privatisation to mainstream NHS management. But the administrators' arguments are worth considering as they have helped shape the nature of contracting out.

Overall, the various professional organisations do not share the unions' outright opposition to privatisation. Indeed, they see that stance as the mirror image of the government's, and call for caution. We have already come across the condemnation of Forsyth's pamphlet by the official journal of the Institute of Health Service Administrators. Echoing the DHSS working party, the *Hospital and Health Services Review* called for

> experiments which will remove the discussion from theory or misleading foreign examples. This will take time, because it is not just a question of whether a good contract can be drawn up or whether things go well in the first weeks but how it works in the longer run.[9]

Similarly, the *Health and Social Services Journal* has cast a caustic eye over NHS privatisation. Its response to the draft Circular of February 1983 was: 'a blind prejudice against the health unions and a somewhat ill-defined desire to increase managerial efficiency are the motivating forces behind this piece of lunacy'.[10]

In July 1981, Derek Harvey, Treasurer of Warwickshire Area Health Authority, compiled the evidence from a survey carried out by the Association of Health Service Treasurers.[11] The AHST found that most Health Authorities 'wish to continue to organise and manage directly-run services of their own' and that in the past the use of contractors had been only in part due to any savings made possible:

> Some of the issues which led to the use of commercial firms in the first place have now diminished, ie more trained domestic managers exist and staff recruitment is easier, and these issues could seriously influence thinking in future back towards a directly-provided service.

Domestic managers had been consulted and identified four main drawbacks to contracting out:

> (i) A very rigid service is provided, restricted to a literal interpretation of the contract. This often leads to 'demarcation' type disputes from the staff;
> (ii) selection of a contractor could be hit and miss and it is difficult to get rid of an unsatisfactory contractor quickly;
> (iii) there were constant disagreements on standards of service with contractors reluctant to erode profit margins by eliminating any low standard brought to their attention;
> (iv) the service provided by a contractor was as good as the local manager and, where there was a good manager, he tended to move on quickly.

Derek Harvey was not against contracting out in principle but did not believe that it would achieve all that its adherents claimed:

> Certainly, we see no purpose in a national move towards commercialisation because we do not see this as a universal panacea for greater economy or efficiency on these services; but we do envisage that in certain specific circumstances such moves could solve local problems.

Richard Dyson, Chair of the Hospital Caterers' Association, has questioned whether privatisation of NHS catering would improve efficiency:

Is there an appreciation by our Lords at the Department of Health and in Government, that such catering departments now feed 600,000 customers daily, an increase of 10 per cent since the last reorganisation? But that during the same period, catering staff numbers have reduced by 9.4 per cent ... In 1975, catering expenditure as a percentage of the total NHS revenue expenditure was 7.3 per cent, but by 1980 this had fallen to 5.6 per cent ... the provision costs per patient day have fallen, even allowing for inflation, from £1.17 a day to £1.09 a day.

Contract catering was far less common than in the past – in 1965, 34 catering departments were run privately but by 1983, only two remained – which 'suggests to my Association that the success and suitability of contractors is very questionable'.[12]

Some Health Authorities have openly defied the government's policy of compulsory competitive tendering while others have insisted that contractors honour Whitley scales of pay and conditions of service. And many of the complying Health Authorities have also expressed severe doubts about the policy.[13]

Health Authorities were strongly opposed to the revocation of the Fair Wages Resolution on the ground that it would damage morale and industrial relations as well as giving outside contractors a competitive advantage not related to gains in efficiency. Indeed, Southmead's District Administrator argued: 'Cheap labour has never been regarded by economists as tending towards efficiency.' Trafford DHA considered that the 'principal effect' of competitive tendering would be 'to lower morale in the NHS still further and delay the reconstruction of good industrial relations' following the long dispute in 1982. The South Western Region's Supplies Working Party complained of a 'complete lack of appreciation of industrial relations implications of the proposals'.

Health Authorities were horrified by the administrative task facing them. Their administrative staff were recovering from the 1982 NHS reorganisation, and would now have to prepare detailed specifications of their 'ancillary' services. In-house tenders would have to be prepared and compared with bids from the contract companies. This task would inevitably displace other NHS objectives. Health Authorities also doubted whether they had the necessary expertise. The position of Grimsby District may have been all too typical: 'Only one of the Authority's officers has any personal experience of competitive tendering for support services and even then the contact was peripheral.'

Many Health Authorities also considered that the inherent advantages of in-house services had not been taken on board. Contract cleaners were less likely to become part of the 'ward team' and East Dyfed 'considers it essential that it should not be obliged to adopt, purely on cost grounds, any form of organisation which would break up or interfere with the multi-disciplinary approach to in-patient care'. Similarly, West Cumbria Health Authority insisted that domestic

> staff often do make a significant contribution to patient welfare, particularly in specialties like psychiatry, mental handicap and geriatrics and it is important that they are enthusiastic and highly motivated.

Contract companies would not be happy to take on unforeseen tasks which would narrow their profit margins. As Oldham pointed out:

> In a contracted-out service it may not be possible to stipulate every eventuality in contract terms. This poses questions of negotiating for additional items with a contractor in a monopoly position which (a) could be expensive and (b) is likely to take time for which service needs cannot wait.

Moreover, the contractors would need to be carefully supervised in order to forestall a deterioration in standards. This might well involve more administrative effort than controlling in-house staff, and require skills not enjoyed by NHS staff.

Health Authorities were also concerned that companies would put in tenders which were not economically viable in order to gain a foothold in the market. Usually called 'loss leaders', these subsidised bids were described by the Wessex Regional Health Authority as a 'legitimate marketing policy employed by many large public companies in the private sector'. The problem was that the contract company might massively increase its fee when the contract came up for renewal. The Health Authority might find it difficult to revert to in-house provision, especially in the capital-intensive laundry and catering services, and might also find little effective competition from other contractors, especially in rural areas. The same problems could arise when a contractor went bankrupt or proved unwilling or unable to secure high standards of service. Wessex Region acknowledged:

> The ability of the NHS to change back to in-house services is a cause of widespread concern, repeatedly mentioned by Districts and needs detailed consideration ... Where there is little competition between prospective tenderers, great care will have to be taken to avoid monopoly situations.

Health Authorities were also concerned about the effect of privatisation on their own staff, many of whom would be made redundant while those workers taken on by the contract companies would often face lower wages, poorer benefits and harsher employment practices. East Dyfed Health Authority made the general point forcefully:

> To suggest that commercial considerations alone should determine whether ancillary services continue to be provided by the Authority's staff, many of whom will have a long and distinguished record of service is, in this Authority's view, not conducive to good industrial relations and is poor management practice, which would be deprecated by any good employer inside or outside the public sector.

Many Health Authorities argued that the DHSS had provided no serious evidence that, as the 1983 draft Circular claimed, 'The scope for savings in domestic, catering and laundry services is potentially high.' The District Management Team of Leeds Western Health Authority remarked:

> The draft circular raises a mixture of philosophical, financial and practical issues. The team has considered it appropriate to concentrate on the last two categories, although the Authority may wish to express a view on the first, which underlies much of the 'thinking' behind the circular ... The basis for the

government's belief in the cost-effectiveness of using contractors is not indicated.

DHAs certainly felt that the disadvantages of contracting out needed to be carefully looked at. Contracting out was no guarantee of expertise and efficiency, according to Doncaster DHA: 'Some Authorities have already tried and been forced to abandon such arrangements because of their proven unreliability.' The government argued that savings would free resources for 'patient care', but Health Authorities pointed out that the so-called 'ancillary' services were in fact involved in providing that care. Indeed, of the various services contributing to 'patient care', it was by no means clear that most waste or inefficiency was found in the 'ancillary' services. To quote East Dorset Health Authority:

A general point of concern to many managers is that of all areas of expenditure, Ancillary Services have been most satisfactorily contained in recent years, and the perceived need is to concentrate limited administrative and finance time on those situations where expenditure has grown substantially and where budgeting effects [sic] have so far proved ineffective, in particular clinically related services such as Drugs, Medical and Surgical Supplies and Diagnostic Departments.

So NHS administrative staff and the Health Authorities themselves have expressed a wide range of objections to compulsory competitive tendering, objections of practice rather than principle. To some extent, the administrative staff 'would say that, wouldn't they?' However Health Authorities express similar objections (and we should remember how few socialists or trade unionists sit on the DHAs and RHAs). The dominant attitude is not that privatisation runs against the socialist principles of the National Health Service, or even that in practice it has drawbacks which will have to be faced by Health Authorities rather than the Ministers or the DHSS. Underlying these objections is the frustration felt by NHS managers and other staff on the ground at repeatedly being forced into initiatives instigated by politicians whose political prejudices have been developed in other fields but are being applied to medical care. Or, as Swindon puts it: 'The Circular ... has all the appearance of specious argument based on premisses which have not been properly thought through and which are not supported by persuasive facts.'

Health Authorities' Experience

Faced with little alternative, nearly all Health Authorities have co-operated to some extent with the DHSS and have drawn up programmes for putting their 'ancillary' services out to tender.

By March 1986, Ministers were claiming that competitive tendering was saving the NHS £42 million a year. The figures are not, however, unambiguous evidence of gains in cost-effectiveness achieved through privatisation. The 'savings' have been achieved in many cases without privatisation and at the expense of the rosy view of contracting out peddled by Michael Forsyth and others. In many cases, the in-house tender has been successful. Then again, sometimes the service was already contracted out and the result of competitive tendering was merely that a different company took over. If savings were evidence of efficiency gains, such switches would praise some contract companies only by damning others. Ministers would, however, point out that the savings were the result of the tendering policy and argue that they are happy to see in-house services where these are more efficient: there was, after all, a change in line between the draft circulars entitled 'Use of Commercial Contractors in the Provision of Domestic, Catering and Laundry Services' and the formal circular entitled 'Competitive Tendering in the Provision ...'

There is no doubting that 'savings' running into millions of pounds have resulted from competitive tendering. But there is certainly room to doubt whether cost-effectiveness has been improved. For one thing, there have been significant costs involved in the exercise. Some Health Authorities – like Medway and Mid-Downs – have paid out major sums due in redundancy payments. Secondly, competitive tendering has been a major administrative burden on Health Authorities, displacing progress towards goals. Few HAs are able to cost this work, which is very convenient for the government. Thirdly, the policy has had serious effects on the morale and therefore commitment of the 'ancillary' staff and has led to

industrial action in Health Authorities such as Medway,
Cambridge and South Tees. The unions have been in no
doubt that competitive tendering is aimed largely at them and
have done their best to fight back. Again, the impact on
industrial relations is unquantified and apparently ignored by
Ministers.

So there are significant costs to Health Authorities from
competitive tendering. There are costs to the workers too.
Redundancy is the most serious threat, followed by the
slashing of hours and then the loss of fringe benefits and
productivity deals. 'Ancillary' staff were already very poorly
remunerated. Yet the successful tenderers have still managed
to achieve savings through increased exploitation rather than
increased efficiency. We cannot take much comfort from the
fact that Ministers appear unable to see that distinction.

Perhaps the most important question is whether competitive tendering has led to lower standards. Certainly, the
hours devoted to the services have been reduced, in many
cases to a breathtaking extent – by 44 per cent in Medway and
53 per cent in Mid-Downs. In theory, that could be evidence
of the enormous inefficiency of the service previously although
it is hard to believe that with recent financial restrictions
hospital administrators would be that oblivious to waste. In
a survey, Frank Dobson MP did ask whether standards had
dropped and in most cases the respondents expressed
satisfaction. (One District Administrator expressing satisfaction was Peter Chapple of Cambridge. Yet just nine days
before writing to Mr Dobson, Mr Chapple had been quoted in
the *Daily Telegraph* saying: 'We are not satisfied with the
cleaning standard that we are getting.') Medway had lowered
the specification, the statement of standards to be achieved,
Milton Keynes was not satisfied that the specification was
being met and in Hounslow and Spelthorne HA the standards
had dropped in both respects. But Hammersmith Special
Health Authority and North Warwickshire reported improvements following privatisation.

The available evidence does not allow us to conclude
whether competitive tendering has resulted in genuine gains
in efficiency. But it does expose the bogus nature of the
'savings' claimed. Counterbalancing any gains have been the
losses through redundancy payments, administrative burden,

lower morale, industrial action, increased exploitation and unemployment and, for some Districts at least, lower standards.

The Threat of Privatisation

This chapter has been fairly dismissive of the claims made for privatisation by the companies involved and their political supporters. Does this mean that the threat is minimal, not requiring firm and thoughtful opposition? Unfortunately, this is far, far from the case.

True, contracting out made little progress in the first years of Thatcherism, as the following figures indicate:

Percentages of the Relevant Current Expenditure Paid to Private Contractors[14]

	Laundry	Domestic/Cleaning Services	Catering
1979-80	14.1	2.4	0.2
1980-81	12.0	2.5	0.3
1981-82	11.7	2.1	0.2
1982-83	11.5	2.0	0.2
1983-84	9.7	2.0	0.2
1984-85	11.0	2.2	0.3
1985-86[1]	12.2	5.0	0.8

[1] provisional figures

Note: The figures are not strictly comparable over the whole period as VAT on contracted out services became reclaimable by health authorities on 1 September 1983 thus lowering later percentages. The figures for 1985-86 do not include expenditure by Family Practitioner Committees, following their separation from health authorities on 1 April 1985. The form of Family Practitioner Committees' accounts does not permit a similar analysis but their total expenditure on contracted out services in these categories was a little over £200,000.

But the policy of compulsory competitive tendering has only recently got under way, so the above table is a poor guide to the future. More relevant is NUPE's tally of developments:

Contracts Awarded prior to August 1986

	Laundry	Domestic	Catering	Total
In-house	81	398	221	700
Privatised	31	207	13	251
Total	112	605	234	951

To claim that privatisation is making progress might be thought to imply that existing in-house teams are less efficient than private companies. There is, as we have seen, no hard evidence of this. The movement of staff numbers suggests that the efficiency of the 'ancillary' services has been improving in recent years. During the 1970s, according to official statistics, nursing staff in the National Health Service increased by 54 per cent, medical staff by 63 per cent, professional staff by 82 per cent, administrative staff by 103 per cent – and 'ancillary' staff by 2.6 per cent. In 1980, 22 per cent of NHS employees were 'ancillary' compared with 32 per cent in 1970.[15]

The service most resistant to privatisation has been NHS catering. Richard Dyson's arguments set out above are surely impressive and Kenneth Clarke, then the Health Minister, said he expected contracting out to be less widespread here than in the domestic service.

The position of NHS laundry facilities is less clear. In the past, the companies have done much better than the contractors for the other two 'ancillary' services now up for grabs. It would, therefore, seem churlish not to acknowledge that some companies at least can cope with NHS work, although the trade's *Laundry and Catering News* warns:

All who have had any real dealings with the hospital laundry sector agree that the work is far from easy, and that there are very special requirements not found elsewhere. This is reflected in views reported from major companies that if sizeable work loads are taken on, contracts of some eight to ten years would be necessary to justify necessary investment in new plants. It would seem unlikely that such terms would be granted. Exposure to the rigours of competition is the factor which is believed to ensure efficiency in private industry. This would not come into play with such long contract periods.[16]

However, laundries are very capital intensive, with high running costs, particularly on steam. Keeping laundries full is therefore essential and private companies may offer to do NHS work at cheap rates. The other danger comes with the run-down of NHS laundries, especially those built in the 1960s. Ministers have repeatedly forbidden Health Authorities to invest in new laundries, even when nothing was to be gained from contracting out. This is a serious threat, and one which applies to a lesser extent to the catering service as well.

The greatest damage has undoubtedly been done to the in-house domestic teams, although the proportion of NHS cleaning contracted out in recent years has been tiny compared to the figure for laundry. But many contracts have now been awarded to private companies. The Contract Cleaning and Maintenance Association calls upon the member firms of its health section to pay fair wages. But this does not apply to NHS benefits or conditions of service. John Hall, Secretary General of the CCMA, has gone so far as to argue: 'The only way we can save the health service and the government money is to quote prices that cut out the frills.' The in-house tenders must respect the nationally agreed Whitley rates and benefits, although locally negotiated bonus schemes are under severe threat and widespread privatisation will undermine Whitley: there is less point in campaigning for increased wages if few Authorities are paying them and any increases provide further boosts to privatisation.

So the contractors have one great advantage over the in-house bids. Can they in addition provide a more efficient service than the in-house teams? Clearly, many of the companies cannot offer the professionalism and expertise implied by Forsyth's phrase 'specialist contractors'. Indeed Forsyth himself acknowledges: 'A small and inexperienced company might well bid low to gain a contract and then find itself trying to cut corners later.'[17] Leading lights in the contract world, Graeme Crothall and Jim Derham, stress: 'The greatest danger the whole privatisation concept faces is incompetent tenders with inadequate man hours costed in, resulting in inadequate services.' They recommend that hospitals specify minimum wage rates lest contractors bid wage rates too low to attract or retain the calibre of staff needed ... In three or four years time when contracts are re-tendered, and the 'cowboys' have been weeded out of the hospital cleaning industry, removal of a floor on wage rates may be appropriate.

It is, in truth, impossible to say whether there has been significant 'over-manning' in the NHS domestic departments. New tenders from both private companies and in-house teams have involved drastic cuts in total hours spent on cleaning, involving more intense work and, arguably, lower standards. But it may not be good enough to point to deteriorations in cleaning standards. Health Authorities keen to remain in the good books of the DHSS, and desperate to find 'savings', may turn a blind eye to falling standards or, worse, lower their expectations. Ministers have made it all too clear that Health Authorities have the right to see standards drop. The deterioration of the NHS's cleaning, catering and laundry would increase the attractiveness of private hospitals.

The domestic contractors do face a problem in trying to keep up a reasonable image in the context of cut-throat competition and with Health Authorities desperately seeking ways to make ends meet. On the other hand, the 'cowboys' should be exposed over time while the other companies will learn from experience. Most likely, tenders from contractors and in-house administrators will continue to increase unemployment among NHS cleaners, drive down pay and conditions, and seriously threaten standards of patient care. This will entail other costs such as increased claims on social security, lost tax revenue and the illness which is caused by poverty and distress. But such factors will cut little ice with either Health Authorities or a Thatcherite government.

Notes

[1] Quoted in William Laing, 'Contracting Out in the National Health Service', *Public Money*, December 1982.

[2] Draft DHSS Circular, *Health Services Management: Use of Commercial Contractors in the Provision of Domestic, Catering and Laundry Services*, May/June 1982.

[3] DHSS Circular HC(83)18: *Competitive Tendering in the Provision of Domestic, Catering and Laundry Services*, 1983.

[4] Evans and Forsyth quoted in *Observer*, 11 September 1983.

[5] Davis quoted in *Reflection*, No.1, 1983, Contract Cleaning and Maintenance Association.
[6] Michael Forsyth, *Reservicing Health*, Adam Smith Institute, 1982.
[7] DHSS, *A Study of Potential Savings in the Provision of Domestic Services in the NHS (England)*, unpublished.
[8] 'A Case for Contractors?', *Hospital and Health Services Review*, June 1982.
[9] Ibid.
[10] Quoted in NHS Unlimited, Memorandum 7, *Contracting Out 'Ancillary' Services: The Health Authority View*, November 1984.
[11] Derek Harvey, 'Commercial Services in the NHS', *Public Finance and Accountancy*, July 1981.
[12] Dyson, speech to a TUC Conference on the Privatisation of NHS services.
[13] The following section is derived from NHS Unlimited, op.cit.
[14] *Hansard*, Written Answer, 24 November 1986.
[15] *Hansard*, Written Answer, 12 November 1982.
[16] *Laundry and Catering News*, 30 September 1983.
[17] Forsyth, op.cit.

PART THREE
THE MEANING OF COMMERCIAL MEDICINE

Chapter 9

The Medical Market-place

It has been an awkward and often embarrassing fact for Conservative Ministers, some of whom, like Enoch Powell, Minister for Health between 1960 and 1963, would have otherwise favoured the unfettered actions of the market-place, that they have had to declare their public support for the NHS and most, if not all, of its works. Indeed, from Powell's own thoughts on this topic, it seems that familiarity with the National Health Service acted both to pull him away from his free market ideology and to attempt to justify the NHS in terms of that ideology. The process of change in the NHS, reflected Powell, many years after relinquishing his post, was not the result of so many actions by a monolithic bureaucracy, but rather by a mixture of factors, including population movements, changes in medical practice and medical fashion, and environmental changes, noting that these bore 'much more resemblance to that in areas outside public provision and within the scope of market forces than is commonly supposed'.[1] One fellow right-wing observer wrote of Powell:

> Those in charge of socialist institutions must become socialists themselves – socialists *pro tem*, socialists *ex officio*. Even Mr Powell looked for a time, as director of the National Health Service, a socialist though he was not one before and he is not one now.[2]

Such pragmatism in the face of 'socialised medicine' has been an unpalatable deviation for many on the right. Even

175

more unpalatable, and a daunting obstacle for right-wing populism, has been the high regard in which the NHS is held throughout British society. Like the proverbial holy cow, the NHS has lived in the public mind as a peerless, if shabby institution which has remained dependable and unchanging despite frightening social change. Almost alone among the institutions of social democracy, the NHS has managed to retain a powerful legitimacy.

This fact alone accounts for the fact that the radical right approach the issue of public support for the health service with some temerity. 'Health care is a very emotional topic for most people,' says Davis from the Adam Smith Institute, 'and in Britain we tend to be very conservative in our views about it.'[3] This arises, he says, for virtuous reasons, including pride in British achievements, the high esteem in which we hold our physicians, and natural caution.

Equally infuriating for the right is the unpalatable fact that really radical alteration in the NHS seems so far off that they are often having to make do with second best. Although the growth of private medicine is presented as proof positive of the correctness of their views, it is still some distance from the goal of market-based services. The political ring fence around the right-wing ideals explains much of the weaknesses of their thought on private medicine. For Conservative wets, the expansion of private medicine is enough by itself. Even then it should be limited in its influence. But for the radical right, the NHS has usurped the moral restraints created, and rightly found, within the market mechanism.

The right-wing critique has therefore played the role of gadfly, picking out the weak parts of the NHS, with always the implication not far behind, that if it were fully private these failures would not be experienced and medicine would allow greater choice and certainly greater freedom. Running alongside this polemic has been an academic style of argument. This says, very simply, that the NHS, without prices to filter demand, and without management able to shape its operations and to adapt it to new methods, is necessarily both wasteful and inefficent.

US Reactions to the NHS

Right-wing Americans have taken even greater exception to the National Health Service than their British counterparts, presenting the NHS as just the example they need to correct the growing belief fostered by American liberals that only strong and decisive government intervention can solve the endemic American health care crisis, a crisis that took the form of the pauperisation of the sick elderly in the 1950s, the spiralling of costs from the mid-1960s, and, though few official commentators speak of it, the failure to treat the uninsured poor in the 1980s. The American public needed to be told that British 'socialised medicine' was a monumental failure, and, *sotto voce,* the British public needed to be informed of the private alternative.

Whereas, then, British right-wing commentators have been rather discreet in their criticism of the NHS, American writers are certainly not. Harry Swartz, former medical correspondent of the *New York Times* asserts:

> The fact is that by American standards the NHS is a meagre and spartan medical system, many of whose economies would be regarded as inhuman brutality if applied to Americans.[4]

Congressman Philip Crane, a one-time member of the Republican Party's Health Task Force writes:

> Great Britain has adopted a system of socialised medicine. It can serve as an example of the deterioration of medical care and increase in medical costs that would befall the United States were such a programme to be adopted.[5]

Crane approvingly quotes Professor John Jewkes's views that the growth in private medicine was the result of a desire to receive prompt medical treatment (which is true), but points to the size of waiting lists in December 1950 as proof of its failure. This implies that in the two years since the creation of NHS there had been a massive increase in unmet need. A second major failing of socialised medicine, says Crane, reiterating a familiar conservative theme, is that state provision of services reduces individual self-reliance, or, in more academic jargon, that it results in moral hazard – people use the services because they are there, not because they are needed.

Not only is socialised medicine expensive, says Crane, but it also constitutes a 'a real threat to the freedom of doctors, patients and druggists'.[6] Doctors are forced to comply with standard diagnoses and regulations interfere in the doctor-patient relationship. Far more serious dangers lie ahead, says Crane, suggesting that talk of euthanasia is also a result of government interference. There is a long history of American attacks on the NHS, some of which have been financed by the drug companies, others by professional associations or right-wing pressure groups. Much has been discovered which can be criticised. According to John Goodman of the Fisher Institute, the central problem is that the NHS is not responsive to consumer demand: 'The average British citizen consumes less health care than his American counterpart, and the health care that is consumed is of a lower quality.'[7]

Goodman's critique of the NHS is not dissimilar in tone to Crane's, but he attempts to marshal far more evidence. Like Crane, he uses the views of British (and American) conservatives to represent mainstream academic opinion. However, whereas Crane is content to castigate the NHS for its expense, in Goodman's eyes it is both too expensive and 'disastrously cheap':

> Most Americans have the vague impression that health care costs have soared under the British system of socialised medicine. In terms of nominal spending, that is correct.

However, he says, Britain's health spending 'still ranks among the lowest in the world'. Perhaps acknowledging that this might have caused the reader some confusion he explains:

> ... part of the price the British pay for so little NHS spending is that they are often denied medical care that doctors admit they need. Those who receive medical care often do so at considerable cost – including months, and even years, of waiting while living in pain.[8]

Goodman asserts that the source of the problem is the statist nature of the NHS. Give it over to private people to run and things would improve. Goodman's main sources are conservative economists and virulently anti-NHS journalists. However even conservatives like Enoch Powell and Dennis

Lees are not sufficiently critical of the NHS for Goodman's taste. In a chapter entitled 'The Trend Towards Private Care' he takes issue with them for suggesting that private patients might not get better clinical care than public patients (as they so clearly do in the USA). Are we to believe, asks Goodman, that private patients would settle

> for the standard of care meted out to the average British patient in an NHS ward? Are we to believe that they would travel thousands of miles and spend thousands of dollars to be treated outside of London in worn-out, ill-equipped, nineteenth century buildings serviced by an inadequately-manned and undertrained staff, where most of the consultants have no merit award at all, and where most of the doctors are poorly trained emigrants [sic], to be operated upon by whomever the random luck-of-the-draw produces? The claim that private patients get the same clinical care received by the average NHS patient is too ludicrous to be taken seriously.[9]

Goodman's strength of feeling on this matter is no doubt due to the prevailing consumerist ethic common to the USA that providing you pay enough money you can get the best person for the job. Even Milton Friedman's tongue lashing of the American Medical Association for its monopoly control of medicine contains the somewhat naïve notion that consumers can best determine their medical needs or choice of physcian on personal reputation, rather than, say, qualifications. However, as Marcia Millman revealed in her study of American cardiac surgeons, smart surroundings and high-flying reputations (acquired many years earlier) are used by doctors whose interest in increasing their incomes had long taken precedence over developing their craft.[10]

Goodman's lack of balance is unfortunately compounded by his failure to see any wrong in American health care. Not all writers on the American right, however, defend existing institutions and practices; for some, like George Gilder, one of the chief popularisers of Reaganite doctrine, American medicine too is tainted by do-gooding welfarism:

> ... there is little difference in the economic character of the medical transactions going on between doctors and patients in the two countries. The combination of regulated private

insurance with Medicare and Medicaid operates in more or less the same way as the British National Health. [11]

America too has been slipping down the slope towards socialisation, and bracing, morally uplifting measures (such as repealing welfare legislation which induces 'dependency') are necessary to stop the rot.

Setting aside the many and various claims that each piece of regulation leading to health insurance for the elderly or health centres for the poor represents creeping socialisation, convergency between Britain and America in health care was first noted by Rosemary Stevens. The reasons she gave were mainly technical and bureaucratic in emphasis. Both societies, despite the 'lingering rhetoric' of the welfare state in Britain and free enterprise ideology in America, were going through technical changes in medicine and specialisation which required intervention to enforce general standards, to assure a regional balance of services and to provide a limited degree of consumer protection. [12]

Thatcher's Dilemma

Political goals appear more refined and subtle when filtered through the gauze of academic respectability, and certainly an historically important role has been placed on the economists and others to explain why society remains unequal and why the arrangements under which people labour reveal such a lack of democracy. Nevertheless it is important not to exaggerate the influence of ideologues. The threat to welfare capitalism posed by Reagan in America and Thatcher in the UK did not emerge in the academy. Indeed, the intellectual ideology of the free market, perhaps the key fiction of any economics course, is not accorded much relevance in health policy matters. The 'free market' when spoken of in the context of health care is no more than a fashionable term, since it has never operated and, without the abandonment of the professional practice of medicine, never could.

Nevertheless some of the libertarian baggage carried along with free-market views has certainly been an influence on the marketing of policies both by Thatcher and by Reagan. In both cases they were required to restate the compassion traditional to conservatism, yet come up with policies suitable to the dominant economic interests. The central, if daunting, task in the case of the NHS was publicly to support the dominant social symbols but privately plan for its liquidation.

David Hart, writing in the *Times* in an article headed 'Time to Sell off the NHS', argued that if the Conservatives took action on the National Health Service, their popularity 'could slump'. He went on to recommend the scrapping of the tax financing of the NHS and its replacement by compulsory private health insurance for all except the very poor, who would be provided with government-purchased cover. Hospitals, he suggested, should be sold off, with those facilities left over (perhaps the older facilities, psychiatric hospitals and so on) handed over to a nationalised concern. When profitable, they too could be hived off. These actions would not only improve efficiency, they would return decision-making into the hands of the consumer:

> Only when the resources that the nation devotes to health care are distributed through the free market will decisions be returned to the consumer, where they belong, and only then will the pound that the individual puts in deliver the maximum care to the patient when it comes out.[13]

Hart, one of the government's advisors during the miners' strike, is more ideologist than theoretician. In fact, as many on the free-market right have come to recognise, this type of suggestion could never be countenanced while public support for a tax-based service remained so high. This makes it all the more important to develop respectable academic arguments for privatisation. Unfortunately the outpourings of the Adam Smith Institute or the Bow Group were seen as too closely tied to the Conservative Party or as simply not academically respectable.

The Attack in Britain

More sophisticated thinking had been mapped out by right-wing intellectuals over some years and is credited with influence on the Thatcher Cabinet. Despite the formal acceptance of the welfare state within mainstream Conservatism, a small number of right-wing writers continued to fight 'a rearguard struggle' against the policies and the practices of the welfare state. The chief source of critical right-wing thought on the NHS was the Institute of Economic Affairs. It is underpinned by a preference for 'individual choice' over what was seen as an inefficient, morally degrading and paternalistic state intervention. Behind an outwardly libertarian philosophy lay the dismal credo of market-place economics. In a sense, Institute members were declaring that nothing had been learned since the days of Adam Smith, and argued that the Victorian age had been unfairly criticised. Beneath the libertarian rhetoric lay an aversion to policies of social redistribution and state provision and, for some of its members, a simple class hatred of groups like council tenants and other recipients of public provision, collectively denounced as 'scroungers'.

The concept of a National Health Service financed from taxation was attacked in a series of pamphlets by members and supporters of the Institute. The 'new' critique was based on a reheated form of eighteenth-century economics, applied in the rather different conditions of the second half of the twentieth century. It thus differed from that of the 1950s since it was not particularly concerned with the supposed 'burgeoning' costs of the NHS, nor did it reflect the nostalgia of reactionary doctors. The new critique was economic, at least in the sense that those advancing it were professional economists.

While the economists attacked the NHS's apparent absence of guiding economic criteria, behind them lay the more complex ideas (of equally conservative hue) of Friedman and Hayek. Friedman's *Capitalism and Freedom* is an attempt to demonstrate that government welfare and regulatory activity undermine individual liberty and freedom. To maximise freedom, he argues, governments should be allowed to handle only those matters 'which cannot be handled through the market at all, or can be handled only at so great a cost that the use of political channels may be preferable'.[14]

Friedman's arguments regarding the organisation of medical care follow a different tack. Rather than centring his concerns on state intervention in medicine, Friedman sets his sights on the (American) medical profession, which he accuses of being perhaps the strongest trade union in the country.

Friedman's solution is to remove licensing requirements and leave the development of health care to the market. British economists, in seeking to present US medicine as the alternative to the NHS, ignored the incipient monopoly character of medicine, suggesting that all that was required to create market freedom was the elimination of third-party interference between the buyer and seller. What Friedman and his British supporters failed to see was that the intervention to improve the position of the American medical profession was not state inspired.[15]

The ensuing debate between the supporters of market-place medicine and the Fabian defenders of the NHS in the 1960s took place at a time when the course of history seemed to be running in favour of the latter. As Friedman commented: 'There is still a tendency to regard all existing government as desirable [and] to attribute all evils to the market ... The proponents of limited government and free enterprise are still on the defensive.' The NHS's opponents occupied the comfortable position of being able to criticise and propose alternatives knowing full well that they would not be taken up. The more junior among them even went so far as to suggest that sources of blood could be more efficiently and cheaply supplied under a free market.[16] This absurdity was tackled by the central figure among the Fabians, Richard Titmuss, who pointed out that in those countries where blood was a commodity there were even greater problems of supply than under the NHS.[17] On the other hand, the defence of the NHS made by the Fabians was far from faultless. Although people like Titmuss were critical of professional control over the NHS, they were hardly in the vanguard of the movement for user control and better redress against medical malpractice.[18] Although a critic of the private market, Titmuss never opposed private practice *within* the NHS.

In the 1940s US sociologists like Talcott Parsons built up arcane theories of social stability based on the idea of a special relationship between patient and doctor and between patient and 'family', liable to be undermined by explicitly profit-seeking activity on the part of the providers of medical care. Certainly patients do expect (even if their expectations are mistaken) that providers of medical care have higher motivations than just money-making. And medical care in Britain is not a business industry in the usual sense that the relationship between providers and consumers is monetarised (or, as Marxists would put it, subject to the usual rules of capitalist economic exchange).

In the USA, Parsons's views would today seem rather old hat, since the American establishment accepts that the words 'competition' and 'health care' run together. But in Britain, several decades of the NHS render the conjoining of these concepts rather less acceptable. Nevertheless, health economist Alan Maynard claims that: 'There is little doubt that the attributes of competition are attractive.'[19] Unfortunately, competition also produces expensive consequences. In any truly competitive market, the established interests might lose out, and so might the patients, since competitive behaviour among doctors could lower medical standards. In fact, because the dominant interest groups stand among those with most to lose, any enforcement of the principles of competition would be limited.

Only some groups in the medical care industry are therefore likely to benefit from more open competition, and even then the benefits would be likely to be temporary. Supporters of truly 'free' markets, either in bubble gum or in medical care, are not as thick on the ground as academics and right-wing policy making groups would like to think, although the lure of the free market is certainly a strong one.

A Free Market for Medical Care?

David Green, of the Institute of Economic Affairs, maintains that a free market for medical care can exist, and moreover has existed in the past.[20] Citing 'working-class' medical provision from the 1830s to the First World War, Green argues that state interference acted to enhance professional power, rather than undermine it. 'Compared with the market-place,' says Green, 'the state offered hugely increased opportunities for the exercise of professional power.'[21] In the nineteenth century doctors were contracted to working men's associations and clubs, and attempts to push up fees beyond levels the clubs would meet were in the main unsuccessful. Using the state as an ally, however, the profession managed thereafter to break the power of the consumer. The state was not, in Green's view, a 'countervailing power' to the medical profession, but its main prop.

Green has a point, although his own recipe for 'consumer power' – a 'return' to arrangements akin to a free market – need not be accepted. The American physician/health-writer Milton Roemer has observed that the suggestion that a free market in health care would work to everyone's benefit flies in the face of historical development:

> We contend that the current health care systems in the United States and other capitalist countries have survived to the present day only because they have been continuously modified by planning and regulation. Without these modifications, the effects of the free trade dynamics would have been so disastrous, so unacceptable politically, that these systems would have collapsed long ago, and been replaced by completely planned and regulated health care systems.[22]

The health economist Anthony Culyer once sided with those who view the market as the solution to the problems of health care but has since described his former allies as seekers of the 'never-never land of the perfect market', where 'the outcomes will be whatever individuals want and are prepared to pay for'.[23] He also describes anti-marketeers as romantics for not accepting the inevitability of making choices on technical means or resource restrictions. Naturally enough, David Green takes the strongest exception to these views. In fact, Culyer supports private medicine for his own, rather idiosyncratic, reasons. The NHS functions best, he says, alongside an active and competitive private sector, for the National Health Service

> offers the potentiality for effective control of the medical professions and industries in the interests of more clearly specified collective concern for the health of the nation, while the private sector will be there not only to provide the ineffective treatments but also always to compel the public sector's attention towards the not altogether unimportant point that patients are people.[24]

Certainly, the history of the development of public health, even in America, confirms the view that the state was forced into enacting measures to stem the causes of disease or to avert social problems or political unrest.[25] The nature of the problem, and the nature of the response, varied from one time to another and from place to place. But the development of a more regulatory environment occurred in spite of ideological trends which favoured either the status quo, or emergent economic and political interests or the 'free market'.

In fact those who champion the role of the British private medical sector are less concerned with the ideological purity of solutions based in the market-place and more interested in establishing public-private links. Says Hugh Elwell, who may come closest to being the strategist of private sector thought:

> I do not see private medicine as being at any time either a threat to or competitor of the National Health Service; what I would like to see is a very much closer working relationship between the management of the NHS resources at the District level and that role that the private sector can play in that district.[26]

This pragmatism is shared even by academic writers such as Haywood and his associates, mildly hostile to private medicine. They argue that there are potential gains (as well as losses) from the growth of private medicine. The positive effects they mention are those trumpeted by the private sector itself, in particular that it draws in extra cash and resources, could be a source of innovation and attracts foreign patients.

'So often,' these academic writers observe, 'discussion fails to proceed beyond familiar calls to defend the faith, either of socialised or private medicine.'[27] In the case of opponents of private medicine, this would lead them to underestimate the regulatory powers at the disposal of public authorities (such as health authorities and local authorities) and the extent to which private resources can be put to use for agreeable social ends. The experience from the USA, they say, shows that it is better to 'anticipate and regulate' before the event than to try to remedy deficiencies afterwards. But the more enduring lesson from the USA is that regulation of private medicine is expensive and haphazard, that regulators are apt to be 'bought off' by the regulated and that the regulators fail to receive the backing they need to make their actions effective. While Roemer is correct to say that regulation is inevitable, it is also inevitably undermined. There are examples of more or less effective regulatory activity in the health care field, for example in the area of pharmaceuticals. But the graveyard of failed regulatory efforts spans the field of health planning, of rules governing the acceptance of poor patients to hospitals in receipt of Federal grants, of professional standards, and of government health insurance. Since the NHS is so poor at monitoring private medicine within its own hospitals, it would be unlikely to be any more effective at monitoring it on the outside.

The larger the private sector grows, the smaller the likelihood that public regulation of commercial medicine can be effective. Indeed, the privatisation of public services is desired by the right precisely because this would avoid government interference in the 'industry'. As Minford confidently asserts, freeing up the market would create competition in each geographic area: 'The new private owners of hospitals will themselves take the action necessary to be profitable in the face of stiff competition.'[20]

Certainly, the NHS is in dire need of assistance. The financial problems that descended on the National Health Service in the 1970s, as well as the pervasive aura of crisis throughout public services, have been building up steam over a long period. The NHS, as Goodman correctly observed, was beset with an ancient stock of buildings designed for a different medical era, and now faces growing numbers of the elderly, an unworkable managerialism that has been thrust upon it and a new set of priorities – more preventive services, more so-called cinderella services and resources equalisation, requiring massive inputs of extra resources.

There is a substantial amount of academic literature, by no means all linked to the right, which seeks at least to accommodate private medicine and market-based perspectives. The current academic (and Ministerial) game is not to attack the NHS head-on, but to suggest ways of making it more 'efficient'. A number of different panaceas have emerged. That which finds the broadest approval, and bridges the gap between the comprehensiveness of a National Health Service and the competitive workings of the market, is the health maintenance organisation (HMO).

Health Maintenance Organisations

The concept of the health maintenance organisation has been seized by the *Economist* magazine a decade or so after it was first picked up by one of its American rivals, *Fortune*. *Fortune*'s championing of the HMO was explicable enough. Quite correctly, they diagnosed that American doctors were claiming too high a price for their services because they controlled the entry of doctors into the profession. HMOs, however, took advantage of the fact that many younger doctors emerged from medical school looking for immediate work, and the HMO, offering them a salary or share, could imbue them with a new style of medical practice before they became tainted by the fee-for-service system of payment with its large fees and inefficiency. But the HMO concept was more than this. It was also about offering a more or less complete package of care to subscribers or their employers, with the claim that their premiums would be lower than any rival insurance. One other aspect of HMOs generated the enthusiasm of the business magazines: HMOs saw themselves as businesses rather than charities (even if only about one quarter of them were actually profit-making), and they set themselves up in competition with other suppliers.

We still need to ask why business people and economists did not prefer the medical care corporations to HMOs. After all, the corporations were the true bearers of the spirit of capitalism. The explanation is that the corporations aimed to maximise their income from the insurance companies, just like other medical care providers. Although they too had the incentive to be efficient, their relationship to each and every patient was an isolated act. They had no interest in developing comprehensive care for patients. Although the corporations may have been the darlings of Wall Street, they did not find great favour with those executives who negotiated the benefits packages for employees.

The most enthusiastic academic fan of the health maintenance organisation concept is Professor Alain Enthoven of Stanford University. In the USA, Enthoven's name has been chiefly associated with the concept of the 'consumer choice plan', an attempt to harness the taxation system, company welfare benefits and government insurance to reduce the consumption of the most expensive medical care. His ideas have drawn the attention of a British audience through the medium of the *Economist* and the Nuffield Provincial Hospitals Trust.

Enthoven rejects as politically unrealistic the possibility of radical change sweeping away the present fundamentals of the NHS, in particular its adherence to free care at the point of demand. Nevertheless, he recommends

> large employers or trade unions to sponsor HMOs, in a scheme in which each subscriber could designate that his actuarian-determined per capita cost to the NHS (considering his age, sex, health status) would be paid to his HMO. If the HMO cost more, the subscriber would pay the difference. In the case of poor people, the government could subsidise part or all of the difference. If this development went well, NHS districts might be allowed to become HMOs and to compete to keep their patients.[29]

Second best is an approach he terms 'market socialism' (as distinct from privatisation) which has the aim of increasing the scale of monetary incentives and introducing market competition between NHS districts.

> Under my experimental proposal, each district would receive a RAWP-based per capita revenue and capital allowance. Each DHA would continue to be responsible to provide or pay for comprehensive care for its own resident population, but would get current compensation when it provided services for other districts' residents. It would be paid for emergency services at a standard cost, and non-emergency services to outside at negotiated prices. It would control referrals outside its district and it would pay for them at negotiated prices. In effect, each DHA would be like a Health Maintenance Organisation.[30]

At first reading, if this is all that is required to create HMOs in the NHS, then the suggestion would find few objectors. Health Authorities, particularly teaching authorities in urban areas, face large cross-boundary transfers, in some cases importing the majority of their patients. But Enthoven intends something more than this. Prices are to be negotiated, not fixed, and Health Authorities would have the option of purchasing private sector provision. After some years of application of internal markets Health Authorities would become purchasers of services as much as providers, and the concept of a *national* service would be eroded by local competitive behaviour by Health Districts.

Enthoven's suggestions fail by being insufficiently informed or imaginative. The only suggestion he does make which would increase patient power is to force consultants to justify their waiting lists to patients, something they are at present under no obligation to do. Sadly, Enthoven fails to address the issue of incentives. Although he is correct to say that professional power and unassertive management do represent problems in the service, he offers no remedy for increasing consumer power over them. His 'consumer choice' theory, transposed to the British context, is merely one more management model for the running of the service, and a form of approach, moreover, which bears the stamp of American preference for acute services over prevention.

In the USA, the HMO might be a useful stop-gap measure in the absence of a National Health Service, since it is part of the movement towards more comprehensive treatment of patients, and towards greater cost-effectiveness. The *Financial Times*, reviewing HMOs in the USA, says:

> There is something essentially American in the concept of publicly-quoted, profit-seeking medical care corporations, which raise money on the stock market and issue prospectuses and earning reports.[31]

Equally, there are dangers for patients contained within the HMO strategy, including the potential for patient selection, i.e. refusing cover to the sick, undertreatment, and, on occasion, fraud.

In the British context, the application of this approach would take the NHS further away from the concept of a national health service in which the priorities were set by social need, and towards a service where the primary motivations of the leading actors (as in commercial medicine) were set by financial factors. As the Adam Smith Institute observes:

> It is most likely to spring up in an atmosphere where private insurance is widespread – and therefore the principles of

subscription medicine and private practitioners are common – than from the bedrock of socialised medicine.[32]

The days of the full-frontal academic assault on the NHS are over, an irony, perhaps, since the NHS is under greater immediate danger than ever before. Today, the more important right-wing challenges appear in sheep's clothing. Yesterday's threats are today's good ideas. The new conventional wisdom is that new methods have to be found to improve health service efficiency, and that standards of good practice exist in the private sector or abroad. Economists of the right have woken from their free-market dreams to play a more practical role in steering the NHS towards the sober financial realities. No longer wishing to appear as the opponents of the National Health Service, the current right-wing stance is that they just, to use the words of one medical corporation executive, 'want to help out'.[33]

Notes

[1] *Times Health Supplement*, 13 November 1983.

[2] Colin Welch in Arthur Seldon (ed.), *The Rebirth of Britain*, Pan Books, 1964, p.47.

[3] Dave Davis, *Public Hospitals/Private Management*, Adam Smith Institute, 1985.

[4] Quotation from John Goodman, *National Health Care in Great Britain: Lessons for the USA*, Dallas, 1980.

[5] Philip M. Crane, 'Let's not Wreck American Medicine' in Marjorie Holt (ed.), *The Case Against the Reckless Congress*, Creen Hill Publishers, 1976, pp.95-104.

[6] Ibid.

[7] Goodman, op.cit.

[8] Ibid.

[9] Ibid.

[10] Marcia Millman, *The Unkindest Cut*, William Morrow and Co., 1978.

[11] George Gilder, *Wealth and Poverty*, Bantam Books, p.185.

[12] Rosemary Stevens, 'Governments and Medical Care' in G. McLachlan (ed.), *Medical Education and Medical Care: A Scottish/American Symposium*: Nuffield Provincial Hospitals Trust, 1977, pp.159-70.

[13] *Times*, 5 December 1983.

[14] Milton Friedman, *Capitalism and Freedom*, University of Chicago Press, 1962, pp.149-60.

[15] See Howard Berliner, 'A Larger Perspective on the Flexner Report', *International Journal of Health Services*, 1975, pp.573-92. E. Richard Brown, *Rockefeller Medicine Men: Medical Care and Capitalism in America*, University of California Press, 1978.

[16] See M. H. Cooper and A.J. Culyer, *The Price of Blood,* Institute for Economic Affairs, 1968.

[17] Richard M. Titmuss, *The Gift Relationship: From Human Blood to Social Policy*, Allen and Unwin, 1972.

[18] Titmuss suggests that the large number of malpractice claims lodged against American doctors results from the dominance of commercial values. While this claim is not without substance it would be mistaken to claim, as he does, that the absence of legal conflict is a sign that wronged patients would not sue if they could. On this point see: S.Law and S.Polan, *Pain and Profit: the Politics of Malpractice*, Harper and Row, 1978.

[19] Alan Maynard, 'Privatising the Health Service', *Lloyds Bank Review*, April 1983, p.32.

[20] David G. Green, 'Doctors Versus Workers', *Economic Affairs* (Supplement) October-December 1984, p.iv.
It might be noted that it is unusual for the right to criticise the medical profession so openly. More typical is the approach of the Adam Smith Institute: 'the medical expertise of the BMA is unquestioned'. See: *The Omega File: Health and Social Services Policy*, ASI 1984, p.1.

[21] Ibid., p.v.

[22] Milton Roemer and John E. Roemer, 'The Social Consequences of Free Trade in Health Care: A Public Health Response to Orthodox Economics', *International Journal of Health Services*, Vol.12, No.1, 1982, pp.111-29.

[23] J. Culyer, 'Public or Private Health Services?' in *Journal of Policy Analysis and Management*, Vol.2, No 3, 386-402, 1983.

[24] Culyer, cited in US Department of Health, Education and Welfare, *International Health Costs and Expenditures*, US Government Publishing Office, 1976, p.113.

[25] John Duffy, *A History of Public Health in New York City*, Russell Sage Foundation, 1974.

[26] *Independent Medical Care*, August 1983.

[27] Philip Chubb, Stuart Haywood and Paul Torrens, *Managing the Mixed Economy of Health: Policy Considerations for the National Health Service in Dealing with the Expansion of the Private Sector,* University of Birmingham, 1982.

[28] Patrick Minford, 'State Expenditure: A Study in Waste', *Economic Affairs* (Supplement), April/June 1984.

[29] Alain Enthoven, 'National Health Service: Some Reforms Which Might be Politically Feasible', *Economist*, 22 June 1985.

[30] Ibid.

[31] Terry Byland, 'Wall Street's Growth Area', *Financial Times*, 13 February 1985.

[32] ASI, *The Omega File: Health and Social Services Policy*, p.33.

[33] Ronald Marston, Head of Hospital Corporation of America (Europe) interviewed in the *Financial Times*, 10 July 1982.

Chapter 10

The Attractions of Going Private

Private practice is beneficial to both providers and users, offering financial, social and psychological rewards. While the expansion of the private sector in medicine depends upon political and economic change, the material and social basis for that expansion exists in a complex matrix of ambitions, frustrated expectations, deteriorating working conditions, anxieties and class prejudices. Consultants are attracted to the 'clinical autonomy' of private practice, while low pay in the National Health Service promotes the drift of other NHS professionals into commercial health care. Users seek a combination of availability and exclusivity, blending the real material advantages offered by the commercial sector with an air of excellence and importance.

Money

Financial reward is the most obvious attraction of commercial medicine for professional workers. Consultant surgeons and physicians, highly paid by UK standards, can achieve incomes closer to their West European and US colleagues by adding private practice earnings to their NHS salary. A surgeon testifying to a House of Commons Select Committee in 1971 put it succinctly:

> I am doing one patient a week who brings me in approximately £75 to £100 per week for 52 weeks of the year, something like £5,000. I have expenses admittedly, but I am giving up £800 and earning £5,000. I am giving up about three hours only of my professional time to private practice.[1]

Since then opportunities for private practice have increased, in part through government initiatives, so that specialists can enter the commercial sector with little or no detriment to their NHS salaries.[3] The pickings can be very rich indeed, as public scandals in 1984 and 1985 revealed.

Similar opportunities exist in general practice, but on a smaller scale. The GP lacks the specialist's status, and cannot command the specialist's high fees, but his/her contract is less specific in its demands than the consultant's and the secrecy of the consultation allows ample scope for commerce. Cash pressed into the hands of obscure general practitioners is harder to monitor than cheques paid to eminent surgeons, and without records of patients seen and fees pocketed, general practice is a humble but potentially profitable area for private medicine.

Doctors' enthusiasm for money can be a problem for the commercial sector. Health insurance organisations and private hospitals complain about the demands of 'wallet-motivated consultants', and any expansion of insurance protection into general practice threatens the hidden, over-the-desk cash transaction with the paperwork and public scrutiny of mainstream commerce.[3] Unchecked greed threatens cash-flows and confidence, provoking the very regulation of medical practice that doctors seek to avoid by undertaking private work.

Autonomy

Private practice takes the professional workers away from the administrative control structure of the NHS. At last they can work as they want, as their own boss, using personal skills freed from rules and regulations, being guided by 'conscience' alone. The professionals' responsibility to the individual patient or client overrides any collective responsibility to all actual or potential patients, to taxpayers or to government nominees. Medical practice, with all its social ramifications, can be reduced to the small problems of the consultation, where the unequal power and knowledge of the participants gives the professionals the opportunity to dominate. For the surgeon or the psychologist this is an enormous change for the better. No committees have to be endured, no resources shared, no long and complicated political manoeuvres sustained, no back seats taken. The professional is the key figure, unchallenged by bureaucracy and unhindered by competing professional interests. Power, or at least the illusion of power, lies where it belongs – in professional hands. The user of the service reinforces this by paying for it, but may also challenge it. This partly illusory professional power is inflated by the economic status of the client or patient. Those who pay to see the professional can almost always pay for the consequences – blood tests, X-rays, medicines. No rationing of investigative and diagnostic services disturbs the professional's decision making. Hospital beds are available in the commercial sector, and operating theatres are readily prepared. Over-capacity comes to the aid of the customer's purchasing power, turning the process of caring and curing into a streamlined, efficient process orchestrated by the professional worker.

The regulator in this process is the conscience of the professional. 'Conscience' makes professional workers act in the best interests of their customers, and (in theory) allows them to avoid the belief that the paying customer is always right. The judgements included in 'conscience' may be narrowly technical (is tonsillectomy worthwhile?) or broadly social (why is this person depressed?), but they are made on the basis of the professional's own education, experience and personal development.

The child offered for tonsillectomy will have his/her tonsils examined by the surgeon, and surgery arranged if it seems appropriate. The relevant question may be: 'Why does anyone want this child's tonsils removed?' The answers may concern absence from school through repeated infection, or a patient's perception of surgery as a solution to a relatively minor problem. The crucial element in the surgeon's 'conscience' would then be his/her ability to distinguish between social and organic causes of problems, given his/her training in surgical technique and anatomical structure. In reality sound judgements are hard even with wide knowledge of people and their circumstances, and everyday medicine is full of errors of judgement made despite ample information and impressions from multiple sources. In the private consultation, when money motivates and power shapes the process of problem-solving, professionals employ a concept of 'conscience' that is inappropriate to modern health care.

The professional health care workers are drawn to private practice because it increases their income and power, and because it does not demand more than a minimum of collaboration or of subordination of personal ambition and expectations. Individuals trained to exercise personal power find power-sharing and co-operation difficult, even to the extent that they exist within the NHS. Their escape into the autonomy of private practice provides personal material compensation and psychological relief for this social and structural problem.

In this sense the development of commercial medicine may highlight problems within the health service that need attention. The greedy surgeon has little to offer the NHS, but he or she does remind us of the immense power of the specialist and the rigidity of medical training. His/her sensitivity to some patients may alert us to an issue relevant to all patients. Moreover, the private psychologist and psychotherapist, the midwife in private practice or the nurse working in a private hospital may have a lot to tell us that we should want to hear.

Private by Default

The private sector also includes some health workers who are poorly served by the NHS, and others who are excluded from state funds, so jealously guarded by the established professions. Psychotherapists and psychoanalysts are largely outside the NHS, as are virtually all 'alternative practitioners'. Most adopt the one-to-one relationship as the only possible style of work, and some analysts insist on a cash transaction as the basis of their therapy, taking it as evidence of the client's commitment to a painful struggle to change. Although increasingly fashionable to the middle classes, 'alternative' (or to use its preferred term, 'complementary') medicine is not yet a significant part of the commercialised sector. Those disenchanted with mainstream medicine may see these alternatives as suitable replacements for orthodox practice, even though the change would be one of technique rather than of power relationships. Public funding for psychotherapy on the NHS, for example, has established a limited network of psychotherapy units and won the allegiance of some psychotherapists to public service, although the impact on the public's health is difficult to measure. However, the incorporation of, say, homoeopathy and osteopathy into the health service seems unlikely, and would depend on political pressure for such a change rather than on any sudden awakening to their therapeutic powers. Such pressure seems more likely to influence the organised commercial sector, which could extend its franchises and insurance benefits to include 'alternative medicine', if the figures worked out right. As yet neither the public sector nor the commercial networks in medicine have decided to snap at this bait; some forms of therapy are not yet too important nor too profitable to be left to small traders.

Other categories of health worker commute between public and commercial medicine, or defect into the commercial sector, because of financial and administrative problems inside the NHS. Clinical psychologists are produced faster than jobs become available, and so create niches for themselves in industry or in individual private practice, using part-time NHS work (if they can get it) as their base. Chiropodists can retreat from the immense demand for NHS care into better paid and less pressured private work. Doctors unable to find NHS hospital posts or suitable vacancies in general practice provide a pool of casual labour for the larger private hospitals in the South-East of England. Managers short changed in successive administrative reforms of the NHS, or wearied by its internal politics, step sideways into the cost-conscious efficiency and industrial harmony of well regimented commercial hospitals. In their thousands, nurses make their exodus from public to commercial medicine, staffing nursing agencies, running private hospitals, nursing homes and clinics, and providing home nursing services.

Over 50,000 nursing posts exist in the institutions of the private sector, 9,000 of them in 'acute' hospitals geared up for surgery. The 'whole-time equivalent' figures are significantly lower because part-time work is one of the attractions of the commercial hospitals. Nurses are drawn into the commercial networks by packages of better pay and improved conditions. Wage rates are determined by market conditions, including the viability and prestige of the hospital, the strength of local competition (including the NHS), the need to recruit and keep specialist nurses, and local commercial sector policy towards pay-parity.[4]

The commercial sector prefers to be flexible in its approach to pay. Nursing homes can exploit the pool of unemployed nurses and may get away with wage rates lower than the health service. The Nuffield Hospitals maintain a 'good neighbour' policy towards the NHS by paying Whitley Council rates. Corporation-owned hospitals may be less sensitive to NHS goodwill and more willing to outbid the public hospitals. Despite this flexibility, the commercial sector relies upon low pay in nursing to provide incentives for nurses trained in the NHS to defect to private hospitals. An increase in nurses' pay, and an expansion of the number of NHS nursing posts available, would have a serious knock-on effect on all parts of the commercial sector, hitting the nursing homes and the for-profit hospitals hardest.

Fringe Benefits

Fringe benefits are the second temptation offered to nurses by the commercial hospitals. Inducements can include: good quality accommodation, sometimes subsidised, compared with often austere NHS nurses' homes; more tolerable work rates with less commitment to 'unsocial hours'; cheap food, comfortable rest and recreation areas and adequate clothing; direct contact with a management that apparently takes a personal interest in staff. These benefits can have a negative side – the undemanding work may provide little satisfaction, the patients may treat nurses as personal slaves, and management's interest may be financially motivated – but the balance of advantage must lie with the private sector.

The third temptation of the commercial sector is the escape route it offers for those unable or unwilling to tolerate, or work against, the deterioration in working conditions or standards of care inside the NHS. Private practice is naturally attractive to those who have retained the least motivation, enthusiasm and commitment to meeting health care needs through public service. In this sense the commercial sector may recruit the 'worse' professionals whose overall motivation, enthusiasm and commitment are minimal. This seems particularly true in the current development of new nursing homes for the

mentally ill and elderly infirm. Nurses working in large
mental hospitals can see these homes as a personal way out of
the institutionalised and degrading environment of back
wards, and no one should be surprised that so many staff are
willing to invest their savings and their residual energy in
opening DHSS-sponsored residential homes. Just as we
should question the ENT surgeon's judgements in private
practice, so we should ask whether demoralised nurses have
the appropriate skills and necessary enthusiasm for looking
after elderly, infirm and irremediably ill people 'in the
community'.

Consumer Choices

The National Health Service does not meet all needs, and
cannot meet all wants. People use the wide range of private
services for a variety of reasons involving necessity, custom
and choice. Private medicine may be all that is available, may
appear to be more accessible than the NHS, and may be more
acceptable to some. Just as the complex motives of those who
work in the private sector tell us much about the functioning
of the NHS, so we can learn a great deal about the use of
medical care from the private sector's customers.

Private facilities may be the only service available. Half the
therapeutic abortions done in the UK are performed outside
the NHS by charitable organisations and commercial clinics.[5]
The fixed charges of the charities restrict the fees demanded
by the clinics, and the sympathetic counselling offered by the
charities may be an advance on much NHS provision, to the
benefit of many thousands of women with unwanted
pregnancies.

The nursing home 'boom' engineered by the Conservative
government demonstrates that the official NHS policy of
promoting 'Care in the Community' without the allocation of
sufficient extra resources can be implemented by the private
sector but only at the expense of the central concept of the
policy. The idea of encouraging elderly, infirm, disabled and
mentally ill people to live in an ordinary neighbourhood,
contributing to it according to their abilities and drawing from
it according to their needs, depends on social networks
adaptive enough to accommodate problematic people and on

back-up services strong enough to step in whenever special attention is needed. The new nursing homes provide no such resources, but they do preserve social peace by permanently protecting the able, competent and busy from the mad, the demented and the incontinent.

Eligibility

Even where the NHS does provide adequate medical services, individuals may not be eligible to use them, or may believe they are not eligible. Regulations for charging those 'not normally resident' in the UK for hospital care came into effect in 1982, despite evidence that the use of hospital services by overseas visitors created an insignificant workload, whilst collecting fees from them generated considerable administrative costs.[6] Questions about eligibility for services from hospital staff who may be ignorant about names or prejudiced about skin colour can divert demand into the commercial sector, as individuals avoid the confrontations, interrogations and racism possible in this vetting procedure by 'going private'. Doubts about eligibility may be sufficient to make an individual into a private patient, without any first- or second-hand experience of rejection by the NHS. An EEC national working in Britain, paying national insurance and accustomed to fee-paying medical care is an easy client for the private GP or specialist. General practitioners, who are not governed by the eligibility rules applied in hospitals, may choose to create their own rules and charge likely customers rather than register and treat them under the NHS as they are entitled to do.[7]

Eligibility for services could become an important issue for the NHS as regional variations in the way the health service works increase. Budget restrictions may impel Health Authorities to examine residence qualifications for NHS care. One RHA has already publicly considered this idea and although this may have been part of a political manoeuvre to embarrass the government and wring more funds out of the DHSS, the idea could be relaunched if needed.[8] The lesson for those who move home frequently, or travel as part of their work, may be that investment in private health insurance will provide a better passport to medical care than an NHS card.

Buying Time and Choice

Contact between the user of the NHS and health professionals can be brief, inconclusive and frustrating, while the time spent waiting for such contacts can be, or seem to be, uncomfortably long. This is not always true, even in the busiest parts of the health service, and the persistent high regard for the NHS recorded in opinion polls may be a measure of the service's success in satisfying wants.[9] It may also be evidence of low public expectations being easily met by cursory attention, and some of the private sector's growth could be attributable to changed expectations being frustrated by unchanging public provision.

The ward round that stops only briefly at each bed, the seven-minute consultation with a general practitioner and the new face behind the desk at each out-patient visit, are common enough to have become formalised as myth. Prolonged, personal contacts with ward nurses and orderlies, with health visitors or with physiotherapists, do not necessarily offset the impression of hurry and impersonality in a service defined by medicine and doctors. Nor can any health worker easily use time, attention and discussion speedily to abolish full waiting rooms, the list of pending operations or the rising workload of out-patient clinics. In an effort to provide more services, or even to maintain services at the same level, within limited budgets, the NHS is speeding up to accommodate more patients in less time. As the NHS shifts into a higher gear to cope with increased demand without a comparable increase in resources, its flexibility decreases. With less slack to use in periods of stress, responses become less sensitive to changes in demand. Waiting lists show how the NHS has lost its capacity to compensate for the effects of industrial action by NHS workers.

The pattern of stress and strain within the NHS works to the advantage of commercial medicine. A lengthy consultation with a specialist, rapid referral for further investigation or treatment by other specialists and follow-up by the same doctor are all possible for paying customers. The patient who can meet the private specialist's fees may be able to escape waiting a long time for an initial appointment, being briefly assessed by a doctor in a training grade, waiting again for investigation, admission, or out-patient treatment, and being reviewed by a different member of the NHS consultant's team. The paying patient does not have to negotiate, and renegotiate, the terms of his/her treatment with a succession of doctors. Nor does s/he become an educational audio-visual aid for the benefit of professionals in training. By paying the consultant's fees, the paying patient aims to extract any element of 'practice' from private practice.

The advantages of paying for private care depend upon the commercial sector's flexibility and capacity. A degree of over-provision in the commercial sector compensates for the relative or apparent under-provision in the NHS. The balance between the two sectors is crucial if this advantage is to be exploited; too much traffic through the commercial sector could overload parts of it faster than it can expand, creating stresses and strains similar to those experienced in the NHS. The commercial screening service providing full physical examination and an impressive-looking array of tests for its customers may come to be experienced as an impersonal medical conveyor belt motored by monetary gain, because the opportunity for a long discussion is not included in its programme. The private midwife providing personal, high-quality care sensitive to the desires of women wanting childbirth at home can become so exhausted by long hours and unforeseen problems that her concentration slips and a serious error of judgement is made.[10] A dramatic collapse of NHS services would create an enormous problem for commercial medicine, which cannot afford to maintain substantial surges in demand. We should not be surprised – or fooled – when representatives of commercial medicine defend the NHS or advise caution in the expansion of the private sector.[11]

Accessibility

Commercial services may co-exist with the NHS, and compete with it, at a local level because of the former's tangible advantages. The financial barrier to medical care can be outweighed (for those with means) by the convenience of commercial provision. This convenience may be geographical, as in the case of the commercial casualty unit in London's

West End, where a huge population of office-workers and shoppers can drop in for medical attention in the course of a normal working day. It may also be a convenience in time, allowing non-urgent surgery for perhaps hernia repair or removal of varicose veins to be done at a time suitable for the sufferer, rather than for the service. The surgery can often be done in one day, avoiding an expensive overnight stay and allowing recovery to occur at home and even work to be continued (for white-collar workers).[12]

This convenience is economically important. Busy business people believe that 'time is money' and place a high premium on correct timing. Workers on oil-rigs cannot stop work and return to land because their local NHS hospital anticipates having a free bed in two days' time, without losing pay. Industries and trades unions cannot be expected to avoid the positive advantages of the commercial sector's accessibility when economic decline intensifies competition for orders, jobs and profits.

Getting the timing right also puts the user of the service in charge of events. The patient becomes the important person, not one of many on a waiting list, experiencing rationing of time and attention. Other people are excluded, and the medical process concentrates on the individual without making him/her subordinate other problems – like work – to matters of health. Convenience is an issue because of the market's emphasis on self and self-reliance.

Acceptability

Paying patients believe that they are buying the best. Value for (personal) money in commercial medicine comes from more than specialist attention, convenience and speedy responses. The paying patients may purchase a paradoxical egalitarianism in the consultation, whilst demonstrating their individual superiority and significance to others. And anonymity of a kind which is almost impossible in the state institution of public health care can be bought, easily and in some cases without question.

A patient whose hernia is repaired in a BUPA hospital, or who is seeking a consultant's advice in his/her private rooms, is at the same time escaping from the lower orders who fill out-patient clinics and GPs' waiting rooms. There will be fewer unseemly interruptions by midnight admissions, attempts at cardiac resuscitation on the other side of the ward, efforts to guide or control unruly psychotics, or snotty whining children shepherded by exhausted looking women. There will be more of the privacy, gentility and pot-plant environment so typical of good quality living. It is true that working-class men and women may occupy adjacent beds or seats, but their presence will be diluted by patients of some breeding and they will be living up to their new-found opportunities and status.

The private patient will expect due consideration, even deference, and to an extent will receive it, in the form of time, courtesy and congenial surroundings. If there is distress about, it is to be the patient's alone, uncontaminated by the madness, illness and poverty of masses of people competing for attention. Commercial medicine changes priorities for people of quality, who work hard, take responsibility and live decently. Such people – professionals, managers, business people, sensitive and intellectual souls, even skilled workers – are extracted from the crowd. Key groups of people, whose production is expensive and whose abilities are not to be wasted, are given the special treatment that allows them harmonious, friction-free lives. Commercial medicine offers further reinforcement of their social status and ideology, whilst repairing their hernias and diagnosing their discomforts.

Paradoxically, movement away from social sharing permits greater egalitarianism in the individual consultation. Both doctor and patient can relax a little, for they are more likely to be similar people when money changes hands than in the hectic public clinic. Both value private medicine, its time-scale and its personal qualities. The payment of fees creates a mutual dependence that levels the relationship between the doctor and patient in a way that consultation in the state's time and at the state's expense could not. Those who take the trouble to escape from their inferiors are unlikely to welcome being treated as inferiors or even as claimants themselves. The commercial consultation evens the odds a little, as specialist speaks to specialist, and entrepreneur to entrepreneur.

Payment, and the understanding it buys, can also produce anonymity. Shameful and stigmatising problems can be discreetly resolved by the commercial sector, which will avoid storing and distributing information about psychotherapy and psychoanalysis, drug abuse and alcoholism, sexual problems and abortions. The patient comes in with a clean sheet, and leaves with one too. A brief report to a general practitioner may be the only record of the event, outside the doctor's own notes. Voluminous files are not stored in some huge room, to be extracted, abstracted, amplified and copied by clerks, doctors, nurses and secretaries. Medical histories are not constructed from a sequence of judgements and recollections, following their owners round as they move from place to place, or problem to problem. The paying patient – the customer – may be treated quite literally as a commodity, a machine with a fault but with no other significant problem. Private medicine excels at creating this anonymity, which reaches beyond confidentiality into conspiracy, the erasure of memory, and the rewriting of personal history.

Notes

[1] Donald Gould, *New Statesman*, 7 April 1972.
[2] See the regular series on money matters by P.F.Hepburn in the *British Journal of Hospital Medicine*, especially the issues of September to November 1984.
[3] *The Health Services*, 11 February 1983.
[4] *Rates of Pay and Conditions of Service for Nurses in the Independent Health Sector*, Royal College of Nursing, 1984.
[5] See the annual Abortion Statistics published by the Office of Population Censuses and Surveys and HMSO.
[6] *Hansard*, 16 November 1983.
[7] Examples encountered by one of the authors working in an inner London general practice.
[8] 'Oxford and the Collapse of Planning', *Medicine in Society*, 1983, 9:2, p.17.
[9] *Daily Telegraph*, 22 October 1984; *Health and Social Services Journal*, 30 May 1985.
[10] Both examples come from people known to one of the authors.
[11] See, for example, Derek Damerell, BUPA Chief Executive, in *Living*, 5 October 1983.
[12] Day-care surgery did not increase in the NHS between 1975 and 1981, despite its economic advantages. OHE Compendium, 3:14.

Chapter 11

US Health Care: The Public Consequences of a Private Market-place

As in Britain, so in America, public and private services are intertwined and interdependent. The present patterning of services in the USA is simply not the result of the autonomous development of the private sector: it represents a complex symbiosis between public provision and financing and private interest, against the backdrop of an ever-shifting power structure and technological change.

The chief characteristics of the American medical market-place are the co-existence of monopoly and commercial activity, a curious form of market competition, systematic inequality and a high degree of distortion of the medical task. Furthermore, the technical, social and economic aspects of this highly complex setting are overlaid by ideological gloss highly favourable to the status quo. Historically, government intervention has been both reluctant and deficient. However the overall structure of the American 'medical market-place' is chiefly defined by government policy – either through the form of positive intervention (financing, direct provision, regulatory policy) or negative intervention (allowing interest groups to shape the market-place).

This chapter outlines the form of the public/private relationship in America and some of its consequences for recipients. We will show how American medicine has always been profit-oriented, but that the recent phenomenon of corporate health care has fundamentally changed the character of American medicine, bringing it much closer to the mainstream of corporate society.

The Medical-Industrial Complex

In modern America, the charitable impulse which led to the founding of so many American hospitals has all but evaporated. Many charitable agencies remain charities in name and legal status only. The single most remarkable process presently occurring in medical care politics is the convergence between the for-profit commercial system and the formally non-profit hospital system. This is resulting in the steady emergence of what has been identified as the 'medical-industrial complex'. This is not, to repeat, an autonomous process. The recent changes that have occurred in American medicine have been nurtured, indeed underwritten, by federal government policy.

As with Britain's NHS, the make-up of American health services is the result of many historical factors. The most recent federal policies draw from the extremely rapid process of cost inflation that occurred in the 1960s and has continued until today. However, the federal government has been merely one component in this process: the current form of the American medical-industrial complex has been established through a continuous process of professional, technical and social transformations. We will now establish the nature of these changes, beginning with the dominant organisational mode of medical care delivery – the hospitals.

The Hospitals

Historically, both public and private hospitals were institutions which provided food and shelter for the impoverished sick – the well-to-do were treated at home by private doctors. It was not until the late nineteenth century that private charity hospitals – the voluntary hospitals – began to attract middle-class patients. With the advent of anaesthesia and antisepsis, work could be done in a hospital setting that was not possible before. In consequence, the private hospitals began to provide services which distinguished between paying and non-paying patients, and provided private rooms to encourage local physicians to admit their patients.[1]

By the end of the nineteenth century private-patient revenues had become important supplements to philanthropy, and hospitals began to reduce their charity wards and increase their paying services. The burden of caring for the sick poor was increasingly thrown onto the shoulders of the public hospitals, and the charity hospitals began to demand government reimbursement.

In many cases public institutions were drawn away from competition with the voluntary hospitals. For example, local societies of doctors had limited public medicine, by law, to the service of the poor. Organised medicine insisted that health care was a private affair, so that when whole populations suffered the ravages of epidemics, including tuberculosis, and women were dying in their hundreds through faulty medical treatment, medical societies continued to insist that such matters were not the affair of government.[2]

Genuine therapeutic advances often occurred in public hospitals and public laboratories. However the operation of America's political and class system meant that public facilities were always too limited, too underfunded and deprived of status.

Voluntary hospitals relied on philanthropic endowments, but as costs rose, these formed a declining proportion of revenues. In Britain the financial crisis endured by hospitals in the 1930s drew them ever closer to the state. In the USA certain factors militated against this. The American medical profession was not, as in Britain, split between the hospital doctor and the primary care physician. By the 1930s the dominant group within the medical profession was made up of fiercely anti-state private practitioners.[3] The voluntary hospitals found that they could obtain government finance while retaining their autonomy.[4] Furthermore, the federal political system meant that the roots of political patronage were local as much as national, forming an additional obstacle to a nation-wide system of health insurance.

Apart from a brief period early in the century, therefore, reformers were never able to mount a serious campaign for health insurance or any other kind of effective government activity in health care (the sole exception, perhaps, being the work of the Federal Drug Administration). The lack of a workable coalition around either an expansive insurance system, or a health service, also explains why government policy in the health field has been so subject to interest groups, or else half-hearted and inept.

By the 1930s the structural characteristics of hospital provision were set. Local governments provided services for the poor, public health and teaching facilities; state government provided psychiatric hospitals; federal government ran military hospitals, while the private sector was divided into a non-profit voluntary sector and a commercial or 'proprietary' sector.

The Depression was a major watershed in the relations between the public and private sectors. In 1935 the total income of short-stay hospitals (excluding those operated by the federal government) was about $448 million. The government's share was about one-quarter, private payments accounted for more than three-fifths, and philanthropy contributed around 13 per cent ($60 million).[5] Although the economic crisis had led many hundreds of municipalities into bankruptcy, public hospitals were in a generally more stable financial condition than the voluntary hospitals. These experienced falling patient revenues, their charity care was drastically reduced and private fees increased. Not surprisingly, occupancy slumped. Logically, the reverse was true of public hospitals, which saw occupancy rates shoot up.

In their search for a solution to their financial difficulties, voluntary hospitals initiated an insurance system of their own – later known as Blue Cross. Initially, revenues provided through Blue Cross were fairly limited, but in the post-war period, with insurance increasingly being offered as a fringe benefit of employment, insurance quickly overtook other sources of income.[6]

However in the immediate post-Depression years, hospitals remained chronically underfinanced in terms of capital resources, and underprovided in regions of new population growth. At the end of the war, a federal insurance plan was touted as the solution to the rising costs facing patients, but, however bland in conception this proposal represented the 'thin end of the wedge of socialism' to the American Medical Association, which with mounting political authority born of scientific advance – and a massive propaganda war chest – became the most effective lobbying group even seen in Washington.

The failure to create a viable funding system for the

payment of hospital costs presented those Americans inflicted by illness with a bitter choice. At the start of the 1950s around 20 per cent of US families owed over $100 each to doctors, dentists and hospitals, and loans for medical payments constituted the biggest item of the small loans business. The elderly were the most heavily affected, since major medical expense inflicted pauperism on even those who had best provided for themselves.

However, one part of the failed reform proposals did meet with the approval of the medical establishment – a programme of financial support for hospital construction, known as Hill-Burton. This programme devoted federal funds (if matched by funds from other levels of government and from private sources) to the construction of public and non-profit hospitals, health centres and other facilities. By 1960, three-fifths of the total federal funding of health care – $1.45 billion – went to the private sector, although the majority of hospital beds were located in the public sector. The Hill-Burton programme was supposed to result in a better geographical distribution of doctors and hospitals and to provide access to care for non-paying patients. It mostly helped suburban areas, and the charity care dimension was ignored – in sum, the programme was so much free money to private hospitals.

The second major piece of federal assistance to the medical sector also boosted the fortunes of private hospital medicine. From the early 1950s the federal government began to invest heavily in medical research, and most projects were established with the private medical school system. By 1957 over $126 million was being pumped into medical research, most of it going to medical schools, hospitals and private laboratories.[7] Naturally, such research boosted the private sector's prestige, but it also upset the traditional system of medical training based within public hospitals. Traditionally, public hospitals had played an important role in tuition and research, and access to public wards was prized by medical trainees. As research contracts poured into the medical schools, the medical mainstream became more firmly established in the private medical centres, starving public hospitals of staff. The result was that by the late 1950s in cities like New York, municipal hospitals were forced to go cap in hand to private medical schools and contract staffing at inflated fees. To this day, many public hospitals have little control over their own medical staffing, and the clinical priorities are determined by medical school teaching programmes.

The third major intervention by the federal government, again of enormous benefit to the private medical sector, was the passage of the Social Security amendments of 1965. These federal reforms created Medicare, which was essentially a financial package which paid the major portion of medical expenses for the elderly, and Medicaid, a programme run in partnership with individual states, which met the expenses of the blind, disabled, handicapped and, depending on individual state coverage, certain categories of the poor.

These programmes allowed many Americans routinely denied medical treatment to gain access to it. However, Medicare and Medicaid were deeply flawed. In mimicking the organisational structure of existing systems of private insurance, which reflected the needs of hospitals, they gave encouragement to acute medicine and hospital-centred treatment. Also, while they bent over backwards to be generous to medical care providers, benefits to their recipients could best be described as parsimonious. Furthermore, because their administration was almost totally privatised, they almost immediately ran headlong out of political and financial control. They were seriously abused by doctors, while the supposed regulators formed, to use an American idiom, 'sweetheart' contracts with the industry.[8]

Such programmes represented what has been termed the 'conservative assimilation of reform', that is to say change did occur, but the question is who benefited most. The AMA devoted approximately $7 million to defeat the Medicare Bill, much of the money spent on friendly politicians.[9]

American health policy has supported the individualistic and entrepreneurial character of medical care, and left doctors, hospitals and other providers remarkably free of obligations. Objective data suggest that many surgeons viewed Medicaid as merely yet another way of exercising their scalpels and enlarging their bank accounts. One Congressional enquiry, for example, revealed that Medicaid patients were more than two-and-a-half times more likely to undergo surgery than the general population.[10] No proof was offered that they were two-and-a-half times more in need of it.

America is today even further away from national health insurance than it was 30 years ago, a major reason being that public 'intervention' has been discredited, while a more collective vision of public health and social equality of access has to some considerable degree been overtaken by consumerism. In the 1960s and 70s, liberals looked to the British National Health Service for inspiration, but by the late 1970s the reformist current was in retreat. The pace for the industry was now being set not by the medical schools buoyed up by federal research contracts, but by the high-profit, high-growth medical care corporations.

The term 'military-industrial complex' was used in the 1960s to describe the economic, social and financial links between Washington, the military and the arms suppliers. The medical-industrial complex had arguably been in existence for many years too, but, as the hospital system started to look towards Wall Street for a test of its worth, rather than towards epidemiology, the term came to have a more sinister meaning. The complex involves the interrelation of private and state power, as wielded by the medical, pharmaceutical, and supply corporations, large voluntary hospitals and medical schools, professional interest groups and the separate departments of government.

As it had emerged by the late 1970s, the character of the 'new' complex contrasted with the old. Even in the 1960s, the system had been underpinned by administration of byzantine complexity, the main function of which was to determine 'eligibility' for treatment, in other words to maintain the operations of the American class system in the delivery of care. With its means-tests, its privatised operation and its variability from state to state, insurance plan to insurance plan, this massively wasteful system presents great problems for the American state. By the late 1970s this system had become allied with management science, computers and marketing. The hospital sector, once defined as a cottage industry, was coming of age.

The Medicare/Medicaid Boom and the Aftermath

The new 'medical-industrial complex' is a creation of the liberal 'Great Society' programme and its aftermath. Beside

Medicare and Medicaid, which were its key policies, the federal government released a welter of reforms, from preventive health policy and health centres – often effective but always at the margins – to health planning and the regulation of medical work. Potentially, the increase in federal funds to the health sector could have improved and upgraded public facilities. In fact, the opposite happened.

In the late 1950s, 2,000 out of a total of approximately 6,800 hospitals were publicly run. The largest number of beds were contained in the state mental hospitals, while federal and local governments had about 200,000 beds each. Altogether, the number of public beds exceeded those in the private sector. Total spending on hospitals averaged $6.4 billion of which 40 per cent ($2.5 billion) was spent by the government, and went for the most part into public provision. In cities like New York the public hospitals, run as a department of city hall, were a massive public enterprise, and together with the public health department provided hospital care, emergency services and preventive care to a large proportion of the population.

Prior to 1966, the year Medicaid began operation, three out of every four public health care dollars were spent on care provided at municipal locations. The remaining dollar went to the voluntary hospitals for public charge patients. Ten years later, the flow of funds reversed. More than half of the aggregate public outlay for hospital care went to private institutions while municipal hospitals remained dependent on the city's withering tax base.[11] Coming on the heels of the influx of increased subscriptions to private insurance in the 1950s, public insurance unleashed the amazingly inflationary capacities of the American medical system. Almost from the outset, the new system was subject to incredible scandals. Medicaid was charged for services never given, patients given unwanted repeat appointments or referred unnecessarily to other doctors. Although the system marginally improved access to general practitioner services, only a minority of doctors were willing to treat Medicaid patients, mostly because the payment rates were well below what they could get from their paying patients. Medicare was the more adequate of the two programmes, largely for the reason that it retained a uniform character thoughout the country. Medicaid, on the other hand, varied from state to state. One state – Arizona – even refused to implement it.

Many of the liberal planning measures, since they failed to
tackle the essentially private nature of the system, were ineffective at reining in cost or creating – in the fashion of the time –
a more participatory system. Health planning which was
supposed to involve consumers was run at the behest of private
hospitals, the attempt to improve medical standards suffered
through being controlled by doctors, while the means-testing
formulae for insurance eligibility tightened every few years.

By 1969, the attempt to 'buy' America's poor participation in
'mainstream', i.e. private, medicine was coming to its close.
And since President Nixon announced that the health care
system was in 'massive crisis', an alternative strategy has
gained currency in political and academic circles. Instead of
further regulations of the system, which would lead to a larger
government role, policy should be redirected to make health
care more businesslike.

Henceforth, those organisations which were smart enough to
play the system, to follow the increasingly complex rules of
hospital reimbursement and planning controls, and to reduce
their overheads and generate surpluses or profits, could prosper. Other parts of the system, including the public hospitals
with large numbers of uninsured patients, small voluntary
hospitals and individually owned proprietary hospitals were
now deemed to be anachronistic. Henceforth corporate
activity, or its voluntary sector surrogate form, was presented
as the medical future.

The Origins of Corporate Health Care

In 1928 there were 2,435 'proprietary' hospitals, constituting
around 36 per cent of hospitals of all types.[12] By the mid-1950s
this had dropped to 1,000 and by 1968 to 769. By 1980 the
figure was back over 1,000, except that whereas in the 1950s
these had all been independently owned, by 1980 almost
nine-tenths of profit-making hospitals were owned by one of
38 hospital chains. Half of these are owned by half a dozen
market goliaths, including Hospital Corporation of America,
American Medical International, National Medical Enterprises and Humana Inc. Furthermore, over 260 non-profit
hospitals were managed by proprietary chains.

Company ownership is often interlocking. 18 per cent of Beverley Enterprises, America's largest nursing home operator, with over 57,400 beds, is owned by HCA, while Hillhaven, the third largest operator (16,500 beds), is wholly owned by National Medical Enterprises.[13] These companies have also staked off other fields in search of 'horizontal integration'. In terms of profits, the hospital chains dramatically improved their return on common equity each year, rising from 10.3 per cent in 1971 to 20.4 per cent in 1980. This matched the profit level of the drug industry and came a close second to the tobacco industry, with a 20.6 per cent return. Not surprisingly, the Chief Executive Officers of two of the major corporations rank within the 20 best paid men in America. In the mid-1960s, the more far-sighted businesses and entrepreneur physicians realised that modern business methods, including marketing, franchising, portfolio analysis, product standardisation and employee incentives, could be employed in medicine to generate profits attractive to outside investors.

The corporations became particularly effective at selling themselves and dropping the normal rules of the medical market-place to suit more efficient operation. For example, Humana's Sunrise Hospital in Las Vegas experienced low demand on Sundays and peaks of demand at other times. The management responded by offering discounts on Sundays. Hospital Corporation of American became adept at selling its management service to public hospitals which were losing money. Politicians, trustees and others later appeared in HCA advertisements to say what a fine job the company had done.

Under Medicare, the federal government paid a hospital's costs, plus allowances for depreciation, interest and 'return on equity' (profit). The commercial chains bought up hospitals or entered into mergers and then revalued their new assets. In the last five years the number of hospitals owned by the big chains increased from 439 to 755, and each time a hospital changed hands the government had to pay increased depreciation allowances. The federal government therefore paid hospitals to merge, which hardly smacks of free competition.

One official document circulating in Washington studied the Hospital Corporation of America's takeover of the

Hospital Affiliates International chain in 1981. In the year after purchase HCA claimed that its assets had grown by $55 million, a portion of which could be claimed back from the government. The Congressional Budget Office estimated that the government could save some $830 million over five years by putting an end to this practice, something the corporations have been fighting tooth and nail to prevent.

The 'Non-Profit' Response

By the mid-1970s, with attempts by states and the federal government to clamp down on burgeoning medical costs, it became evident that, although the commercial hospitals had to pay taxes on their income, they could still generate fabulous profits while an increasing number of voluntary hospitals struggled to make ends meet. The competition, together with the very desire to survive in an increasingly regulatory environment, meant that voluntary hospitals began to ape the commercial competitors.

Recognising the benefits of operating in groups, the voluntary hospitals linked together. Recognising the benefits to be gained from employing business graduates with marketing expertise, they sought them out. Many of the hospitals even gained a liking for profits, forming subsidiary corporations to manage hospitals.

The Demise of Public Services?

American public hospitals are now in dire straits. It was openly acknowledged within the upper circles of the medical establishment that the costs of President Reagan's cuts in the health budget would be borne by the public hospitals. Reports from most states indicate that 'patient dumping' – that is, for-profit hospitals refusing treatment to the poor – is on the increase. The Reagan Administration's health cuts have come in several packages, all of which have had a significant impact on the poor.[14] Eligibility for Medicaid has been tightened, and state health programmes have suffered funding reductions. The Administration toyed with the idea of introducing what it called a policy of 'competitive health care'.

The Reagan Administration held a number of people within

its ranks who hold strongly free-market views on the issue of health provision. Martin Felstein, the President's former economic adviser, has been the chief advocate of this view for more than two decades. David Stockman, Reagan's former budget director, holds the view that health care is a marketable product like any other and should be organised accordingly. These advisers argued that medical insurance should be taxed – in 1982 the revenue loss was $28 billion – and that cost-based and unrestrained fee-for-service reimbursement should be replaced by an alternative, free-market delivery system. Hospital care also should be reduced.[16] The sharp end of this policy is swingeing reductions in public programmes.

Even the administration of the programmes is privatised. In Georgia the scheme is run by the Prudential Company; in Nebraska by Mutual of Omaha (who are also competing in the British medical insurance market); in Nevada by Aetna Life. These companies have an appalling track record when benefits paid out are compared to premiums received.[17]

The State of Arizona was granted the right to experiment for 40 months with a system in which doctors, hospitals and other providers of health care would compete to provide all-inclusive medical care to the poor for a fixed, prepaid monthly fee. Those organisations which agreed to care for patients at the lowest per capita cost were awarded contracts. By early 1984, 150,000 of Arizona's 2,860,000 residents (who were required to be very poor, disabled or elderly) were enrolled in nineteen plans. Thirteen of the plans were operated by commercial groups, two by counties, three by hospitals and one by a university. The administration of the project was contracted out to the McDonnell Douglas Corporation, the aircraft company which also administers the huge Medicaid programme in New York State. Privatisation does not come cheap. The first piece of bad news was that McDonnell Douglas raised its management fee from $8.2 million to $35 million. It was also disclosed in the Arizona press that a state politician instrumental in starting the programme was on the payroll of the largest commercial operator, and that this group also had offices in Chicago and was claimed to have links with organised crime.

As one might expect, the Reagan Administration has

softened its line on full-blooded competition, and adopted Diagnosis Related Groups, designed to give hospitals a financial incentive to provide care efficiently. Under this system, hospitals are no longer reimbursed the costs incurred in treating the patient but according a set cost schedule (covering 467 diagnoses). American hospitals have suffered as a result of the Reagan cuts, indeed several of the largest commercial chains began to lose money in 1986. Several companies, including AMI, cut back expenditure, dropped loss-making divisions, in particular insurance, and laid off staff. This will not slow up the process of commercialisation. It simply means that the adverse consequences for the poor and publicly insured patients begin to show up earlier.

These changes do not really add up to the type of market freedom recommended by David Stockman. Although the words 'competition' and 'consumer choice' are freely used they have an ambiguous content. The new language of American medicine is not patient care but marketing strategy. As Jeff Goldsmith, one of the academic health pundits popular with the corporations put it, the hospital of the future will be a

multicorporate, diversified health services enterprise – only one division of which will be a conventionally organised hospital. I believe that hospitals will offer a wide range of ambulatory and aftercare services through different corporations and alliances with physicians in private practice.[18]

We are witnessing, in America, the emergence of a true medical-industrial complex, with the erection of impenetrable partitions between rich and poor. This has occurred, with the financial and political support of the state, fronted by a neo-conservative party of the government.

The words 'health care' no longer apply. The more appropriate term in the late 1980s is 'health business'.

Notes

[1] Charles F. Rosenberg and Morris J. Vogel (eds), *The Therapeutic Revolution: Essays in the Social History of American Medicine*, University of Philadelphia Press, 1979.
[2] D.M.Fox, 'Social Policy and City Politics: Tuberculosis Reporting in New York City', *Bulletin of the History of Medicine*, Vol.45, 1975, pp.169-95.

[3] Ronald L. Numbers, *Almost Persuaded: American Physicians and Compulsory Health Insurance*, John Hopkins University Press, 1978.

[4] E.Ginzberg (ed.), *Philanthropy and Public Policy*, National Bureau of Economic Research, 1962. pp.73ff.

[5] ibid.

[6] Sylvia A. Law, *Blue Cross: What Went Wrong?*, Yale University Press, 1974.

[7] L.Sobel (ed.), *Health Care: An American Crisis*, Facts on File, 1979.

[8] Judith M. Feder, *Medicare: the Politics of Federal Hospital Insurance*, Lexington Books, 1977.

[9] R.M. Harmer, *American Medical Avarice*, Abelard-Schuman, 1975.

[10] Subcommittee on Oversight and Investigation, Committee on Interstate and Foreign Commerce. *Cost and Quality of Health Care: Unnecessary Surgery*, US Congress, Washington DC, 1976.

[11] N.Piore, P.Lieberman and J.Linnane, 'Public Expenditures and Private Control? Health Care Dilemmas in New York City', *Milbank Memorial Fund Quarterly*, Vol.55, No.1, 1977, pp.79-116.

[12] Arnold S. Reiman. 'The New Medical-Industrial Complex', *New England Journal of Medicine*, Vol.303, October 1980, pp.963-70.

[13] E.F. Kuntz, 'Systems Scoop up Nursing Homes', *Modern Healthcare*, Vol.12, 1982, pp.101-2.

[14] Gerealdine Dallek, 'Who Cares for Health Care: The First Two Years of Reagan Administration Health Policy', *Health Policy Advisory Centre Bulletin*, Vol.14, No.1, 1983.

[15] D.Stockman, 'Can Fee-for-Service Private Practice Survive Competition?', *Forum on Medicine*, January 1980, p.35.

[16] Walter McClure, *Reducing Excess Hospital Capacity: A Report Prepared for the Bureau of Health Planning and Resources Development*, USDHEW/Interstudy, October, 1976.

[17] S.T. Mennemeyer, 'Effects of Competition on Medicare Administrative Costs', *Journal of Health Economics*, No.3, 1984, pp.137-54.

[18] Jeff Goldsmith, 'The Health Care Market: Can Hospitals Survive?', *Harvard Business Review*, September-October 1980.

Chapter 12

In Defence of
The National Health Service

The NHS and commercial enterprise are interlaced and interlocked. The National Health Service operates in a capitalist economy and inevitably consumes privately produced goods and services. Its long standing reliance on private pharmaceutical and medical-technology companies is an area of particular concern, as is the recent privatisation of 'ancillary' services. General practice is not truly 'socialised', and this places limits on its very real benefits. Finally, private practice was built into the NHS. The relative importance of NHS pay beds is declining but the staff of the private hospitals are trained by the NHS, while the overwhelming majority of doctors in private practice are moonlighting NHS consultants. The NHS is not, therefore, a pure socialist island, and has negative features over and above those that can readily be attributed to its capitalist environment. But it is worth defending.

The grounds of that defence are not straightforward, however. Comparing the National Health Service with the right's ideal model of a perfectly functioning, competitive capitalist health sector is tortuous indeed: their theories soon get abstruse if not obscure. Comparing the NHS to socialists' ideal model would be less precise as the left has never closely defined what exactly it wants. It is more useful to compare the NHS first with medical systems in other countries – especially those like the American which are closest in structure to our commercial medicine – and secondly with the comparatively small private sector in Britain.

The criteria by which medical systems are to be judged also need to be established, if only because the yardstick cannot be the health of the public. 'Health' itself is difficult to define, let alone measure. Most analyses do not even try to use figures for sickness or 'morbidity' and refer instead to the prevalence of death or 'mortality'. But this is a very rough and partial measure. Also, mortality rates cannot be attributed primarily to the countries' different medical systems. The factors explaining why people in one country (or for that matter one class) are more healthy than those in another relate more to their life-styles and to their economic and social environment than to their access to any form of medical care. The available statistics suggest that the British are healthy, except that, relative to other nations, death rates among babies and children are high. As Kenneth Clarke, the former Conservative Health Minister, put it: 'We come fourth, and a good fourth, not far behind Sweden, the Netherlands and Switzerland.'[1] But this has little to do with the NHS.

Neither Clarke, who often paid tribute to the National Health Service, nor his successors Hayhoe and Tony Newton, are committed to the far-right denigration of the system. Thatcher's Health Ministers, like Enoch Powell years before, came to understand some of the simple virtues of the Service. Norman Fowler has pointed to the increasing productivity of the NHS and concluded: 'It reinforces the argument that the NHS when working full-out is one of the most cost-effective systems in the world.'[2] Similarly, Beric Wright, Medical Director of BUPA, once said:

> Due to the structure of the Health Service, the distribution of health services is reasonably good, and there is relatively little waste – particularly when this is compared to America. The benefits of what they used to call socialised medicine, disparagingly, seem to be inescapable.[3]

However, measures of efficiency such as the length of time patients spend in hospital are ambiguous, and socialists are wary of notions of 'efficiency', especially in an enterprise as labour-intensive as the NHS. Academic studies and official statistics are problematic sources. Definitions of particular aspects of medical care differ from country to country and study to study and produce apparent inconsistencies. Some of the studies are highly polemical, verging on diatribes against the National Health Service. Also, the statistics are often quite dated.

The basic characteristics of the NHS are that it is financed from government funds and provides 90 per cent of medical care in the UK. Those funds are, primarily, taxes and they are collected and allocated centrally in the first instance (although the NHS budgets in Wales, Scotland and Northern Ireland do not come under the control of the Social Services Secretary). Hospital doctors are salaried, while GPs' remuneration is more complex, but is based partly on the 'capitation' principle – that is, the more patients they can claim to have on their books, the more they are paid. (Dentists, by contrast, are paid on the 'fee-for-service' basis – that is, the more procedures they carry out the more they are paid.) Above all, the UK medical system covers everybody in the nation, although a tiny minority may choose not to use it at all (far fewer than the 9 per cent or so who have private medical insurance) or may have difficulty obtaining medical attention (particularly down-and-outs). The NHS is also, more or less, free at the time of use.

Other medical systems come in a variety of forms, differing in the extent to which the services are provided by private institutions; are paid for by private money; are financed on the insurance basis or the tax basis or through charges to patients; are staffed by doctors paid a salary or by capitation or on the fee-for-service system; are funded centrally or through local government. Even American medicine has some virtues: the boundaries between the 'professions' are less fiercely defended and in some places local services do genuinely try to cater for ethnic and cultural differences. Patients there are more conscious of their rights and the law is balanced more in their favour than in the UK, although this is a positive aspect of their judicial rather than their medical system.

The case for the NHS rests on three main arguments. First, the National Health Service is an effective system for rationing medical care. Secondly, there are reasons for believing that the NHS can provide services more cost-effectively than its competitors. Thirdly, the profit motive is especially inappropriate in health care.

Rationing Health Services

It is almost universally acknowledged that medical services should be distributed according to need, not according to ability to pay. Only New Right theorists openly and unashamedly support the development of a two-tier medical system, while Hugh Elwell, a former marketing director of BUPA, has presented this prospect as 'a danger' in private sector growth.[4] Even Patrick Jenkin MP argued (before he became Social Services Secretary): 'Market forces are pretty ineffective in balancing the need for health care and supply of services.'[5]

The need to ration scarce resources is not something that applies only to state-funded services. In market systems services are rationed by the price mechanism, and entirely unsatisfactorily. The fairness of a price system depends very much on the fairness of income distribution. Also, in medical care information is very complex and confusing, and therefore price is not a good guide to the quality of the product. Thirdly, when services are being actually used, the patient is often covered by medical insurance, which can bring the actual cost of treatment down to zero. Because use is not controlled, medical services and their costs therefore rise out of control. In the US health care system, the result is an inflationary spiral, with the priorities of the hospitals and doctors determined largely by the insurers' reimbursement patterns. By contrast in the NHS as in the Canadian system:

> Providers cannot play one reimburser against another, or charge patients for amounts insurers refuse to pay. The 'cost-pass-through' of the decentralised, fragmented private system, in which the costs of expenditure increase fall on the consumer of the product made by the firm which paid the premium which funded the insurer which paid the claim by the physician who directed the care that Jack received, is not available. And the 'sole source' is at a level of government with sufficient expertise and political credibility to confront and constrain providers.[6]

This explains why Norman Fowler decided after all not to replace the NHS by an insurance-based system. Ironically, at first glance it appears that searchers for unresricted access to health care should opt for the American system and not for the NHS.

In fact, Americans do not get everything they want or need from their medical system. Insurance secures abundance only in particular fields, and millions have no insurance at all. In many areas, the National Health Service does better. But clearly, two questions must run through any discussion of the rationing of health care. First, does the NHS ration too harshly (or, indeed, not harshly enough)? Secondly, within the budget limits, is the rationing appropriate or could the money obviously be spent better? The record can be examined from three points of view – rationing by social class, by geographical area and by type of medical service.

Rationing by Social Class

Socialists are fearful lest the NHS is becoming the lower part of a two-tier medical system. In fact the two-tier idea does not bear a close relationship to medical systems elsewhere in the world and may be based uncritically on a highly simplistic model of capitalist class structure. Government-financed safety-nets do exist throughout the West and the inequalities are found in gradations of health care rather than in distinct tiers.

The National Health Service covers all British citizens and is used by nearly all of them at some point in their lives. It is free at the time of use, and avoids the complexities of insurance forms and the indignities of means-testing (except for prescription and dental charges). The British do enjoy free access to medical care, and this is not strictly rationed at the primary point of contact with the patient – that is, the general practitioner's surgery. So there are no financial barriers to the use of medical services and broadly speaking they are utilised irrespective of social class. Working-class people tend to be in hospital and to consult their GPs more often than middle-class people, because they tend to be less healthy, but middle-class people make much greater use of preventive services.[7] Moreover, the quality of the care received by working-class people is often inferior, and their GP consultations certainly are shorter than those for middle-class patients.

But before the NHS is condemned for these inequalities its record should be compared with that of the United States. There some insurance cover is provided for the old through Medicare, and for the disabled, blind and some of the poor through Medicaid. These reforms of the early 1960s did improve access to medical services among these groups.[8] But the care for poor and old Americans is under increasing threat. The financing of Medicare has been changed in response to the soaring costs of the programme. Instead of government meeting all 'reasonable' costs, fixed levels of reimbursement for different types of procedure have been introduced. Commentators feared this would mean that poorer, and therefore less healthy, patients might find it harder to find care; that less 'efficient' hospitals would end or reduce their treatment of Medicare patients; and that hospitals generally would be less willing to provide 'indigent' care (that is, free services for those who are not insured).[9] Secondly, the criteria for coverage under Medicaid are again being tightened up.

Commentators are also concerned that the level of 'indigent care' may be threatened as the corporations take over more and more public and voluntary hospitals and as the voluntary hospitals, the non-tax paying 'charity' hospitals which provide the bulk of medical care, act to stem financial losses.[10]

In any case, and despite Medicare and Medicaid, 25 million Americans have no insurance cover at any time while 34 million are not covered for some of the year. One poor American in four has no insurance cover. Despite 'indigent care', the

> uninsured make 41 per cent fewer visits to physicians and are less likely to be admitted to hospital ... in 1982 over a million families were refused care ... Cook County Hospital in Chicago receives more than 7,000 economically motivated patient transfers from private hospitals each year.[11]

In one survey of US hospital administrators, 69 per cent said they believed that patients were putting off medical treatment because of its cost.[12]

The NHS is not perfect. Indeed, in a class society it is inevitable that the privileged and the powerful should get more than their fair share of medical services, and one comparative study found that class inequality in medical care for adults was more pronounced in Liverpool than in Helsinki, Lodz, Baltimore or Saskatchewan.[13] But the universal coverage provided by the NHS, and the fact that services are free at the time of use, make the UK medical system the model for all who believe that money should not be the passport to better or quicker treatment.

Rationing by Geographical Area

The geographical distribution of services is largely but not wholly a matter of class. There are great regional differences even in the NHS provision. For many years, the NHS failed to challenge the distribution of hospitals inherited in 1948 – largely because of inadequate capital expenditure. In 1976, however, the Labour government introduced a new approach to financial allocation – the RAWP system – whereby extra funds go to Regions deemed particularly needy. While criticisms can be made of the precise calculations and of the implementation of RAWP in a no-growth health budget, broadly speaking its priorities are defensible.

As GPs are fiercely 'independent contractors' it has been less easy to improve their distribution around the country, although incentives do exist and some improvement appears to have been made in recent years. Nevertheless, to a disturbing degree Tudor Hart's 'inverse care law' still holds:

> In areas with most sickness and death, general practitioners have more work, larger lists, less hospital support and inherit more clinically ineffective traditions of consultation than in the healthiest areas; and hospital doctors shoulder heavier case-loads with less staff and equipment, more obsolete buildings and suffer recurrent crises in the availability of beds and replacement staff. These trends can be summed up as the inverse care law: that the availability of good medical care tends to vary inversely with the need of the population served.[4]

But we should ask how other countries fare, especially those with more private medicine. The Black Report points out that in Britain the region with most physicians has 1.4 times as many as the region with least. Other countries have worse records – the figure in Germany is 2.1, in France 2.2 and in the Netherlands 2.3.[15] Rural areas and poor inner cities are always avoided by private physicians. Harlem, for example, with a population of over a million, has less than 80 registered physicians.[16] On the other hand, the geographical distribution of hospitals in America has been improved by millions of dollars in subsidies from the federal government to hospitals built in rural areas.[17] Overall, Rudolf Klein reports:

> If the NHS's record in moving towards geographical equity is disappointing when measured against the expectations of its architects, it is a striking success story when measured against the achievements of most other countries ... one exception must, however, be made to this assertion. In the case of general practice in Britain geographical variations in the distribution of doctors have persisted throughout the history of the NHS.[18]

Turning to the present distribution of services, rather than their change over time, the General Medical Services Committee reports:

> The evidence is that general practitioners are evenly spread in the United Kingdom. This contrasts with the uneven distribution of hospital based staff. And the primary care services in this country are better spread than in France, Germany and the USA.[19]

It does appear that the geographical distribution of medical services is as least as good in Britain as elsewhere – although far from perfect.

Rationing by Type of Medical Services

It is not possible to discuss the distribution of resources between one type of medical service and another without bringing to the fore the question of the severity, as opposed to the justice, of NHS rationing. The services which the NHS provides less extensively than other countries come in two main categories: high-technology care and routine surgery. Both are encouraged by the fee-for-service payment of consultants and by the open-ended reimbursement of competing commercial hospitals by insurance plans, the premiums of which are typically paid not by the individuals covered but by their employers. On high-technology medicine, Aaron and Schwartz report three main findings.[20] First, in relation to life and death emergencies, the British system tends to provide as much care as the American. Haemophiliacs receive top quality treatment, bone marrow transplantation is as common as in the United States and megavoltage radiotherapy is widely available. On the other hand, the British do only a third as much dialysis (having accounted for the smaller population), only a quarter as much total parenteral nutrition and spend 70 per cent less on chemotherapy for cancer patients. However, in the last case the difference is due to the NHS not 'treating' incurable cancer victims. One British surgeon is quoted as believing in prolonging life, but not in prolonging dying. Also, the United States has at least five times as many intensive care beds. Another study found that in 1975 over 40 per cent of American hospitals with less than 100 beds had intensive care units. This is undoubtedly a waste of resources, caused by competition between hospitals as opposed to planning by clinical need.

Secondly, Aaron and Schwartz find that the British devote far fewer resources to relieving pain. For example, the Americans do ten times as much coronary artery surgery. Surprisingly, however, the UK carries out at least three-quarters as many hip operations as the USA. Aaron and Schwartz suggest the long NHS waiting lists for this treatment may be exacerbated by consultants' desire to promote their own private practices.

Thirdly, the British spend far less on diagnostic procedures. The Americans carry out twice as many X-rays and use twice as many films per examination. At the high-tech end of the scale, they have six times as many computerised axial tomography scanners. Again, many British experts and consultants would argue that the American system encourages more, and more expensive, diagnosis than is justified.

British restraint in the use of medical high technology is due in part to the effective use of randomised control trials, which justify medicine's claim to be a science rather than merely a craft based on tradition and intuition. A survey conducted by the US Congress's Office of Technology Assessment reported on the varying employment of medical trials in different countries.[21] The USA spent most (not unexpectedly), but the UK had the best record. The DHSS has a genuine interest in making sure that clinical trials are undertaken since this may delay a technique's introduction during the initial period of enthusiasm. British medicine has traditionally been more research-based than its American counterpart. British doctors, as the Aaron and Schwartz study implies, are relatively cautious. When American surgeons were jumping headlong into cardiac surgery and calling for the creation of cardiac care units, British doctors were coming up with findings which suggested that patients might fare as well by staying at home.[22]

Undoubtedly, British waiting lists for non-urgent operations reveal that need is not being met and other countries do more in this area. Bunker found that America has twice as many operations per head as England and Wales,[23] the difference being largely attributable to 'discretionary' operations.[24] But it is certainly arguable that in this area again countries with insurance-based, fee-for-service medicine treat not well, but too well. One Congressional study estimated that in 1974 2.4 million surgical procedures had been unnecessary and 11,900 deaths avoidable.[25] Ivan Illich inveighs powerfully against tonsillectomy, even if overstating his case:

> Non-technical functions prevail in the removal of adenoids: more than 90 per cent of all tonsillectomies performed in the United States are technically unnecessary, yet 20 to 30 per cent of all children still undergo the operation. One in a thousand dies directly as a consequence of the operation and 16 in a thousand suffer from serious complications. All lose valuable immunity mechanisms. All are subjected to emotional aggression: they are incarcerated in a hospital, separated from their parents, and introduced to the unjustified and more often than not pompous cruelty of the medical establishment.[26]

Tonsillectomy is not the only operation often carried out without good reason, especially under medical systems where, in Brian Abel-Smith's words:

> The highest financial rewards go not to the best doctor but to the quickest and to the doctor with the least professional scruples about responding to the financial incentives of the payment system.[27]

So, Britain performs fewer routine operations and carries out less 'high-tech' relief of pain than other countries. But broadly speaking the NHS does provide costly treatment in life-and-death situations. The British also avoid many unjustified 'elective' operations and the excessive duplication of newsworthy but ethically dubious medical technology.

The NHS provides some services to a greater extent than other medical systems. The most important is general practice. A report from the profession's General Medical Services Committe, *General Practice: A British Success*, points out that GPs

> treat around 90 per cent of all the episodes of ill health which are presented to the NHS ... over 70 per cent of consultations take place within a day of the patient seeking help ... over 90 per cent of people find it easy to get to their doctor ... Over three-quarters ... [have] been registered with their general practitioner for over five years.[28]

GPs can thus offer a continuity of care not available in many countries. As it is their responsibility to refer patients to consultants, unnecessary consultations with specialists are minimised. At their best, GPs also act as the base of effective preventive medical care. Certainly, British general practice is far from perfect and far too reliant on harmless – and harmful – drugs. GPs are also excluded from hospitals, so the continuity between primary and hospital care is frequently poor. Nor are they obliged to undergo regular retraining. But overall the UK system of general practice is a bonus. To quote the NHS Consultants' Association:

> Not all countries with private health insurance systems bypass primary care: in Belgium, for example, 50 per cent of doctors are GPs and there is a rich development of home nursing services. However, in general, private medicine encourages a concentration on specialisation to the neglect of general practice. This is certainly the case in France, Germany and the USA. In West Germany there were only 14,000 general practitioners left in 1976, as compared with 26,000 in Great Britain. (Germany has a larger population and many more doctors overall.)[29]

The NHS's services for the old, the chronically ill and the disabled may be an indictment of Britain's claim to be a caring, civilised society. But other countries have worse records. In the USA, according to the Inter-Governmental Health Policy Project at George Washington University:

Medicare is geared toward episodic, short-term, acute illness rather than the chronic, long-term disorders prevalent in the elderly population. Therefore, many of the greatest needs of the elderly, such as custodial care, dental care, and eye care, are not covered at all.[30]

While the USA has far more nursing-home beds, the care provided by some of those homes has been widely criticised. While the USA has a huge private market in psychiatry and commercial hospital chains provide services for middle-class drug addicts, alcoholics and the short-term mentally ill – and also house many 'patients' who are not genuinely ill – the market is not an effective mechanism for dealing with the chronic problems of mental (or physical) handicap.

More generally, the range of services provided by the NHS is impressive when compared with other countries' medical systems (which belies the propaganda claims for 'choice' in commercial medicine). To quote the NHSCA again:

> We too often take for granted the existence of antenatal clinics, geriatric and terminal care, well developed pathology services, accident and emergency services (including ambulances), home visits and so on. Elsewhere, some of these services are not so available and not of such high quality; some may not even be available at all ... The NHS would appear to be outstanding in the level of its provision of services in the patient's home or within the local community. The work of Health Visitors, District Nurses and closely related social services such as Home Helps is particularly important in antenatal and child care and the care of the elderly.[31]

Unfortunately, this wide range of services has been cut back since the 1979 election. Certainly, there is a grey area where 'health services' shade into 'social services', but the former term should not be restricted to those medical techniques designed to cure the physically ill: preventing illness and caring for the incurable are vital functions, too often neglected in private practice.

As a system for rationing limited medical resources, the NHS's record compares favourably with systems elsewhere, but critics argue that the rationing system is too strong. They suggest that central control of NHS budgets, with tax-financing and payment of doctors by salary and by capitation, leads to fewer services being provided than are demanded by British public opinion. Britain spends less on health care than other industrialised countries – about 6 per cent of GDP compared with 11 per cent in the USA, with the other Western European countries somewhere in between. On the one hand socialists point to this as evidence of the cost-effectiveness of the NHS, but on the other hand present it as an indictment of the spending priorities of Thatcherism in particular and British capitalism in general. Indeed, some would question whether medical services should be rationed at all, especially as there is no evidence that higher spending on health prevents wealth-creation – the richer countries tend to spend more on medical care than the poorer. So maybe societies should strive to 'universalise the best' in medical care, as Bevan put it, and pay whatever it takes.

Technological advance in many fields lowers costs, but the scientific advance of medicine nearly always has the opposite effect. Governments concerned to control their own expenditure, and to control the costs facing the economy, are less and less likely to allow all technically feasible treatment to be available to everyone, given other claims on available resources. Certainly the development of public housing, transport and social services could have a major impact on the nation's health.

In Britain, the size of the private medical sector is at present unregulated. The Conservative government's ideological hostility to public spending leads it to treat the NHS as a burden and commercial medicine as a boon. However, as the private sector grows – and company-bought medical policies threaten profit levels – these Thatcherite blinkers will become increasingly unhelpful. In America, the pressures for the rationing of medicine are driven by the desire of companies to limit the volume of their spending on employee benefits.[32]

There are other, less pragmatic, reasons for placing 'limits to medicine', forcibly identified by Ivan Illich. His argument, in short, is that the medical establishment has become a major threat to health. It is not simply that too many unsafe operations are performed and drugs prescribed. For Illich, iatrogenesis – that is, illness caused by medicine – has three levels:

Iatrogenesis is clinical when pain, sickness and death result from medical care; it is social when health policies reinforce an industrial organisation that generates ill health; it is cultural and symbolic when medically sponsored behaviour and delusions restrict the vital autonomy of people by undermining their competence in growing up, caring for each other, and ageing, or when medical intervention cripples personal responses to pain, disability, impairment, anguish and death.[33]

If this perspective is valid, the question becomes where to set the limits on medicine. Illich regards even the NHS as over-blown.

The NHS is, then, a reasonable system for allocating medical services. Perhaps as important, the National Health Service is broadly speaking comprehensive and free at the time of use. Largely for these reasons, it commands enormous popular support, despite its strict rationing of medical services. And it is this popular support which enables it to ration. American right-wing commentators criticise the NHS as an all-pervasive monopoly. But the British are perfectly free to go private. They must 'pay twice', true, but even so they end up paying less than Americans paying just once. To a large degree, it is because the NHS is seen as a just rationing system that it is able to ration as justly and as strictly as it does. It is impossible to say whether this is too strict. Certainly the NHS could spend more. Its very low expenditure is not an inevitable result of its centralist, tax-based structure. There is some room for manoeuvre. Even under Thatcherism, spending on the NHS has increased by a quarter when measured against the Retail Price Index and services are significantly better resourced in Scotland than in England and Wales. It is debatable whether the NHS could spend as much as the American medical patch-quilt. But that is not necessarily a criticism.

The Medical Cost-Effectiveness of the NHS

The NHS is comparatively cheap not simply because of the limits placed on its provision of high-tech medicine and 'elective' (that is, not urgent) surgery. The low expenditure of the NHS is due to the costs of the inputs to the system as well as to the volume of its output.

Despite the right's criticism of 'bureaucracy' in the NHS, the British spend comparatively little on administrating their medical system. While different studies define 'administration' in different ways and come up with different figures, the NHS figure is consistently low. Indeed, the British may spend too little because administrators or managers are needed to plan and to mobilise staff time and resources. But the NHS has a major cost advantage as it is funded through taxes, centrally allocated. Systems which are insurance-based need to survey their physicians more closely, they need to check their patients' cover, they need to reimburse the money and so on. Also, in private systems the competing insurance carriers further put up the administrative costs.[34]

The NHS is not only almost a monopoly in the provision of medical services to Britons. It is also, in consequence, almost a monopoly buyer (or monopsony) of medical supplies, giving it great market influence. Certainly, despite the misuse of drugs by British GPs, our pharmaceutical budget is low. Robert Maxwell estimates that the percentage of GNP spent on drugs varies 'from approximately 0.75 per cent ... in Canada, the United Kingdom and Sweden to more than twice that in West Germany, France, Italy, the Netherlands and (probably) the United States'.[35] This appears to be due to the price of the drugs as well as the extent to which they are used:

> it is unlikely to be coincidence that the three countries ... with the lowest costs relative to GNP all have government-dominated systems of health funding ... with an opportunity to use government influence in negotiating prices.

Maxwell's figures cover drugs bought over the counter as well as those prescribed by doctors. Kenneth Clarke's 'limited list' has brought down the latter at the expense of pushing up the former.

The NHS also enjoys monopsony powers in regard to medical staff, although these are counter-balanced by the intrinsically monopolistic nature of the medical profession. But the NHS has another advantage here, as the British do not pay their doctors by fee-for-service. Certainly, this helps contain doctors' incomes. According to OECD figures for fourteen Western nations, in 1974 the average British doctor earned 2.7 more than the average production worker. Only the figure for Norway (2.4) was less. Doctors earn at least six times as much as production workers in France, Germany, Italy and the Netherlands (and 5.6 times as much in the United States).[36]

Doctors are relatively privileged in British society, even taking into account the hours they work and the exploitation of junior hospital doctors. So socialists would see their relatively low incomes as a cause for congratulation. But the NHS also relies on paying very poor rewards to nurses and to 'ancillary' staff. On the other hand while lower grades of health service staff are no doubt paid more in wealthier countries, it is questionable whether they are paid significantly more relative to other workers in those societies. Also, trade unionism gained strength in the NHS during the 1970s, and the right would argue that restrictive practices and 'over-manning' have overly protected NHS workers. The Tories' policy of privatising NHS 'ancillary' services has turned back the gains of that decade. In so far as it is increasing the exploitation of 'ancillary' staff through market competition, the privatisation policy suggests that the NHS has not relied upon monopsony powers in relation to these workers. Indeed, in this case, the NHS has few if any monopsony powers at its disposal. While hospitals are the only institutions in which you can carry out surgery, they are not the only institutions which need to be cleaned, fed or laundered.

Finally, the NHS is comparatively cheap partly because its component parts do not need to generate profits for shareholders, interest for money lenders or custom for advertising agencies.

The Profit Motive in Health Care

The argument that it is wrong to make profits out of ill health is greeted with scorn by the private sector. Their representatives point out that capitalist enterprises meet many of people's basic needs without this causing outrage. They point out also that NHS staff make their living from treating illness. In any case, many private and voluntary hospitals are not profit-making in the sense of having to show a return to shareholders.

These are objections to the argument that profits as strictly defined have no place in medical care, but they miss the real issue which is the commercialisation of medicine. While NHS staff make a living from medicine, they are not driven by the pursuit of monetary gain. This is much less the case in fee-for-service private practice. However harassed its doctors, the National Health Service provides them with a structure in which they can act as professionals, and see their patients as clients. In commercial medicine, doctors are entrepreneurs, hospitals are businesses and patients are consumers. British GPs may despair at their inability to change the social realities that too often make people ill, but while GPs' habits are shaped by pharmaceutical advertising, they do not have a direct financial interest in administering drugs, unlike the chemists who may well gain from the 'limited list'. The argument has been put forcefully by Paul Torrens:

> If the creation of a private health insurance plan shifts the emphasis from comprehensive family care towards an item-by-item, high-technology, entrepreneurially oriented health-care system, it will ... not be worth the price to the country. The present system is remarkable in its devotion to people as people, not as interesting scientific problems to be tackled organ by organ; it is remarkable among health-care systems of the world in its devotion to family practice and the values inherent in that devotion. Anything that would move the value system from that more humane, more personal approach would remove much of what is best in the British system today.[37]

Rationing Health Services

The international evidence, then, provides a sound case for the NHS as an appropriate, cost-effective and comparatively just health care system. Does the British private sector share the same drawbacks as the fully-fledged commercial medicine found in other countries?

The prevalence of private practice varies greatly from one geographical area of Britain to another, and this variation is largely but not wholly determined by the areas' wealth. Every available measure – shows the very uneven spread of commercial medicine around the country.

Turning to the rationing of different types of medical service, British private practice largely consists of routine surgery. More than one in eight 'elective' operations in this country is private. For hip operations, the figure is one in four. There are as yet no major studies of the prevalence of unjustified surgical interventions in British private practice, although the issue has been raised in relation to child-birth. Also, private psychiatric clinics house residents who are not mentally ill.

High-tech medicine is not a characteristic of the British private sector, although the Wellington, the Cromwell and the larger AMI hospitals provide expensive medical techniques, and the development of in vitro fertilisation ('test-tube baby') procedures has been largely within the private sector (after initial development within the National Health Service). Also, private and charitable funds have tended to finance expensive equipment such as CT scanners and lithotripters (machines for dealing with kidney stones). On the other hand, few private clinics have intensive care units and the NHS is certainly the prime provider of life-saving, high-tech medicine, even where there are clearly shortages. Tory MP Michael McNair-Wilson pointed out:

> Since last January I have been the victim of a rare kidney disease. Without kidney dialysis, I would be a dead man. In the months during which I have been receiving treatment in hospital, I have cost the National Health Service tens of thousands of pounds – much more than I could have afforded privately; and, although I am a member of BUPA, it is a service that it does not provide because of the expense. Had my treatment depended on my ability to pay, I would not be alive today. The NHS met my need for treatment without requiring me to show that I had funds to pay for it. It operated on supply and need not supply and demand. That is why it is such a precious asset to us all.[38]

The British private sector provides a large number of beds in nursing homes: 40,397 in 1985, according the Association of Independent Hospitals.[39] However, to a large extent these homes are financed by public money; many of the patients are placed there by Health Authorities and local authorities, and others have their nursing home charges met by the Department of Health and Social Security. Nursing homes enjoy 100 per cent rate relief under the 1978 Rating (Disabled Persons) Act. Private nursing homes, hospices and so on have little to do with commercial medicine in the restricted sense.

Few of the patients are covered by private medical insurance and the medical care is provided by local GPs on the NHS and not by consultant geriatricians almost all of whom work solely for the NHS.

The UK private sector does not share fully the priorities of commercial medicine elsewhere, primarily because it is operating in the context of the overwhelming predominance of the NHS. Where NHS provision is good, as in medical emergency care and general practice, there is little demand for private treatment. Where the NHS falls short, as in long waiting lists for routine surgery, care for the elderly, services for the childless or abortions, private companies can move in and reap their profits. If the NHS declines then private practice will become more like its grown-up siblings overseas.

Turning to rationing by class, the typical private patient is clearly more affluent than the typical NHS patient. In 1983, 13 per cent of 'in-patient stays' by 'professional' people were private and 16 per cent of stays by 'employers and managers'. The figure for the 'unskilled manual' category was nil.[40] On the other hand, it would be wrong to assume that private medicine is superior to NHS treatment. Private clinics are typically very small and not well equipped. Only one in three has a resident doctor providing 24-hour medical cover. The close commercial relationship between a private patient and his or her doctor means that junior doctors and other staff are less willing to intervene in the consultant's absence. As the Consumers' Association (publisher of *Which?*) gently puts it, this 'can mean an unpleasant delay for the patient'.[41]

While the safety standards of private clinics are improving the British do not yet have two tiers of health care in terms of the quality of the treatment, but they certainly do in terms of access to 'elective' surgery.

Cost Effectiveness

The administrative costs of British private medicine are double those of the NHS. In 1983, 10 per cent of BUPA's expenditure went to 'administration' and another 6 per cent to 'provision for administrative systems'; PPP spent 11 per cent of its expenditure on 'operating expenses'. It is also certainly true that consultants are paid well in private practice – the insurance companies pay up to £145 for a 'minor' operation and £1,720 for a 'complex major' operation. In 1980, David Bolt, then leader of the consultants' negotiating body, estimated that 'the average consultant earns about £5,000 from private work'.[42] Given the growth of commercial medicine since then and the inflation of doctors' private charges, the figure must be £10,000 today.

The Profit Motive in Health Care

There is no doubt that British private practice is becoming more and more commercial. In January 1986, BUPA's Chief Executive Robert Graham complained that 'The recent injection of commercialism goes against the grain of tradition in this country where the care of the sick has always transcended commercial interest.'[43] Not, however, that the problem is entirely new: the Royal College of Physicians was founded in 1485 'to curb the audacity of those wicked men who shall profess medicine more for the sake of avarice than for the assurance of any good conscience'.

Conclusion

This, then, is the case for the National Health Service: it is a moderately effective system for rationing medical care, it has low costs and it facilitates a relatively humane form of medical practice. Certainly it has defects: these would be major if the NHS were put next to an 'ideal' system rather than next to other actual systems. But one of its basic characteristics is the strength of its centre which means that defects can, to some extent, and only over time, be corrected: despite the undesirable effects of RAWP or of 'Care in the Community', as general trends towards the redistribution of limited resources they are evidence of the ability of the NHS to respond to politically defined need. Other initiatives taken by the centre in recent years may have little to recommend them: compulsory competitive tendering is one more episode in the Conservatives' class struggle, while the limited drug list was a cheap and clumsy alternative to a rational generic drugs policy. But they show that the National Health Service can be changed, certainly with more ease than other medical systems. Already, the NHS is one of the best systems in the world. It has the potential to become genuinely first-rate. Unfortunately, the strength of central government means that it also has the potential to become the lower part of a two-tier health care system as unjust and irrational as any of its rivals.

Notes

[1] Quoted in *Times*, 10 October 1984.

[2] Quoted in *Daily Telegraph*, 11 March 1983.

[3] Quoted in International Federation of Voluntary Health Service Funds, *Conference Proceedings*, London, 4-8 September 1972.

[4] Quoted in William Kay, 'Queue for Private Health', *Sunday Times*, 13 September 1981.

[5] Quoted in National Health Service Consultants' Association, *What's Good About the NHS?*, no date.

[6] R.G.Evans, 'Health Care in Canada: Patterns of Funding and Regulation', in Gordon McLachlan and Alan Maynard (eds), *The Public/Private Mix for Health: The Relevance and Effects of Change*, The Nuffield Provincial Hospitals Trust, 1982.

[7] National Child Development Study survey cited in Peter Townsend and Nick Davidson (eds), *Inequalities in Health: the Black Report*, Penguin, 1982.

[8] Karen Davis and Cathy Schoen, *Health and the War on Poverty*, The Brookings Institution, 1978.

[9] Emily Friedman, 'The Dumping Dilemma: The Poor Are Always with Some of Us', *Hospitals*, 1 September 1982; Emily Friedman, 'The "Dumping" Dilemma: Finding Out What's Fair', *Hospitals*, 16 September 1982; Den Balz, 'Urban Public Hospitals in US Carry the Burden of Cuts in Medicaid', *International Herald Tribune*, 31 August 1982; K.Wrenn, 'Sounding Board: No Insurance, No Admission', *New England Journal of Medicine*, 7 February 1985; A.S. Relman, 'Economic Considerations in Emergency Care: What are Hospitals For?', *New England Journal of Medicine*, 7 February 1985.

[10] Davis and Schoen, op.cit.

[11] David U. Himmelstein and Steffie Woolhandler, 'Pitfalls of Private Medicine: Health Care in the USA', *Lancet*, 18 August 1984.

[12] Bill Jackson and Joyce Jensen, 'Home Care Leads Rising Trend of New Services', *Modern Healthcare*, December 1984.

[13] D.S. Salkever, 'Economic Class and Differential Access to Care: Comparisons Among Health Care Systems', *International Journal of Health Services*, Summer 1975.

[14] Quoted in Townsend and Davidson (eds), op.cit.

[15] Ibid.

[16] Health Systems Agency of New York, *The Health of Harlem*, The Agency, 1979.

[17] Lawrence J. Clark, 'The impact of Hill-Burton: An Analysis of Bed and Physician Distribution in the United States, 1950-1970', *Medical Care*,

Vol.18, May 1980; Judith R. Lave, and Lester B. Lave, *The Hospital Construction Act: An Evaluation of the Hill-Burton Program, 1948-1973*, American Enterprise Institute, 1974.

[18] Rudolf Klein, *The Politics of the National Health Service*, Longman, 1983.

[19] General Medical Services Committee, *General Practice: A British Success*, BMA, 1983.

[20] Henry J. Aaron and William B. Schwartz, *The Painful Prescription: Rationing Hospital Care*, The Brookings Institution, 1984. Also: R.W. Evans, 'Health Care Technology and the Inevitability of Resource Allocation and Rationing Decisions', *Journal of the American Medical Association*, Vol. 249, 1983; M.A. Baily, 'Rationing and American Health Policy', *Journal of Health Politics, Policy and Law*, Fall 1984; Council for Science and Society, *Expensive Medical Techniques*, London 1982.

[21] Office of Technology Development, *The Implicatiion of Cost-Effectiveness Analysis of Medical Technology: Background Paper 4. The Management of Medical Technology in Ten Countries*, Washington DC, 1980.

[22] H. Mather *et al.*, 'Acute Myocardial Infarction: Hospital and Home Treatment', *British Medical Journal*, 7 August 1971.

[23] J. Bunker, 'Surgical Manpower: A Comparison of Operations and Surgeons in the United States and England and Wales, *New England Journal of Medicine*, Vol.285, 1970; J.P. Bunker, D. Hinkley and M. McDermott, 'Surgical Innovation and its Evaluation', *Science*, Vol.200, 1978, pp.937-41.

[24] J.E. Wennberg and A. Gittleson, 'Small Area Variations in Health Care Delivery. Population-based Information Can Guide Planning and Regulatory Decision Making', *Science*, Vol.82, 1973, pp.1102-8.

[25] Subcommittee on Oversight and Investigation, Committee on Interstate and Foreign Commerce, *Cost and Quality of Health Care: Unnecessary Surgery*, Washington DC, January 1976 and *Background Report on Surgery in State Medicaid Programs*, Washington DC, July 1977. For a British view see: F.G.R. Fowkes, 'Overtreatment in Surgery', *Journal of the Royal Society of Medicine*, June 1985.

[26] Ivan Illich, *Limits to Medicine*, Pelican, 1977.

[27] Brian Abel-Smith, *Value for Money in Health Services*, Heinemann, 1976.

[28] General Medical Services Committee, op.cit.

[29] National Health Service Consultants' Association, op.cit.

[30] Cited in National Health Service Consultants' Association, op.cit.

[31] Ibid.

[32] Louis Kleber, 'How US Companies are Tightening Control of Health Costs', *Financial Times*, 21 October 1985.

[33] Illich, op.cit.

[34] Commercial insurance runs the highest administrative costs, followed by Blue Cross and Medicare. See R.D. Blair and R.J. Vogel, *The Cost of Health Insurance Administration*, Lexington Books, 1975; Kuo-cheng Tseng, 'Administrative Costs of Medicare Contractors: Blue Cross Versus Commercial Intermediaries', *Inquiry XV*, Sec.1978, pp.371-8; S.T. Mennemeyer, 'Effects of Competition on Medicare Administrative Costs', *Journal of Health Economics*, No.3, 1984.

[35] Robert J. Maxwell, *Health and Wealth: An International Study of Health-Care Spending*, Lexington Books, 1981.

[36] Cited in ibid.

[37] Paul R. Torrens, 'Health Insurance in the United States: Implications for the United Kingdom', *Lancet*, 5 January 1980.

[38] *Hansard*, 8 November 1984.

[39] Association of Independent Hospitals, *Nursing Home Beds*, AIH, November 1985.

[40] Office of Population Censuses and Surveys, *General Household Survey 1983*, 1985.

[41] Consumers' Association, *A Patient's Guide to the National Health Service*, London, 1983.

[42] Quoted in *On Call*, 13 September 1979.

[43] Quoted in *Daily Telegraph*, 8 January 1986.

Chapter 13

Private Sector Growth: Benign or Malignant?

There are, as we have seen, good reasons for preferring the National Health Service to the private sector. Nevertheless, for many people these good reasons are not enough, because they argue – or feel – that the private sector, for all its faults, is supplementary to the NHS: as a result of private practice, more medical care exists than would otherwise be the case. We have already questioned one of the underlying assumptions of this argument. The 'limits to medicine' should be recognised – people are not made healthier solely by increasing the number of pills they take or the number of operations available on demand. Also, many people support the NHS in so far as it leads to reasonable equity in the provision of medical care. From this viewpoint, the development of private medicine would be a bad thing if it led to two-tier health care provision, even leaving aside arguments about its impact on NHS services.

In any case, we would also ask whether in fact the private sector adds to the total amount of available medical treatment. If commercial medicine did not exist, the NHS would itself be able to treat more patients. This is for four main reasons: firstly, patients are often treated privately on the NHS without paying the due charges; secondly, the private sector is subsidised by the NHS and by the taxpayer; thirdly, commercial medicine is served by the same doctors who work in the NHS; and fourthly, commercial medicine undermines the support for the NHS, without which Treasury perspectives on state medical expenditure would go unchallenged.[1]

Lost Income

One way in which the NHS has lost out to the private sector is through private patients using its facilities and not paying for

them. Tory Ministers and other apologists for the private
sector often point to the income received from patients who
use NHS pay-beds. This clearly ignores the expenditure
incurred in treating these patients. The NHS can only be said
to gain if a financial surplus is made. The reality is that often
the expenditure is incurred without any income being
received.

NHS staff have long complained of private patients being
subsidised in this way, and also of private patients receiving
favourable treatment, of consultants not fulfilling their
contractual obligations, of waiting lists deliberately kept long
to encourage patients to go private and of other forms of
misbehaviour. Many allegations remain largely unproven –
and necessarily so given the doctors' 'clinical autonomy' and
their seldom challenged authority. But Kenneth Clarke, the
former Health Minister, was clear that waiting lists were an
inaccurate measure of need partly because a long list makes
opportunity for private earnings. And in May 1986 the
Central Committee for Hospital Medical Services felt obliged
to set up a working party to deal with the 'few people' who
were 'besmirching the profession by failing to turn up when
they are meant to'.

The staff concern about private patients not being charged
appropriately was proved well founded in 1984-85. Norman
Fowler felt obliged in May 1984 to send DHSS auditors out to
the Districts to investigate the collection of private patient
charges. 37 Health Authorities were investigated and critical
reports were issued on 21 of these with 'control weaknesses in
the remaining sixteen'. That December, the Health Minister
called for improvements and also issued an NHS Scrutiny
Report which suggested that each year 'some £10 million
potentially collectable income is not being identified and
collected' from private and other chargeable patients. The
following March, the Comptroller and Auditor General felt
compelled to qualify his certificate to the 1983-84 Accounts of
the NHS. He pointed out that auditors had offered estimates
of income lost in thirteen authorities for that year which added
up to £317,000. He was in no doubt that 'serious weaknesses'
had been uncovered. His findings were later supported by the
cross-party House of Commons Public Accounts Committee.

In the media coverage of these 'discoveries', fingers were

often pointed at the consultants. For example, in August 1984, the *Health and Social Service Journal* insisted:

> The corruption of the medical profession in hospitals is so widespread that the situation cannot be allowed to continue. It is commonplace for doctors not to work their full hours, leaving a greater burden on their juniors. It is commonplace for doctors to steal NHS equipment and facilities for use on private patients. Criminal prosecutions are now long overdue.

The consultants' BMA leaders claimed this was all terribly unfair, that it was the NHS administrators' responsibility to collect private patient charges. The Comptroller and Auditor General referred to 'serious and persistent failures to follow departmental guidance'. However, the DHSS and its political masters cannot escape criticism as they have displayed procrastination bordering on complacency. Indeed, in certain respects – for example, in relation to the ease with which patients can avoid charges by opting in and out of private status – the regulations have been weakened. The Public Accounts Committee in any case was clear that: 'All parties – DHSS, Health Authorities and consultants – have been partly responsible for the loss of income due to the NHS.'

The Health Ministers have now acknowledged the scale of the problem, so this form of damage should at least be reduced. However, this will be achieved at the cost of more NHS administrative time and effort being devoted to private practice.

Subsidy

There is a wide range of ways in which commercial medicine can be said to be subsidised by public money, so that less is available to be spent by the NHS.

It has often been suggested – not least by private hospital companies – that NHS charges to private patients are not economic. The Thatcher administration has repeatedly changed the way in which those charges are calculated with the result that they have shot up, even faster than the costs facing the NHS. This weakens the argument that NHS private charges are subsidised at present. However, as recently as June 1986 the Comptroller and Auditor General issued a report saying

that the charges were not always high enough, and this
prompted a DHSS investigation into the issue. This of course
is leaving aside the point that the charges have often not been
levied at all.

The average private clinic, according to the most recent
official figures, has just 44 beds, although the Association of
Independent Hospitals' figures suggest an average of 51 beds.
These clinics are often built near NHS hospitals in order to
make use of their services, and certainly to attract their staff.
Only 38 per cent of private clinics have their own pathology
departments and only 65 per cent have radiology departments. (For the hospitals with which BUPA was dealing in
September 1984, the respective figures were 36 per cent and 83
per cent.) Few have intensive care units. Certainly, some of
the larger central London hospitals are well equipped and
largely self-reliant, but one proposal for a private hospital
development, next to University College Hospital in
Bloomsbury, contained perhaps the best statement of the
reality for many so-called 'independent' clinics:

> The private sector would gain a high quality new hospital, with
> the back-up availability of the full resources of a major teaching
> hospital. For a private hospital the availability of sophisticated
> supporting services and skilled staff within University College
> Hospital would provide a range and quality of services that is not
> generally available within private hospitals and probably could
> not be provided by other means.

Another form of subsidy is the training of private sector staff
by the Health Service at the taxpayer's expense. According to
official statistics, it costs £9,750 to train a nurse and £100,000
to train a doctor.[3] While it is not possible to make a precise
calculation as there are no published figures on consultants'
commitment to private practice, we can safely say that the
taxpayer has invested well over £100 million in training the
personnel of commercial medicine.

The private sector has two pat replies to this argument.
First, representatives point to the negligible amount of nurse
training carried out by private clinics. The reality was
expressed by two NHS Regional Administrators, commenting
on a DHSS draft Circular:

> One view that the (Regional) chairmen might like to consider is that the DHSS should come absolutely clean on this issue and make it clear that they do not expect the private sector to contribute at all to basic professional training.[3]

Secondly, the private sector argues that all capitalist enterprise relies upon education and training provided by the state. But this argument serves only to muddy the waters. The training of medical staff is a special case to the extent that it is carried out largely by the NHS and at its expense. Anyway, the fact that other private companies are subsidised by public money does not annul the taxpayer's investment in commercial medicine. The issue here is whether there is a subsidy, not whether any subsidy is exceptional.

This leads on to another point. Certain basic medical resources are in limited supply. Further supplies will not appear merely because a growing private sector demands them. Medical and nursing staff are one example. It is often alleged that private hospitals 'poach' nurses, leaving staff shortages in the NHS. Health Authorities *have* faced major problems in recruiting and retaining nurses, especially in London, and for nurses with post-basic training – such as operating theatre nurses. With low pay, increased pressure of work due to faster patient throughput and inadequate ward cleaning, their status and accommodation threatened, it is not surprising that some nurses have decided that the private sector's grass is greener. Also, the opening of new private clinics often leads to the temporary disruption of nearby NHS hospitals, as crucial staff desert. In the early 1980s, three inner London Area Health Authorities considered applying for 'designation status', which restricts private hospital development, out of concern about the effects of the private sector. For example, the consultative document drawn up by Lambeth, Southwark and Lewisham AHA referred to high levels of vacancies for nursing staff and commented:

> The existence of a large private sector in Central London, creating an additional demand for skilled and trained staff without increasing the supply, can only increase the problem; and whatever may be the historical situation, further private developments creating a demand for additional staff can only provide yet further competition for this scarce but essential resource.

In 1986, the House of Commons Public Accounts Committee stressed: 'The prospect of a future shortage of nurses, both qualified and in training, is a most serious matter of direct importance to patients.'

Another medical resource in limited supply is blood, which is distributed to NHS and commercial hospitals on a 'first-come-first-served' basis. This means that when shortages occur, NHS operations may be delayed partly because blood is being used by the private hospital up the road.

It is often argued that private practice is coddled by tax advantages and concessions. The main medical insurance companies are 'non-profit-making' and so do not pay corporation tax. Many hospitals are 'charities' which results in advantages in relation to donations, freedom from corporation tax and their rates being halved. No VAT is payable on private hospital charges, consultants' fees or medical insurance premiums. A company which buys medical insurance policies for employees enjoys tax advantages, while any workers earning less than £8,500 can set the value of their policies against income tax. There can be tax advantages in being self-employed, enjoyed by consultants in private practice. Consultants and others have invested in clinics and claimed tax relief under the Business Start-Up and Business Expansion Schemes. The argument here is that these tax advantages are equivalent to grants from the public purse, which leave less for the NHS.

But there are at least two counter-arguments. First, the Conservatives have not felt able to grant special tax concessions to the private medical companies, despite intense lobbying. So, the argument runs, the companies do not enjoy 'concessions' – they are working within the same tax structure as every one else. Perhaps it is true that an 'advantage' too widely shared becomes no advantage at all. But some aspects of private medicine's tax status seem anomalous – especially the charitable status granted to organisations selling a luxury service good to the middle class for the benefit of moonlighting, highly paid public employees.

The private sector also points out that the companies do pay some taxes and rates, which actually increases the size of the public purse. This is in principle a strong point, although we wonder, first, how much they do actually contribute to the

Exchequer considering all the allowances they enjoy; and secondly whether, if private medicine ceased, more money would not be spent on the products of other companies which – who knows? – might pay more in tax than the private medical business.

So it is certainly arguable that private practice is subsidised by the taxpayer to the detriment of the NHS. The annual subsidy runs, perhaps, into tens of millions of pounds. But this must be put next to the turnover of commercial medicine, estimated at £500 million. Clearly, the arguments advanced so far do not seriously dent the private sector's claim to create additional medical services.

Consultants' Commitment

It cannot be over-emphasised that consultants are the lynch-pin of the NHS hospital arch. They have enormous influence – as well as potential destructive power – which they wield through the formal structures of the NHS and through their everyday working relations with managers, junior doctors, nurses, 'ancillary' staff and, of course, patients. Consultants' perspectives shape the NHS and the forces that shape those perspectives are crucial to its future.

One of those forces is undoubtedly private practice. The average NHS consultant earns around £10,000 p.a. – maybe much more – from private work. Roughly 85 per cent of consultants are involved to some extent.[4] What impact does this have on their commitment to the NHS?

There is, first of all, the question of actual abuse and misbehaviour. As we have seen, consultants and their private patients use up millions of pounds' worth of NHS resources each year for which they do not pay. The consultants may blame the administrative procedures, but the fact remains that with sufficient goodwill and effort on the doctors' part those sums would be collected by the Health Authorities. The misuse of NHS facilities is, we believe, endemic (or epidemic). This is white-collar crime writ large.

Abuse is the most exciting issue, but it is not the most important. Private practice hurts the NHS in three more significant ways: firstly, it draws consultants' time away from NHS patients; secondly, it distorts consultants' priorities; and thirdly, it whittles away their commitment to the NHS.

The point about time can be stated very simply: consultants cannot be in two places at once. Most consultants work very hard for the NHS, certainly more than a 40-hour week. The NHS has relied upon this dedication, but has no legal or, arguably, moral right to do so. As private practice grows consultants will be spending less of their time treating NHS patients (or otherwise working for the Health Service). Similarly, as the Medical Research Council points out: 'Serious clinical research is only exceptionally compatible with any significant commitment to private practice for personal gain.'

Consultants might argue that private practice eats into their leisure time rather than their NHS work. Probably, it is a bit of both. We would however point out that even consultants need to 'recreate' and if they do not, their patients may suffer. To quote the Review Body on Doctors' and Dentists' Remuneration: 'The length of the hours that some consultants now work regularly cannot be in the best interest of the standard of care and efficiency in the National Health Service generally.'[5] David Bolt, a former consultants' leader, has put the point more bluntly: 'Some chaps are working themselves into the ground.'[6] It seems totally anomalous that we restrict the hours worked by lorry-drivers and yet encourage surgeons to moonlight.

Commercial medicine has its own priorities, as we have seen: it is biased towards hospital-based surgical intervention, towards the wealthier parts of the country and towards viewing patients as collections of organs rather than as people. The NHS is certainly distorted – to a lesser extent – in these directions. But this is partly due to private practice itself. Medical graduates gravitate to those specialties which provide the best opportunities for the additional earnings and the 'professional autonomy' of private practice. Young hospital doctors drift towards the South-East where the pickings are richest. Top consultants get to play with new toys at the prestigious London private hospitals and then insist that their NHS place of work needs the equipment too. As NHS consultants become more heavily involved in private practice, the priorities of commercial medicine may seep further into the National Health Service.

Consultants wield enormous power and influence not only in hospitals, Health Authorities and the DHSS but also in the 'body politic' generally. The pronouncements of their trade union, the BMA, carry a weight both among the political elite and among the general public which dwarfs the influence of the Royal College of Nursing, COHSE, NALGO and NUPE put together. Most consultants still spend most of their time and, probably, receive most of their income from the NHS. They therefore have a vested interest in its preservation. In recent years, the BMA and other consultants' representatives – from the NHS Consultants' Association through the *Lancet* to the Royal Colleges – have repeatedly called attention to cuts in the National Health Service. These interventions have, surely, moderated the severity of those cuts.

But year by year the consultants' vested interest in the NHS is whittled away by the growth of commercial medicine. It is certainly arguable that the changes in the consultants' contract favouring private practice which were introduced by the new Conservative government in 1979 were partly intended to buy off the profession. But more generally the threat is that the most powerful corporate voice for the preservation, let alone improvement, of the NHS is being silenced.

Support for the NHS

The medical profession is not, however, the only group with a vested – and diminishing – interest in the NHS. We should not forget their patients! 91 per cent of the population are not covered by private medical insurance. 99 per cent probably use the NHS at some point in their lives. Surely, the Treasury would have been more successful in its opposition to the NHS were it not for the reliance upon it of the overwhelming bulk of the population. Against the Retail Price Index, the NHS budget has increased by a quarter under Thatcherism. While this has not been sufficient to enable the NHS to cope with rising costs and needs, it contrasts starkly with the devastation of public housing, for example. If 91 per cent of us lived in council flats and houses, the story would have been very different.

As in housing, so in health care: the more people go private,

the less secure become those reliant on state provision. The
political influence of 'top people' is, of course, absurdly
disproportionate, especially under a Conservative administration, and seldom needs to be open. So if the NHS is to prosper,
its coverage of the middle class and above must be real, not
merely notional.

Yet, even in 1983, 23 per cent of 'professional' people had
private medical cover and the figure was 28 per cent for those
aged between 45 and 64. Sadly, the Register of Members'
Interests does not tell us how many members of the Cabinet,
the government and the respective parliamentary parties have
private medical insurance. But we know Margaret Thatcher
goes private. So does the Chief Nursing Officer at the DHSS.
Victor Paige, the former chair of the NHS Management
Board, has private medical cover, though he now knows he
was wrong to believe 'most people have it nowadays'.[7] It is,
surely, only common sense to agree with the report
commissioned by the American Medical Association, no great
ally of 'socialised medicine': 'The fact that many politicians
and members of "the establishment" do not use the NHS for
routine treatment goes perhaps some way toward explaining
why such defects as long waiting lists are tolerated.'[8]

The elite is important, but not all important. Popular
support for the NHS has certainly played its part – alongside
and often following the medical profession – in reducing the
severity of the monetarist attack on the NHS. But here again,
commercial medicine is undermining the foundations of the
NHS as medical insurance seeps slowly through the
population. Psephologists tell us that the concerns and
perspectives of the lower-middle and upper-working class
groups (especially the 'C2s') are electorally crucial – certainly
more influential than the interests of the unskilled, the low-
paid, the pensioners and the unemployed who simply cannot
afford medical insurance policies.

Commercial medicine undermines popular support for the
NHS not only by reducing people's interest in its preservation.
The enormous loyalty to the NHS – like the loyalty to the
family or the nation – is not based solely on self-interest. It is
based too on ideology or moral principle, on the idea of the
National Health Service as a universal provider ensuring a
right to, and equity in, medical care. That idea is under

increasing threat, as the media sing the praises of medical techniques the NHS cannot – and, arguably, should not – provide 'on demand'.

Also, the ideological support for the NHS must be undermined as memories of the days before the National Health Service fade away and as traditional working-class notions of solidarity – and, indeed, traditional middle-class notions of paternalism – are challenged by contemporary consumerism. And the single most important component of that consumerism in this context is the commercial medical business. Every BUPA advertisement – 'it makes all the difference' – undermines the kind of image of the NHS which largely explains its popularity and without which it cannot be safe, in *any* politician's hands.

We cannot measure the importance of these factors, but their importance is acknowledged by supporters of commercial medicine. They do not necessarily accept that the private sector at present has a harmful impact on the NHS. But some of them fear that in the future it might do so and others argue that while the private sector makes the NHS smaller than it would otherwise be, that consequence is only to be welcomed.

Enthusiasm for private practice has its limits even among the medical profession. Dr Michael Wilson, chair of the GPs' General Medical Services Committee, acknowledges that the NHS is 'eroded' and 'chipped away' by commercial medicine.[9] A BMA discussion paper rejected insurance funding for the NHS partly on the ground that 'any government would be tempted to reduce its contribution to health care if the insurance fund attracted "extra money".'[10] Quite so, and does not the same apply to the gradual growth of medical insurance? Sir Kenneth Stowe, Permanent Secretary at the DHSS, acknowledges that to some degree the private sector substitutes for, as well as adding to, NHS medical care, although: 'It is impossible to say how much of that care would have been provided under the NHS if not bought privately.'[11] Meanwhile, the medical insurance companies defend their business on the ground that otherwise taxes – that is, spending on the NHS – would be higher. This is the line of John Phillips, former chair of PPP, who sees the 'strong development' of commercial medicine as a way of 'reducing the tax burden' through the restraint of 'public expenditure on health care'.[12] David Lock, that company's managing director, points out that: 'Political opinion has moved greatly in favour of self-help and away from a suffocatingly protective welfare state,' and so asks the government: 'Please do not ignore the incentives which would encourage patients to provide for themselves and their families and reduce government expenditure on the NHS.'[13] Meanwhile, BUPA's Bob Graham argues that the abolition of the private sector 'could mean higher taxes on the public'.[14]

Conclusion

Commercial medicine undoubtedly damages the NHS, through the unrewarded treatment of private patients in NHS hospitals, through the subsidies the private sector enjoys, through the conflicts of interest it creates among the medical profession and through its weakening of elite and popular support for the NHS. We cannot quantify these factors. It may be that even after they are taken into account commercial medicine genuinely does increase the total resources devoted to health care. On the other hand, it may destroy more NHS services than it creates private ones.

When the medical insurance companies defend their business on the ground that otherwise taxes would be higher, they are acknowledging that to a large degree (if not wholly) the political question is not whether we want commercial medicine *as well as* the Health Service, but rather whether we want it *instead*.

Notes

[1] For a fuller discussion, see Geof Rayner, John Mohan and Ben Griffith, *Commercial Medicine in London*, Greater London Council, 1985.
[2] Written Answer, *Hansard*, 19 December 1983.
[3] Briefing note for regional chairs reproduced in *The Health Services*, 3 June 1983.
[4] Bob Graham, Chief Executive of BUPA, 'You the Jury', BBC Radio 4, 28 January 1984.
[5] Review Body on Doctors' and Dentists' Remuneration, Eighth Report, Cmnd 7176.
[6] Cited in Gareth Griffiths, 'Business Looking Up?', *The World of Private Practice*, April 1984.

[7] *Guardian*, 14 December 1984.
[8] Economic Models Ltd, *The British Health Care System*, American Medical Association, 1976.
[9] *Observer*, 17 March 1985.
[10] Executive Committee of the Council of the BMA, *Health Services Financing*, April 1982.
[11] Evidence to House of Commons Treasury and Civil Service Committee, *Long Term Trends in Resources and Public Expenditure*, 14 January 1985, HC 109 – iii.
[12] Chairman's Statement, *Private Patients' Plan Report and Accounts*, 1983.
[13] Speech to *Financial Times* Private Health Care Conference, 25 March 1985.
[14] BUPA Press Release, 2 November 1984.

Conclusion:
How To Tackle Banking On Sickness

Medical care, in all societies, is deeply and irretrievably political. Nowhere is there anything approaching a pure market-place in medicine, although the British are fortunate in the degree to which the private interests are under state control. Politicians and political movements have a major impact on medicine (which is certainly too important to be left to doctors), but cannot transform health care overnight to tally with dogmatic assumptions, as Thatcherism has discovered. To a large degree, therefore, the future of the NHS and of the competing and parasitic private interests hinges on the result of future General Elections. A progressive government will have its work cut out in many fields and medicine is one of them. Strategies for tackling the private interests are discussed below, albeit tentatively. If Thatcherism has taught us anything it is that slogans are not enough and that certainty just lands you in a hole.

But before setting out options for policy and campaigning it may be as well to summarise our main themes so far. In the first section, we described the shambles that passed for medical care before 1948 which necessitated major change and in the event resulted in the National Health Service. The political battle to create the NHS was recalled, along with Barbara Castle's attempt to move on from the 1948 compromise over private practice. We analysed the prejudices and policies of Thatcherism in relation to commercial medicine. We described the present constitution of British private medicine: the limited growth of medical insurance and the increasing challenges to the 'provident associations', especially BUPA; the emergence on the scene of the American hospital corporations, their imperialist ambitions and the extent to which they have been able to use their home-grown techniques in this country; and the new British hospital chains, trying to satisfy their shareholders in an environment not wholly to their liking but largely of their making.

In the second section, we turned to the mutual dependence of the NHS and various private interests. We focused in particular on the independent contractor professions of general practice, dentistry, optical care and pharmacy; and on the parasitic and distorting contribution of the pharmaceutical companies and to a lesser extent and in different ways of the companies selling medical high technology. We revealed how the Tories have faced formidable obstacles in reshaping the independent contractor professions and in restraining the demands of the suppliers and contractors, but how they have made significant progress in particular areas – like the winding up of NHS spectacles, the introduction of the 'limited list' of drugs and, last but not least, compulsory competitive tendering for hospital 'ancillary' services.

In the final section, we engaged in some of the most important debates over the private sector. We referred to ambiguities in past academic and intellectual comment and discussed the private sector's attractions to both staff and patients: the obvious ones (such as money and jumping NHS queues) and the less tangible ones too (such as the pursuit of 'professional autonomy' and a sense of social superiority). We considered the advantages of the NHS as a system of rationing medical care and as a cost-effective public service, and described the consequences of the Americans' failure to create a similar structure of health care services. Finally, the reasons for believing that the private sector weakens the NHS were summarised.

What's to be Done?

With political will, it is possible to stand up to the private interests in medicine. Take, first, the case of private medicine itself. The orthodox left demands its total abolition, although this requires some definition. The 'private medicine' referred to is presumably that practised overwhelmingly by NHS consultants, in NHS pay-beds or private clinics, usually performing operations which fall well within the remit of the National Health Service but for which NHS patients usually need to wait. 'Abolition' is a more difficult concept however:

perhaps it involves making private practice illegal, that is specifying procedures which can be performed only within the NHS. Or perhaps the real enemy is not the consultant in private practice but the big business of commercial medicine. In which case 'abolition' would involve closing down the medical insurance and private hospital companies.

Is abolition the course to adopt? Many people would see this as a major infringement of not only 'freedom of choice' but also of a 'fundamental human right'. We would contest this: after all, laws exist – at least in theory – precisely to prevent anti-social or immoral behaviour in which category we would (in normal circumstances) put jumping NHS waiting lists. However, we are not pleading the case for abolition.

Indeed, we find such a course unrealistic. It would involve a major conflict with the medical profession which would destroy any hopes of working with doctors in furtherance of other important goals. Public opinion is clearly against abolition, which should concern us not only on pragmatic grounds but also perhaps on the principled ground that governments should have regard to the wishes of the governed. For abolition to be feasible would require the return of a radical socialist government with massive public support. It may not be wise to count on that in the immediate future.

Government policy certainly has a place in restricting the supply of commercial medicine. Perhaps the most important input in the private sector is the medical profession. The Conservatives promoted commercial medicine by changing the consultants' contracts. They must certainly be changed again, to discourage private practice. We doubt, for reasons set out above, whether it is politically wise to forbid consultants from private practice. We would go further: it may be necessary to stuff the consultants' mouths with gold, again. Consultants who stick with the NHS could be rewarded with a loyalty premium. If merit awards are worth keeping (and many on the left would say they are not) they should go only to those consultants who are unequivocally committed to the NHS. However, it would probably not be possible to take existing awards away from consultants involved in private practice, so this policy would take several years to have any effect. Loyalty may be encouraged by increasing the resources of the National Health Service, especially in the fields of most interest to consultants. But clearly the spending priorities within the NHS should not be determined primarily by the desirability of maintaining the support of the medical profession.

What of the other elements of the commercial medical business? Certainly, there would be widespread support for the phasing out of NHS pay-beds, or for a genuine common waiting list so that private patients could not gain prior access to NHS treatment. Indeed, these moves would be welcomed by the private hospital companies, which should give us cause for thought.

Should private clinics be closed down, or integrated into the NHS? The latter option is occasionally raised polemically, but would (further) distort the spread of NHS facilities in terms of both service priorities and geographical distribution. Perhaps the building of new clinics could be banned. Or Labour councils could be given new rights to prevent developments they find politically abhorent. Or the Health Services Board or a near equivalent could be restored. This, however, would have two major drawbacks (or advantages from the companies' point of view). If effective it might prevent the building of clinics without proof of demand and thus counteract the over-bedding facilitated by unbridled free enterprise. Secondly, it could be uncomfortably close to the American system in which new clinics require a Certificate of Need. This would involve the legitimation of commercial medicine.

Three other possibilities are worth mentioning. There could be far tighter controls on the medical standards of the clinics. For example, it could be laid down that no surgery was legal unless it was carried out in clinics with 24-hour cover by doctors. Such a move would certainly cause havoc in the private sector. However, this would also help legitimate going private. It would hurt the clinics run by religious groups, 'charities' and consortia of consultants rather than the corporation-owned chains. By improving the standards of private clinics, it would in addition move us closer towards the two-tier system we are trying to avoid. There is the option of a special levy on private clinics (perhaps in the form of vastly increased annual registration fee), justified in part by their reliance upon staff trained by the NHS. Lastly, the charitable status of private clinics is surely due for revision.

However, it will not be enough to control the supply of private medicine if there is no control over the demand. We need to dissuade potential purchasers of medical insurance policies. The political fight itself should do some good (at least, it did in the mid-1970s) and so should some of the policies mentioned above: consultants would be less likely to suggest going private; and the higher standards and annual levies faced by commercial clinics would put up the cost of premiums. We would also suggest that medical insurance should be seen as a luxury good and treated as such: that is, subject to special taxation.

That is a negative course – is there no room for improving NHS facilities? The National Health Service can compete with the commercial sector to some extent by improving standards of patient comfort. For example, it is feasible to adapt existing wards to promote privacy and comfort, and new hospitals are being constructed with these aims in mind. Standards of decoration are improving in places, and some Health Authorities are working hard to make hospital food both healthy and palatable. Better staffing levels will improve the communication and support that ill people need so much. Lopping 'ancillary' services off to the lowest bidder is certainly a retrograde development in this context.

In the long run, the NHS can change popular (and some professional) ideas about illness and health. A new model of medicine can grow out of the public service, whilst the commercial sector will offer only the old model in a glossier package. The current preoccupation with cure overvalues that aspect of NHS work and undervalues a more extensive need for caring services. Caring for those with long-term illnesses, for the disabled and for the dying demands commitment and team effort if satisfactory results are wanted. The commercial sector can warehouse the elderly sick until they die, but it cannot rehabilitate them towards a more normal existence – unless they can pay. Only a public service can bring different kinds of expertise to bear on the problems of *all* those in need. Care on such a scale relies on the knowledge, motivation and skills of the ill and disabled themselves, and of their relatives, neighbours and friends, together with a co-ordinated input from a range of therapists, advisers and helpers. It is a collective social process, not an inventory of actions that can be itemised for the final bill.

The same process must develop within preventive medicine, if it is to work. The women most likely to die from cervical cancer are those least likely to use the screening services already available. If the NHS is to reach them it must find out why they do not (or cannot) take up current services and adapt itself to their circumstances. Similar adaptation will be needed if the NHS attempts to reduce deaths from heart disease by concentrating special attention on those families with strong histories of coronaries, high blood pressure or circulatory disease. First, we would have to find such people, by asking everybody. Then the NHS may have to help them change their lifestyles, after persuading them that the effort was worth it. Instructions to stop smoking, take more exercise, drink less alcohol and change eating habits will not be enough. Health workers will have to answer complex questions. How to stop smoking? What kinds of exercise? How much alcohol? What is a healthy diet? Straightforward physical investigations, like blood tests and cardiograms, may be necessary; long-term checks will be inevitable. All this would require more time, organisation and talk than the NHS is used to, and much more than the private sector can afford. The controlled development of the public services in this direction will benefit both the population (through better medical care) and the health professions (through increased staffing), whilst outbidding commercial medicine in the extent and intensity of provision.

Experience will be at a premium as the NHS develops. The present reliance on specialists-in-training for day-to-day work is a feature of NHS hospitals exacerbated by consultant involvement in private practice. As community care and preventive initiatives evolve into the dominant model of medicine, their natural reliance on skilled staff will encourage reform of hospital career structures. More consultants doing more routine work would be beneficial to NHS standards and harmful to the private sector.

However, most private patients are driven by the desire to jump NHS waiting lists. This issue requires closer attention. Typically, the individual waits until s/he considers a symptom worth taking to a doctor; then the doctor may decide to refer the patient; a surgeon assesses the balance of advantage – do the advantages of surgery outweigh the risks? Admission for elective surgery then depends on the balance of advantage as well as the availability of resources (in addition, access may be deliberately delayed to encourage patients to see surgeons privately). 'Waiting' may begin as soon as the individual shares responsibility for the problem with any professional. Referral may be delayed; risks may outweigh gains and the patient may be put on a 'waiting list' until gains outweigh risks; admission may then be delayed through lack of resources.

A number of factors may influence waiting list size and waiting time: the self-perception of 'problems'; changing morbidity in an ageing population; referral thresholds; operating thresholds; the availability of beds, theatres, surgeons' and anaesthetists' time.

The NHS inherited huge waiting lists and they have varied considerably over the years in response to industrial action, but it has never been able to abolish them. Nor is there any realistic prospect that it could, even with an enormous increase in surgical resources. Waiting may become more of a problem if public understanding increases, self-referral or GP thresholds drop (perhaps through increased work-load), morbidity increases (as it is bound to for some conditions, such as arthritic hips) or operating thresholds increase (as surgeons become more cautious or conscious of limited resources).

There are a number of responses the NHS could make to the 'waiting list' problem. First, some medical problems need to 'mature' before surgery becomes effective. For example, operations performed too early on patients with cataracts may be counter-productive. There can be a positive advantage to the patient in waiting, but s/he will often need persuading of this. Secondly, resources for elective surgery could be increased by major additions to the total resources of the NHS, by giving greater priority to elective surgery or by increased efficiency. Thirdly, some of the backlog could be reduced through positive discrimination. For example, a modest increase in resources could reduce waiting time for hip replacement, if this were thought an appropriate use of limited resources. Fourthly, it may be possible to raise referral thresholds to surgical units, for example through specialists working in the community. Fifthly, people referred for surgical opinions could be given an admission date at their first contact with the specialist. This would allow flexibility and abolish the 'waiting list' (but not waiting time). Sixthly, new developments could assist. Day-care surgery could take off given a modest increase in community nursing staff. Minor operations could be performed by selected GPs with the appropriate training in community health centres. Preventive medicine might reduce the need for certain types of surgery. Priority should be given to non-invasive procedures such as those involving ultrasound and lasers in order to reduce the need for diagnostic and curative surgery. Finally, we need to persuade the general public to view the search for 'instant cures' for non-urgent problems as a sign of misunderstanding about health and illness. More generally, the rationing of medical services is a fact of life to which we must become accustomed.

There is another way of influencing the demand for commercial medicine – persuasion. This is a job that we can start now. We should point out the drawbacks to going private, such as the poor safety standards of many clinics and the astronomic inflation of private medical premiums. We should argue for the *benefits* of waiting (as set out above) and against the medicalisation of social problems. Neither should we be afraid of expressing the basic moral objections to going private.

How about the private interests within the NHS? The left's age-old demand has been for the transformation of GPs into salaried state employees. Again, this would be a major battle which could be won only in political conditions wholly unlike those at the time of writing. We also doubt whether this would not be a battle over form rather than substance. GPs' freedoms need to be influenced and impinged, but this may be best achieved by further incentives and barriers within the present structure. The real issues are *accountability* and *planning* and we need to set up mechanisms to move in these directions while keeping a broadly demand-led service. Salaries are not the only option.

Certainly, there is room for improving general practice,

even though it is a 'British success'. Some GPs are ignorant or
lazy and they should be reformed or cut off from NHS
funding. Effective preventive services need to be developed,
but equitably and without the introduction of charges to
patients. More health centres and peer review, along with
serious incentives to continuing medical education, would
spread excellence throughout general practice. GPs form the
primary contact with the NHS for the overwhelming bulk of
actual and potential patients. If that contact meets their needs
and (where appropriate) their wants, if it appears informed,
caring and effective, then 'going private' will lose much of its
charm.

The opticians present different dilemmas. Their role has,
after all, been drastically changed by Thatcherism. It is
essential to retain and develop free access to ophthalmic
screening. However, do we really believe in bringing back
opticians' monopoly over the sale of spectacles? This must be
open to doubt. The end of the supply of NHS glasses was a
mean-spirited act which hit those who could not afford private
frames and lenses. Indeed in this case the Tories could not be
accused of setting up a two-tier service. NHS spectacles were
typically unattractive, so there already *was* a two-tier service.
What Norman Fowler did was kick away the lower tier.
However, maybe socialists should not be committed to
bringing back such an inequitable system. The old system
helped relieve poverty – a noble enough goal in the Thatcher
era – but in the long run the NHS is not necessarily the best
means of achieving that ambition.

Dentistry is different again. Here, the practitioners are paid
on the fee-for-service system and it is certainly arguable that
this has led to unjustified interventions as well as exorbitant
incomes. There is a solid case for dentistry on a capitation or
salaried basis (maybe with fee-for-service payments for
selected preventive services alone). The charges have shot up
under Thatcherism and many patients are unable to tell
where the NHS ends and private practice takes over. This is a
powerful disincentive to preventive dental care. Dentists'
charges need to be reduced and ultimately revoked – probably
more so than prescription charges.

Which leads us nicely to the pharmaceutical industry.
Certainly, there is room for greater restrictions on the

companies' profits and we find it anomalous that the DHSS strives both to promote employment in the drugs industry and to tackle 'over-manning' in the NHS. The drug companies' advertising needs to be far more tightly controlled in both extent and content. For example, 'repeat advertising' should be stopped: all advertisements should include full clinical details (warts and all). Certainly, generic substitution has a place and limited lists may too, at least in principle: it all depends on which drugs are on the list and how easily it can be circumvented. Also, doctors and patients need to be dissuaded from inappropriate reliance on medication. Public ownership of the industry may not give us much advantage in the absence of a planned approach to research needs, education of professionals in pharmaceutics, controls on prescribing and agreed objectives in drug use. (The Treasury will still exist and might urge a nationalised drug industry to manufacture more generic tranquillizers because of their saleability whilst the DHSS urges doctors and the public to use less and less.) Public control may well mean a dramatic reduction in the industry's size which needs to be predicted and planned for.

How about the other suppliers and contractors to the National Health Service? The NHS is bound to rely on goods and services provided by other organisations and as long as it operates in a mixed economy some of those organisations are very likely to be profit-seeking companies. So the knee-jerk option of public ownership is a chimera. As far as medical technology goes, the problem is due in part to the influence of the industry, but also to the demands of the medical profession (always keen to play with new toys) and of commercial medicine (which provides some of them and encourages the NHS to follow suit). A partial answer is the further development of controlled trials of techniques and also of cost-benefit forms of analysis.

The contracting out of 'ancillary' services is in large part an attempt to grind down the NHS trade unions and in the process the standards of the services provided. The next progressive government should end compulsory competitive tendering, put VAT back on private contractors and restore the Fair Wages Resolution.

This is not the place to go in detail into the policy options for all the various fields, but the above discussion should have thrown some light on some of the dilemmas. The general points are worth drawing out. First, we find the orthodox left perspective totally unpersuasive. Slogans have their place and that place is on banners, not in discussion of the policies to be pursued by a government committed to the NHS. In all the fields, we suggest a more pragmatic approach, combining a number of policy initiatives rather than 'abolition' or 'nationalisation'. However, it is also clear that these policies are not enough. In many fields, it is the ideas – of patients and doctors – which need changing, first and foremost. It needs to be *argued* that going private is anti-social and often not in the patient's own interest either; that treatment with drugs, with elective surgery, with high-tech equipment, is very often inappropriate; that NHS workers merit our support. For many reasons, health campaigning cannot be restricted to opposition to hospital closures or to private hospital developments. The great advantage of the pragmatic approach is that it demands more detailed political understanding, more political activity on a wider scale and more co-ordination – so it can act as a mobiliser, provided that political action is not restricted to parliament, council chamber and trade union conference. The NHS can be saved, and improved, if we get the breaks and make the most of them.

Appendix:
The Private Sector in Statistics

In the last few years, the previous dearth of statistical data on commercial medicine has been transformed. In one sense this is an ominous development reflecting the growing objective importance as well as political significance of the private sector. It does, however, mean that we know the nature of the beast better than formerly.

We can start with the financial basis of private practice, namely medical insurance. There have in fact long been statistics compiled on this market, but these have appeared only erratically in recent years.

In 1984, an estimated total of 5,100,000 people were covered privately. BUPA covered 3,140,000 of them, 61.5 per cent of the total. Private Patients Plan covered 19.2 per cent and the Western Provident Association 7.2 per cent. Another five provident associations brought the 'non-profit' total to 4,665,000 or 91.4 per cent of all those covered. Of seven explicitly for-profit companies listed, the largest was Crusader covering 170,000 people or 3.3 per cent of the total. The market, therefore, remains dominated by the provident associations, although this is slowly changing.[1]

Detailed information has been published on the 'Big Three' – BUPA, PPP and the Western Provident Association which together covered 4,302,000 people in 1983 under 1,954,000 separate policies. The subscribers paid in £356,203,000 in premiums and received £291,216,000 worth of benefits. 49.5 per cent of subscribers were in schemes bought by their employers and provided as fringe benefits. Another 22.1 per cent were in group schemes but paid the premiums themselves. The remaining 28.4 per cent had purchased their policies individually. The subscribers paid out £304,778,000 to receive private treatment: 46.1 per cent of that went in room charges, 30.5 per cent went in fees to consultants and others for in-patient treatment, another 16.2 per cent in out-patient fees and 7.2 per cent was classified as 'miscellaneous'. The provident associations paid out £219,216,000, as we have seen, so there was a shortfall of £13,562,000.[2] These statistics are only occasionally made available. However, the Big Three's annual accounts reveal that in 1985 their subscribers paid out £470,701,000 in premiums and received benefits to the value of £416,610,000.

Table 1 shows how the medical insurance market grew in the early Thatcher years. Clearly, the growth has slowed down quite considerably, although the overall growth has been stronger than these figures might seem to suggest, as explicitly for-profit companies have been successfully winning new custom. The market in individually bought policies has not undergone major change, despite widespread media advertising. The most dramatic story relates to the employee-purchase section of the market which grew massively up to 1981, and then started actually to shrink (at least for the Big Three). The progress of the company-bought policy has been similar, although less acute.

Table 1
Medical Insurance Subscribers by Category (1,000)

	1979	1980	% change	1981	% change	1982	% change	1983	% change
Individual purchase	474	507	+7.0	530	+4.5	546	+3.0	555	+1.6
Employee purchase	200	323	+61.5	447	+38.4	438	−2.0	431	−1.6
Company purchase	625	805	+28.8	886	+10.1	933	+5.3	968	+3.8
TOTAL	1299	1635	+25.9	1863	+13.9	1917	+2.9	1954	+1.9

Source: BUPA, PPP and WPA, *UK Private Medical Care: Provident Association Statistics 1982 and 1983*, 1984 and *Provident Schemes Statistics 1981: an Overview*, 1983.

The 1983 *General Household Survey* revealed that 7 per cent of the population was covered by private medical insurance in that year. Coverage varied substantially from one social group to another. To take class first, 23 per cent of the 'professional' group were covered; 22 per cent of 'employers and managers'; 8 per cent of those classified as 'intermediate and junior non-manual'; 3 per cent of the 'skilled manual and own account non-professional' group; just 1 per cent of the 'semi-skilled manual and personal service' and 'unskilled manual' categories. Significant variations – largely but by no means wholly explained by social class – existed between one area and another. 8 per cent of residents of Greater London were covered; 14 per cent of those in the suburban Outer Metropolitan Area; and 10 per cent in the Outer South-East. At the other extreme were the North of England and Scotland, which had just 3 per insured. The survey also revealed widespread variation by age group: 8 per cent of those aged from 16 to 44 were covered; 9 per cent of those between 45 and 64; and just 3 per cent of those aged 75 and over. 12 per cent of the insured reported a limiting long-standing illness next to 20 per cent of those not covered.[3]

Medical insurance is the basis of the demand for private treatment. We can turn now to measures of its supply, in three categories: the consultants involved, commercial clinics and the private use of NHS facilities.

There are no accurate data on the numbers of consultants

Table 2
Contracts Held by Consultants, 1985

Regional Health Authority	WT	M P-T	P-T	H	Total
Northern	69	19	5	6	99
Yorkshire	51	37	6	7	101
Trent	54	30	4	12	100
East Anglia	52	34	5	8	99
NW Thames	34	30	19	17	100
NE Thames	30	29	21	20	100
SE Thames	36	35	14	15	100
SW Thames	34	40	13	13	100
Wessex	48	38	5	8	99
Oxford	42	39	6	13	100
South Western	48	35	6	11	100
West Midlands	53	36	4	7	100
Mersey	53	30	5	11	99
North Western	52	34	5	9	100
English RHAs	46	33	9	12	100

WT is the percentage in the Region with 'whole-time' contracts
M P-T is the percentage with 'maximum part-time' contracts
P-T is the percentage with other 'part-time' contracts
H is the percentage with 'honorary' contracts
Source: derived from Written Answers, *Hansard*, 14 April 1986.

working privately. One industry estimate is that 85 per cent of NHS consultants are involved to some extent. In addition, some 200 or 300 doctors are reported to work solely within the private sector. Table 2, setting out the types of contract held by consultants in each English Region, is some evidence of the wide variation in opportunities for private practice.

In 1985, 46 per cent of the consultants working for English Regional Health Authorities held 'whole-time' contracts. They are able to 'earn' up to 10 per cent of their NHS income from private practice. 33 per cent were 'maximum part-time'. They are expected to give 'substantially the whole of their professional time' to the NHS, but earn 10/11 of the whole-time salary as there are no limits on the extent to which they practise privately. 9 per cent of consultants were 'other part-time'. On average, they are contracted to work 7.4 sessions a week for the NHS, a session being nominally $3\frac{1}{2}$ hours. However, consultants with part-time appointments do not necessarily have particularly large private practice commitments, as they sometimes hold NHS appointments in more than one Region. The percentage of consultants with 'full-time' contracts varies from 30 per cent in North-East Thames to 69 per cent in the Northern Region. Major variations can also be seen when the contractual position of consultants in the different specialties are compared. In 1985 just 22 per cent of general surgery specialists worked whole-time for the NHS, compared with 88 per cent of specialists in accident and emergency work and 91 per cent of specialists in geriatric medicine.

The DHSS started its annual survey of private clinics only in 1982. All institutions registered in England under the Nursing Homes Act 1975 are surveyed. On 31 December 1985, there were 1,833 such 'nursing homes', with 50,985 beds. The Regional figures ranged from 38 institutions with 1,115 beds in the Northern Region to 246 institutions with 6,598 beds in South-East Thames. Altogether 200 of the 1,833 'nursing homes' had operating theatres, and therefore can reasonably be classified as private clinics. Table 3 gives the Regional breakdown.

Unfortunately it is not possible to show the growth since 1979 of private clinics from these official figures. However, surveys conducted by the Association of Independent

Table 3
**Numbers of all Institutions and Institutions with Operating Theatres
and Their Corresponding Beds, 31 December 1985**

	All institutions		Institutions with operating theatres	
Regional Health Authority	*Number of institutions*	*Number of beds*	*Number of institutions*	*Number of beds*
England	1,833	50,985	200	8,634
Northern	38	1,115	3	144
Yorkshire	141	3,749	19	552
Trent	125	3,437	14	517
East Anglia	58	1,306	10	333
NW Thames	68	2,712	16	1,192
NE Thames	95	3,237	32	1,531
SE Thames	246	6,598	17	905
SW Thames	228	6,523	16	732
Wessex	191	4,358	15	540
Oxford	82	2,718	11	436
South Western	222	5,674	9	360
West Midlands	124	3,443	16	603
Mersey	119	3,001	8	315
North Western	96	3,114	14	474

Source: DHSS, *Private Hospitals, Homes and Clinics Registered Under Section 23 of the Registered Homes Act,* December 1986.

Hospitals can help us here. First, Table 4 gives the Regional breakdown for 1979 and for 1986, as well as the figures for Wales, Scotland and Northern Ireland.

Table 5 shows that between 1979 and 1984 the number of private hospital beds rose from 6,614 to 10,007, but that the growth has since levelled off.

According to further figures provided by the Association of Independent Hospitals, the commercialisation of the private hospital sector has been proceeding apace. In 1979, 'charitable' clinics accounted for 71 per cent of all private hospital beds, with the religious institutions providing 28.5 per cent. By July 1986, the 'charitable' clinics were providing just 49.5 per cent of all beds and the religious bodies were down to 15 per cent. Meanwhile, in the explicitly 'for-profit' component of the market, hospital chains have been making progress at the expense of the independent clinics: the

Table 4

Association of Independent Hospitals:
Acute Hospital Survey: Nationary Summary July 1986

Region	1979 Hospitals	1979 Beds	New Hospitals	Closures	Total of New Beds	1986 Hospitals	1986 Beds	% increase in Beds
Northern	1	30	2	–	114	3	144	380
Yorkshire	9	341	6	–	228	15	569	67
Trent	9	286	5	2	190	12	476	66
East Anglia	6	151	5	2	172	9	323	114
NW Thames	13	837	6	2	462	17	1,299	55
NE Thames	24	1,383	5	5	197	24	1,580	14
SE Thames	16	615	7	4	361	19	976	59
SW Thames	12	762	4	1	143	15	905	19
Wessex	7	191	8	1	390	14	581	204
Oxford	7	232	6	–	257	13	489	111
South Western	9	345	2	1	79	10	424	23
West Midlands	12	336	6	3	270	15	606	80
Mersey	5	273	2	1	39	6	312	14
North Western	5	283	7	1	280	11	563	99
Total (England)	135	6,065	71	23	3,182	183	9,247	52
Wales	4	202	1	1	–13	4	189	–6
Scotland	9	265	2	2	149	9	414	56
Northern Ireland	2	82	–	–	4	2	86	5
Total (rest of UK)	15	549	3	3	140	15	689	25
Total UK	150	6,614	74	26	3,322	198	9,936	50

Acute = hospitals with operating theatres. Beds = all beds, not just surgical beds. Figures include cosmetic surgery and termination of pregnancy clinics, and also hospitals such as Benenden and Manor House which are not usually open to the public.

Source: Association of Independent Hospitals.

Table 5

AIH Acute Hospital Survey: Increase in the Independent Sector 1979-1986

Year	Change in Number of Hospitals			Total Number of Hospitals	Total Number of Beds*	Number of Beds
	New	Closed	Change			
1979	–	–	–	150	–	6,614
1980	+ 6	–2	+ 4	154	+364	6,978
1981	+14	–1	+13	167	+832	7,810
1982	+15	–2	+13	180	+792	8,602
1983	+12	–5	+ 7	187	+643	9,245
1984	+14	–2	+12	199	+762	10,007
1985	+7	–7	0	199	–112	9,895
1986 (July)	+ 6	–7	– 1	198	+ 41	9,936
1986/87	+ 7	?	+ 7	205	+470	10,406

[1] Bed numbers include all beds, not just surgical.
[2] Figures include all hospitals and homes with operating theatres (including cosmetic surgery and termination of pregnancy homes).
[3] Figures refer to UK total.
* includes new hospital beds, expansions of existing hospitals, and losses.
Source: Association of Independent Hospitals.

American corportions increased their share from 5.5 to 22 per cent while the British chains rose from 2.5 to 14.5 per cent of the total.

According to AIH, then, in July 1986 the private sector included 25 religious hospitals with 1,508 beds, and a total of 90 clinics with 4,936 beds enjoying charitable status. The American corporations ran 29 hospitals with 2,151 beds. (Incidentally, these figures do not include private psychiatric clinics, some of which are owned by US groups.) British groups owned 34 hospitals which included 1,441 beds. Finally, AIH counted 45 'independent' for-profit hospitals with a total of 1,408 beds.

The DHSS has sponsored a survey of the work of private clinics carried out by the Medical Care Research Unit at the University of Sheffield.[4] The Unit obtained data on 148 out of 153 acute hospitals in England and Wales in 1981. They estimate that 344,008 patients received treatment in private clinics that year. 28 per cent of these cases involved the termination of pregnancy, 92 per cent of abortions being performed in just 15 clinics. Cosmetic operations accounted for another 7 per cent. Otherwise: 'Most of the operations performed on residents from England and Wales were those that characterise NHS waiting lists.' Leaving terminations of pregnancy aside (over 85 per cent of patients coming from Eire and Europe for private treatment received abortions), 90 per cent of patients were resident in England and Wales, although they 'accounted for only 78 per cent of the women undergoing sterilisation and, more remarkably, only 22 per cent of the small number of patients receiving major heart surgery'. 96 per cent of the non-UK residents were treated in the Thames Regions:

> Excluding patients from overseas and abortion cases, nearly a third (31 per cent) were self-financed and 69 per cent were covered by some form of health insurance, 57 per cent through provident associations and 12 per cent through other institutions.

Data on NHS pay-beds have been published in response to Parliamentary Questions. Table 6 gives the figures for 1984 when there were 3,019 pay-beds in England. The occupancy rates were very low. Some, but by no means all, of these beds

Table 6
Pay-beds in NHS Hospitals 1984

Region	Authorised Pay-beds	Average Number Occupied
Northern	105	26
Yorkshire	199	77
Trent	143	37
East Anglian	108	40
NW Thames	292	131
NE Thames	410	172
SE Thames	337	132
SW Thames	194	64
Wessex	120	52
Oxford	180	85
South Western	104	42
West Midlands	276	80
Mersey	123	38
North Western	245	75
Special Health Authorities	183	104
England	3,019	1,156
Wales	52	14
Scotland	109	19
Northern Ireland	149	25
United Kingdom	3,329	1,214

Source: derived from Written Answers, *Hansard*, 4 February 1985 (English data), 21 February 1985 (Welsh data), 1 February 1985 (Scottish data), 1 February 1985 (Northern Ireland data).

would have been occupied by non-paying NHS patients when private demand was insufficient to keep them filled.

Table 7 shows how the Conservatives have increased the number of pay-bed authorisations in England from 2,405 to 3,019. The number of private patients shot up in 1979-80, reflecting the growth of medical insurance, but then fell back to well below 1979 levels as the new private hospitals opened.

The Sheffield Medical Care Research Unit estimated that of the 344,000 private patients treated in commercial clinics in 1981, 162,000 were 'residents of England and Wales admitted as in-patients for elective surgery other than termination of pregnancy'. The Unit estimated that another 57,000 private elective operations were carried out in NHS hospitals. The total 219,000 private elective operations accounted for 13.2 per cent of the total in England and Wales. The elective case-load treated privately varied widely by Region: making up 5 per cent of the total in the Northern Region, but 22 per cent in both NW Thames and SW Thames. The Unit identified five types of operation over 20 per cent of which were performed privately: haemorrhoidectomy (23.7 per cent); hysterectomy (20.9 cent); total hip replacement (26.2 per cent); excision, internal structure of knee (22.8 per cent); and varicose veins, ligation and stripping (23.0 per cent). 'Proportionately, hip replacements were twice as common in the private sector as they were in the NHS.'

Table 7
Pay-beds in England

	Quota	Number occupied	Percentage occupied	Patients
1979	2,405	1,508	62.7	91,128
1980	2,405	1,514	63.0	98,565
1981	2,677	1,469	54.9	97,739
1982	2,919	1,259	43.1	80,686
1983	2,987	1,264	42.3	82,938
1984	3,019	1,156	38.3	77,489
Change 1979-84	+25.5%	−23.3%	NA	−15.0%

Source: Written Answer, *Hansard*, 4 February 1985.

How significant is the private sector when compared with the NHS? The answer to this question depends largely on the measure used. If turnover is taken, and William Laing's estimate that private acute hospital care brought in £475 million in 1984 (excluding NHS pay-beds) used, then the private sector is about 3.4 per cent of the size of the NHS.[5] If bed numbers for all specialties are taken into consideration, the NHS total comes to 325,500 (1985 figures for England) and the private total to 55,000, with 45,100 of the latter figure accounted for by beds in private nursing homes (1986 figures for UK as a whole). In 1985 the NHS in England had 134,500 acute beds while the Association of Independent Hospitals recorded 9,900 beds in private hospitals. The Sheffield Unit found that even in 1981 13.2 per cent of elective operations were performed privately and that this rose to a proportion of one in five in some Regions and for some specialties. Only 46 per cent of consultants – and only 20 per cent of general surgeons – working for English Regions hold 'whole-time' contracts with the NHS. Nearly all consultants are involved in private practice to some extent. While unquantifiable with present data (limited by respect for 'professional autonomy'), this is arguably the most important fact of all about the nature and significance of commercial medicine in Britain today.

Notes

[1] Clive Grant, *Private Health Care in the UK: A Review*, The Economist Intelligence Unit Special Report No.207, 1985.

[2] BUPA, PPP and WPA, *UK Private Medical Care: Provident Association Statistics 1982 and 1983*, 1984.

[3] Office of Populatioin Censuses and Surveys, *General Household Survey 1983*, HMSO, 1985.

[4] J.P.Nicholl, B.T.Williams, K.J.Thomas, J.Knowelden, 'Contribution of the Private Sector to Elective Surgery in England and Wales', *Lancet*, 14 July 1984 and 'Analysis of the Work of Independent Acute Hospitals in England and Wales, 1981', *British Medical Journal*, 18 August 1984.

[5] William Laing, *Private Health Care 1985*, Office of Health Economics, 1985.

Medicine and Labour
The Politics of a Profession

STEVE WATKINS

The British Medical Association is, as its repeated victories over various governments have shown, the most powerful trade union in Britain, but, as a body representing a learned profession, is keen to be seen as 'above' trade unionism. Doctors, as members of a caring profession imbued with the mystique of medical expertise, occupy an immensely influential position which touches on numerous areas of public life. Given this power, it is surprising that the politics of the medical profession have not been put under the microscope before.

The author, himself a practising doctor, looks at doctors' relationship with the labour movement and the special role played by medical schools in the formation of an ideology quite distinct from that of other health workers. As well as discussing the discrimination faced by black doctors in the NHS and the many issues raised for the medical profession by the women's movement and women doctors, he explores the dilemmas posed for doctors working in industry.

By examining the successes and failures of campaigners for civil liberties and nuclear disarmament within the medical profession, and the work of the TUC-affiliated Medical Practitioners' Union, Steve Warkins charts a map of the possibilities and limits which face the left when it intervenes in the politics of a profession.

paperback £6.95

Index